'I love how Mike has added the nature writing and history into his personal story of bikepacking. This book emphasises the importance of being outside in nature and of movement through the environment. It contains great practical and technical information for those starting out, but it is a personal journey – from naïve beginnings to travelling and exploring the natural world – the unconscious competency. This book is so much more interesting than simply going faster, going stronger!'

Rosie Baxendine, she/her, Bikepacking Guide

'This is a book full of information, anecdotes and useful insights, written by a man who has climbed, walked and biked around most of the UK and Ireland. Mike's beautifully written travelogue clearly indicates his intimate knowledge of ecology, geology, history, travel, and a sense of place. A cracking read.'

Iolo Williams, Naturalist and Broadcaster

Riding My Bike
A bikepacker's tales from the trails

Mike Raine

© Mike Raine 2024

The rights of Mike Raine to be identified as the author of this work have been asserted by him in accordance with the Copyright, Designs and Patents Act of 1988.
All rights reserved; no part of this publication may be reproduced, stored in a retrieval system, or transmitted in any form or by any means, electronic, mechanical, photocopying, recording or otherwise without the prior written consent of the publisher or a licence permitting copying in the UK issued by the Copyright Licensing Agency Ltd. www.cla.co.uk

ISBN 978-1-78792-066-8

Book design, layout and production management by Into Print
intoprint.net
+44 (0)1604 832149

Cover illustration: Molly Tong

For Graham and Richard.
Thanks.

Acknowledgements

Without doubt this book would not have happened without Sally. Not only is she ever patient when I'm away, she is supportive and understanding about my need to go on trips. Sally is also my first line of editing and proof checking. I'm very lucky to be married to Sally.

I can't thank Molly Tong enough for the wonderful cover painting.

Graham and Richard have played an enormous role in my development as a bikepacker. I thank them for their support, encouragement and patience. They too have helped with the proofs of this book. Another friend Kenny is my bike encyclopaedia. He's saved me from many a mechanical floundering.

John Mainwaring and Harry Tong have also helped with the text, thanks guys. Thanks to Rosie Baxendine, Iolo Williams and Jethro Jessop for kind encouraging words.

As a child of the sixties and seventies I wasn't taught English formally. By reading lots, I've managed to sneak through life, but work on this text has exposed my shortcomings. Despite the gallant efforts of Sally and Harry to proofread I'm quite sure a few spolling, grammer and punchution eras have crept though! They are entirely my responsibility and if you find any, let me know and I'll tweak them for future editions. Sorry.

Jules, Liz, Chris and the team at Alpkit in Betws-y-Coed have been patient with my demands – and always willing to help. A special mention goes to the team at 4Play Cycles in Cockermouth, who changed my relationship with my bike. And finally, apologies to Graham Watson: honestly, I thought it was just a head cold.

Contents

Acknowledgements 6
Prologue 8
A note on Cymraeg 10

Part One – *Unconsciously incompetent*
1: Learning to bikepack 12
2: A midsummer bothy trip 18

Part Two – *Consciously incompetent*
3: Drinking in the Howgills 24
4: The Outer Cairngorm Loop 29
5: Pushing in the dark 34

Part Three – *Consciously competent*
6: A Covid county boundary challenge 38
7: Chylchdaith Rhinogydd 48
8: The Highland Trail 550 – Part one, northbound 55
9: The Highland Trail 550 (train stress in the Highlands)
   – Part two, southbound 67
10: Midsummer Teifi time 76
11: The Welsh 550/Cylchdaith Cymru 550 79

Part Four – *Unconsciously competent*
12: A winter's loop of northern Eryri 144
13: In camp 147
14: Conwy to Knighton 151
15: Bored on The Trans Cambrian 159
16: Disappointed on the Traws Eryri 167
17: Time travelling in Eryri 175
18: Notes from the Triban Trail 179
19: A couple's adventure 183
20: A tour of the English Lake District 187
21: A winter bothy trip 198
22: The best bike for bikepacking is the one you already own 205

Postscript 217
Your Author 217

Prologue

I see greater stitchwort, soon to be joined by the lesser stitchwort. I see lesser celandine, but never greater. Herb Robert, always, then there are common dog violets and the barren strawberry. I don't ignore the buttercups, or the daisies and I cheer for the dandelions. Every now and then there's a lushness of wild garlic and a cloud of meadowsweet dotted with tiny germander speedwell. The wood vetch leans over into Jack-by-the-hedge and sticky leaved cleavers. I'm enjoying a slow, close encounter with a spring verge in Wales. The verge is a throwback to our long-gone wild wood. It's a place to celebrate, to enjoy, not curse.

There are days, make no mistake, when bikepacking just seems like too much hard work. There are days when the hills are just too steep. There are days when the ground is just too wet and too muddy. Sometimes I look at the map and see the hills and it makes me feel worse. Can I really be bothered? But in the absence of anything else to do, I start to ascend the hill, pedals turning ever slower. Life is now very simple, pedal, eat, sleep and repeat. Often as I begin the climb, my legs slip in to gear and although my mind is weak, my body is strong, and my lungs are fit. I can grind my way up most hills in the lowest of low gears. And in doing so I celebrate the flower-filled verge.

One of the inalienable truths about bikepacking, and indeed mountain biking, is that you spend more time going uphill than you do going downhill. A long grind on an easy angled slope, typically a forest track, can be quite rewarding and should pay dividends with a long gentle downhill. On the other hand, a stubborn steep push can feel rather brutal.

Bikepacking is journeying, journeying with a bike. There are ups and there are downs, both mentally and physically. Pushing your bike, or hike-a-bike as it's often called, is quiet time. It's time for contemplation.

I cycle as far as I can up the hill; it's rarely quicker to walk. No one sees me, no one cares. I have nothing to prove. As my spirit wilts and the pedals get harder to press, I step off my bike and push. I try to not to stop on the hill; I look for a flattening or a natural break to pause for a breather. Sometimes it's a corner in a wall, maybe a gate. Today it's a small copse, on another day it might be a viewpoint. I enjoy the sense of place, of being and of calm; my journey to be enjoyed, not endured. I start again, this time pushing. I push from the left-hand side of my bike with my hands on the handlebars. I switch to the right-hand side of the bike for a bit, just to save a crick in my back. I try pulling on the saddle, just for a change, but it doesn't really make it any easier and I'm soon back to my standard pushing from the left-hand side. I dream about inventing a harness and stabilisers so that I can pull my bike like a sled in the Arctic snow. I embrace the push and keep plodding. I don't mind a walk now and then – it adds variety to the journey.

I live in Wales, and this is a book dominated by bikepacking in Wales and in Wales there are lots of hills. It's not really the big hills that get me down. The big hills are honest, apparent and obvious. They're well-marked on the map, I can see them ahead, so I know what I'm in for. No, it's not the big hills that work me hard; it's the little, pop-up hills that consecutively, and cumulatively, crush me.

I've done the hard work, I'm in the valley. The minor road follows the edge of the flood plain. As the flood plan narrows the road pops over a small hill, steeply up then steeply down. It does it again and again. These are the hills I find hard, short and steep. They spoil my flow. Just one more. That's all I can do today.

Bikepacking is hard; it's slow and tiring. There can be an element of what they call 'type 2' fun and sometimes it's after the event that I will really appreciate it all.

Much of what I read, see and hear about bikepacking is about the race. Outsiders could be forgiven for believing that this is a sport about racing, another branch of cycle sportive. It isn't. It certainly doesn't need to be. Bikepacking is an agreeable way to travel through the countryside seeking out quiet lanes, by-ways and bridleways. I can ride to the horizon and beyond. Famous bikepackers can travel far and fast in a day. I don't need to do that. I take my time, meander, stop and look. It's a simple life. Eat, pedal, sleep, repeat. Slowly.

A note on Cymraeg

Many readers will be slightly bamboozled by the Welsh language. I'm sorry that I live in Cymru/Wales and that Cymraeg/Welsh is still used here. Actually, no I'm not! I'm a proud Yorkshire man so I totally get the pride in your home. In fact, I'm quite jealous that Wales has its own language and Yorkshire only has a dialect. Anyway, fact is, much of the book is set in Wales so you need to work out how to read the place names. Here's a few tips that might help a bit.

With Welsh spellings, you say what you see. A combination of letters has a particular sound no matter where it appears, unlike English, which has silent letters (write, rite and right) and words which share the same letters but sound different (the wind blows as you wind your alarm-clock). Once you have grasped the sounds of Welsh, you will be able to pronounce any written word you see. Most letters are pronounced phonetically as follows – A as in attic, B as in bat and C as in Cat and so on, with the exception of:

Dd	pronounced Th (as in the)
F	pronounced as V (as in van)
Ff	pronounced as F (as in physics)
Ll	similar to Ch (tricky, pop your tongue on the roof of your mouth and blow across the top of it, that'll get you started)
Ph	same as in the English language, i.e. F (as in physics)
R	Welsh people enjoy the letter R so roll it to your heart's content if you can!
Si	as Sh e.g. siop is pronounced shop.
U	tends to be pronounced as Ee
W	is a double U (as in blue or cool)
Y	has several pronunciations: dyn (as in dean but with rounder lips), Llyn (as in tin) and Cymru (as in tee)

Part One
Unconsciously incompetent

1: Learning to bikepack

Around Ben Alder

I think it was Nige who laughed out loud, whilst Graham merely chuckled, and Mat looked bemused. I was eating an apple. Taken from a packet of six. They came packaged in cellophane sitting on a cardboard tray and that seemed to me to be a good way to carry some fruit on my first bikepacking trip. On previous overnight walking trips, it was fruit that I'd missed the most. My thinking was that having the bike I'd be able to carry more stuff and hence some fruit. I was excited about travelling through the mountains and taking real food instead of traditional dried camp food. What I hadn't realised is that when bikepacking my load needed to be even lighter than when walking. Because when bikepacking, we were still mountain biking, and we wanted to be able to hammer down some single-track trails whenever the opportunity arose. Hence, the amusement my apples caused. My bikepacking lessons had begun.

To be fair, this wasn't actually my first bikepacking trip. On my debut, we'd carried even more kit. This was when Sally and I went to climb Squareface, a rock climb in the Cairngorms. I knew the route was a long way from the road. I'd been to the crag before, in winter, when it had been a five hour walk in. It seemed sensible therefore, to cycle in on mountain bikes. We made an overnight camp, did the route the next day then went back to camp and on the third day, enjoyed the cycle out. But what did we learn?

I am a climber. Well, I was a climber. Climbing has been a constant throughout my life but moving towards middle age (and beyond) I wanted to spread my wings and journey in other ways. Another world, a world of travelling by bike had started to open up for me, thanks to my good friend Graham. I need to add here that I mean off-road cycling, in fact what we do is long-distance mountain biking with overnight camps. We call it bikepacking, but others use that same term for different kinds of overnight bike travel. I wasn't particularly good at mountain biking, but it had given me a fun way to keep fit and get out in the winter. I can camp though and have done all my life. I've spent a lot of time camping with groups and walking into remote mountain camps. I wouldn't say I love camping, but it's a frugal means to an end, making multi-day journeys doable (especially when you aren't sure how far you can travel each day). Our plan had been to combine bikepacking, climbing and camping into one journey.

We'd been told to keep the weight on the bike and not on our backs. This seems to be a reoccurring theme when bikepacking: don't carry a rucksack, never carry a rucksack, the last thing you want to do is carry a rucksack, I'm unconvinced. Now, it may be my background as I'm someone who has always carried a rucksack. As a walker, climber and mountaineer a rucksack is standard, so I actually feel quite naked without one. Indeed, even as a mountain biker I'd always carry a rucksack with a first aid kit, some spare clothes and other emergency gear, just in case. It's a good habit we learn as mountaineers and I'm comfortable with it.

Sally and I had bought seat post racks for our bikes, mine was a full suspension mountain bike, whilst Sally's was a hard tail. We'd lashed our climbing gear to the racks in waterproof bags. Packed inside were ropes, climbing rack and climbing shoes; all the paraphernalia associated with rock climbing. Across the front of the bike, we had another bag with our tent, sleeping bag and other camp kit, such as stove and food. I remember we took a tarp as well as a tent and made a porch. We could carry more gear (or so we thought) than we would have if we'd walked. Our plan was to make a comfortable camp high in the mountains from where we'd be able to spend the next day on our climb.

The climb went well, sort of. I suppose it's fair to say the actual climb went well but the access to it was hampered by late season snow and we needed to deploy some mountaineering skills. We had to make sound judgements about steep ground, about route choices and about navigation in low cloud. We had an adventure, and it was great. But cycling out, something needed to change.

The bikes had been prone to tipping on the way in. The seat post rack had been overloaded so that every time we got off the bike the front wheel lifted off the ground. We needed to redistribute the weight. We worked out that it suited both of us to actually carry the heaviest stuff on our backs rather than on the bike. We did this, and we cycled out, mostly downhill to be fair, carrying the climbing gear in our rucksacks. It seemed to go extremely well, and it was a wonderful ride. We paddled through the gossiping Quoich Water in bare feet and descended into the Caledonian Forest before heading back, via the Linn of Quoich, to our car near Braemar. We'd had a great trip. We were still innocent about travelling in the mountains on bikes, but with years of experience of carrying rucksacks we'd concluded that on your back was the best place to put the weight. Turns out, there was more to learn.

A year on and I was bikepacking again, this time just for the sake of it, and Graham and Nige told me I needed to reduce the weight I was carrying. It's not just about the descents, they said, but the ascents are harder the heavier your bike. In the future I would ditch the apples.

We went north of Ben Alder on wonderful estate-built single-tracks. From Loch Pattack it's a fair old climb and each of us found our own space to enjoy the place. Some riding, some pushing, a snow patch and a steep little incline brought us to Bealach Dubh, below Meall an t-Slugain, from where the fun really started. The track beyond here heads through wild and empty landscapes. It's a fast well-maintained track, just at a nice width and marred only by slightly wider-than-I-would-have-liked drainage ditches. Some of the ditches were rollable, some were not, at least not for me anyway. The Ben Alder circuit is a well-known and brilliant mountain bike trip. We regrouped at the Ben Alder bothy.

The route had been planned by Graham. Graham is a long-standing good friend who'd been doing a lot of backpacking. We used to climb together, and he got me into mountain biking, selling me one of his old bikes to get me started. He's from Cleckheaton, like me, so he has an inherent grumpiness about him which we like to call 'dry'. Graham has come to be an authority on bikes and bikepacking. He's done more trips than anybody else I know. He's spent time in Scotland on his own, cycled the length and breadth of the Pennines, throughout mid-Wales and is, therefore, a compendium of bikepacking routes. Graham is the 'Knowledge'. He's 10 years older than me and it's starting to show but he's quick-witted, humorous and chatty. Always good company, Graham is the man with the plan.

The track from Ben Alder bothy along the shore of Loch Ericht is also well known in mountain bike and bikepacking circles, but not for good reasons.

We didn't know anything about it except that Graham had heard it was bad. Cutting inland we pushed our bikes through undulating heather-clad moraine debris. It was tough going. As we drifted closer to the lochside, we started to get glimpses of a decent double track along the shore. We cursed at Graham and sidled over towards the good going separated from us only by a fence. A bloody deer fence. Deer fences are typically about two and half metres tall. Climbing over them with a laden mountain bike is a challenging thing to do. Fortunately, we had Nige and Matt. We stripped the bags from our bikes, then Graham and I stood around pretending to be useful whilst Matt lifted the bikes up high on our side of the fence for Nige, now on the other side, to take hold. Nige lifted each bike clear over the fence and down to the ground whilst never letting up on his banter-filled commentary.

Matt is calm, intelligent and easy company. He's also incredibly strong and, ironically for a vegan, as fit as a butcher's dog. His long limbs never seem to tire. Matt brings another level of engineering knowledge to the party. He does things with aeroplanes and, like Graham, he genuinely understands how those gear things work on bikes. Handy. Matt is principled and one day, when we all wake up to what's going on on our planet and in our bodies, we'll need him to do the expedition food as well as well as fix things and lift things.

It was time to camp. I had visions of a lochside beach and the sun setting slowly over the water, as we reclined in comfort around our campsite. Those of you who have camped in Scotland will be all too well aware that the 'insta' (as in Instagram) camp can be a rare thing. Besides, my more experienced chums were still under the impression that tarps were the way to go, so trees were required. Instead of being lochside in the mizzle we skulked in a conifer plantation like fugitives on the run. My shop bought tarp stretched over my upturned bike and completed the shelter that the trees provided. A decent night was had.

The next day we cycled west through more plantations barely glancing at the freshly built utilitarian metal shed on the north shore of Loch Ericht. A hilltop turquoise coloured pool gave pause for thought and some silly conversation about shades of blues. Nige spun a yarn or too, some with geographical basis (he was a geography teacher) some just silly, but always funny.

Nige is funny. He's from Hull way and has a wonderful accent. Beguiling and popular, he's a gifted people person whose intelligence is baked into conversations. His thoughtfulness for others will always load the humour in a favourable direction, typically against himself. He works hard to keep in shape; his toned body and greying half beard give him a piercing look and that strength frequently comes in handy, especially in a land of fences, stiles and locked gates.

We followed tarmac to Rannoch station where we refuelled our bodies with soup, hunks of bread and fine cakes. Then it was north to Loch Ossian, past the impressive Corrour Shooting Lodge and speedily along the boring Strath Ossian to our next camp below Lochan Earba.

It was Graham who suggested I bring a tarp instead of a tent. Tarps were the order of the day. Now, tarp camping is something that has been heavily promoted on social media. Tarp camping is brilliant on dry summer days when there's no wind and is probably splendid in the Mediterranean, California or Australia. In Scotland it rains, if it's not raining there are midges. I guess the teacher was still learning. In Scotland it can be windy, which is great for keeping the midges away, but not so good when it blows the rain under your tarp. Tarp camping in Scotland can be daft.

Graham and Nige had gone full hog with homemade lightweight tarps held up by wheels removed from their bikes. I was unconvinced. Unsure of how to make a tarp I'd just gone and bought one in the shop. I'd bought one big enough to throw over my upturned bike and make a sort of, erm… tent! It was so good and so big that Matt ditched his homemade effort and slept under my tarp on the other side of the bike. We were, however, still open to the elements at each end. This necessitated that first night being spent deep in conifers. Another problem with a tarp, that we discovered on the second night, is that if there's any slope you will slide down it. We both slid out from under the tarp and into the rain and were woken by wet feet.

Tarps have their place, but you need to be very careful about when and where you use them. It was Nige who observed that if you could attach the tarp to a ground sheet, that would reduce some of those rain gaps and stop the wind coming in. You could then hang a lightweight inner inside your tarp/groundsheet combo to combat condensation and midges. You'd have a sort of stretched out material sleeping edifice for overnight protection. The Latin word for 'stretched' is tent, so tent would seem to work for such a shelter. It might even catch on!

Needless to say, from that trip on I've used a tent. It's a good quality lightweight tent that weighs less than a kilo. It can be used all year round whether it's windy, rainy or midgey.

I had learnt that Scotland is laced with fine tracks for the bikepacker. Well-surfaced, and well-graded these tracks would take me around the hills, and through them, in tarmac-free ways. The contrast with the ups and downs, the roughness and the uncertainty of the bridleways at home in Wales, was pleasing. The mountains are bigger and more serious in Scotland than Wales and as a climber, when the rain and midges are added in, it's a tricky place to visit and success is hard won. The bikepacker however is, presented with lengthy opportunities for easy, off-road mileage. The tracks are often on the hunting/shooting/fishing estates. I don't like the hunting/shooting/fishing way of carrying on, I just don't get it. But I must admit they've created some great tracks for biking in the mountains. And shaped the land to suit their needs.

I vowed to return to Scotland with a lighter load, a tent and time. It would take a while before I was back on those well-made tracks, loving and hating them all at the same time.

Along the shores of Loch Ossian

2: A midsummer bothy trip

Around Pumlumon

Graham is our lead bikepacker. Each mid-summer he's organised a bikepacking weekend, but due to my work schedules I had struggled to attend these. On this occasion, however, I was pleased to be able to join the team, meeting and greeting at a pub, now a former pub, called Y Star (I know, I know it should be Y Seren or The Star, but Y Star is what it was called!) We'd had permission from the pub to leave our cars at the end of their car park out of the way. In return we felt it rude not to enjoy lunch before making a leisurely departure. Sitting outside, in the sun, we swapped yarns of old, though I was keen to get on and learn more about bikepacking.

Our plan was simple and satisfying. A gentle team ride to a bothy and back. A simple overnighter, discovering the bikepacking joys of mid-Wales. I was still new to the game, but I'd learnt enough to keep the weight down. My bike was still a full suspension mountain bike, so I'd bought a saddle bag, strapped a bag to my handlebars and had the overflow in a small rucksack. I've done plenty of camping in the mountains over the years, but I'm not a skilled bike rider and I'm a worse mechanic; it was pleasing to have Graham nearby for support. Map reading whilst on the bike was also proving challenging, I'd struggled to keep track of where we were when moving fast and linking strange valleys with new vistas. Graham was using a map in a map case secured onto his handlebars (it wouldn't take long before phone mapping replaced this system and would even tell you where you were with a handy blue dot.) I was starting to pay attention to the map on this ride as I'd been out with Graham a few times, but despite being an expert map reader, I was still struggling with map management and route finding. I was more than happy, as were the rest of the team, to follow Graham's lead.

We rode across a sheep- grazed hill called Penycrocbren, with its barely noticeable Roman fortlet, then down to the Hafren Forest. Forest tracks led us to the source of the River Severn, the Afon Hafren. A sneaky downhill, alongside the garrulous, youthful Hafren, flowed beautifully. South of here is the Sweet Lamb Rally complex. This place came as real shock. It's like the mountain bike trail centres at Coed y Brenin or Llandegla but for motorsport enthusiasts. I had enormous mixed feelings here, but on balance if they are going to do it then it's brilliant that there is a place like this. Now I know about it, I can keep clear.

Across the road there were more conifers, then we rode up past the raised bumps of Cae Gaer, a Roman Fort, and out on to the open moor of Cefn Groes. We cycled through a wind farm. This was the first time I had been so close to one. It's incredible how tall the turbines are and riding below them is unearthly. They were turning slowly, creaking with each rotation. As I got to do more bikepacking I'd get more familiar with windfarms. On the one hand, they provide clean sustainable energy along with handy gravel tracks to cycle on. On the other hand, they seem to use enormous amounts of concrete to build, and they create a ground disturbance of significant size. On balance, if I can pass through, I'm happy, but I do think they should all keep their gates unlocked and the odd little addition of a cycle track here and there would open up many a sound route.

We dropped into a shady, tree-lined valley and along it to the Nant Sydion bothy. I'm a big fan of bothies. These free to use, always open, basic shelters are usually maintained by the Mountain Bothy Association. Most of them are private, but the association take on the work of looking after most of them. Some bothies do get abused. The remoter they are the better and avoiding the weekends is usually wise. Richard thrives in bothies. Whilst most of the team set up tents outside, Richard and I quickly realised that there was plenty of sleeping space inside; we were the only group in residence. I supported Richard with his wood collection and fire building. Then the midges came. I don't know what it is about midges. They are not dangerous, you don't feel their bites, they carry no disease and they inflict no pain; but my goodness they drive you mad. As the campers drifted indoors, we had a roaring blaze going. Perhaps not needed as it was mid-summer, but it was delightful to spend a little time watching the bothy TV.

Richard is a reliable adventure companion and he's always up for a trip. He does have a busy schedule though. Having been retired for nearly 30 years he's found many ways to keep busy and trips have to be slotted into his saturated programme. We'd recently been on sea kayak expeditions together. In the past we'd skied and climbed and struck up a partnership that flowed without unnecessary banter, just companiable silence interspersed with considered conversations. He is keen to make do and mend his kit, will buy cheap and buy more than twice, but his possessions are not worshiped, they are functional and he's happy to share. Richard likes good company and fine food. He's a master fire lighter and stoker, though his attention can wander should members of the opposite sex be present.

When you arrive at most bothies they always seem dark, a little damp and somewhat grubby. They have cheap plastic chairs upon which, when in school, it was impossible to sit still. But as the temporary abode is cast into darkness and the bothy TV spits and splutters, those chairs transform into comforting armchairs and an evening of idle chat drifts aimlessly by. Life is simple in bothies. I would endeavour after this trip to visit more bothies by bike.

Sunday dawned wet. It's something you just have to get used to. In the summer I've learnt that some quick drying shorts and a waterproof top work fine. In the winter though, I dress up with over-trousers and hiking boots. On this trip I was still learning so over-trousers it was. We headed to the Nant yr Arian mountain bike centre where we had a brew and went against the flow. The trails tend to arrive at the centre from the north whereas we came in from the east so all we did was pedal uphill away from the Centre, on forestry tracks. Somehow though we felt superior. We'd worked hard to get here and being on a bikepacking journey seemed to top trump playing around on the manufactured trails. Crowded purpose-built mountain bike centres can be a bit overwhelming when you are bikepacking. They do, however, provide good cafes, and I'm not averse to using the trails either. I would be back here when heading south on my Cylchdaith Cymru (which was, at the time, not even a pipe dream).

This was my first visit into the green desert of Wales. Hyddgen is a remote and eerie, wild spot. I think I may have watched too many TV dramas which feature such places. I could easily imagine a lonely, disturbed individual wandering here in a menacing and sinister way. It seems an unlikely spot for a battle. In 1401 an English force attacked the armies of Owain Glyndwr hereabouts. It had proved a good spot to hide from the marauding invaders as the Glyndwr's men kept the English at bay, defeated not just by the Welsh but by the eternal bogs of Hyddgen. On the day we passed through, the district was empty, no sheep, no people and certainly no villains. In fact, there wasn't much life at all in those parts. The tracks that traverse it are good going though and it's a grand spot for riding a bike. I suspect that bikepackers are amongst the only people who would venture out here. It's a long way from the road and it'd be a rather dull walk. There are signs of mining, of sheep ranching and it's surrounded by conifer plantations. It's a working landscape that requires few people in the 21st Century.

↑ At the bothy

Descending to Hyddgen ↓

Bugeilyn is another deserted spot. Once it would have been a home for a family, in a time when nearness to tarmac and supermarkets was less important. In a time when you knew who your neighbours were even if they weren't quite next door. A time when community worked together and looked after each other. We barely paused as we passed. One person held the gate open and the others filed through heading for Glaslyn and a quick return to our cars.

It had been a tremendous learning journey for me. I loved my full suspension bike, but I was struggling with the saddle bag as it swayed from side to side. I'd seen how painful it was using maps on the handlebars. I experienced a windfarm, slept in a bothy and discovered mid-Wales. I would be back.

The midsummer team

Part Two
Consciously Incompetent

3: Drinking in the Howgills

It was Graham who had planned this trip. In fact, he'd planned us a wee Scottish trip, but the weather up north did not appeal. We stayed in England. For me this was grand; a chance to visit a corner of my home county to which I had not ventured in many years. We met amongst a Beckside, a Hebblethwaite, a Brigflatts and a Broad Raine. It felt like a homecoming.

Unfortunately, Graham fell ill and was unable to lead, so it became a three-men on three-bikes trip. Nige showed us the way, but I was, by now, managing to keep up with the map work. Mechanicals were definitely in the hands of the other two. The third team member being Richard who would, as usual, take the lead should any charm initiatives, or fire lighting, be demanded of us. We gelled easily and shared the decision making.

We camped the night at the most wonderful and welcoming farm just outside Sedbergh. We'd surprisingly been turned away from another campsite that chose not to cater for single sex groups, even geriatric ones. Our hosts allowed us to leave our cars for the duration of the trip and on return invited us in for tea and cake. It was, I have to say, rather like a scene from a James Herriot book. Nige (also a Yorkshireman) and I revelled in it as these proper Yorkshire folk, strangers to us, lived up to our reputation for friendliness and hospitality. Meanwhile Richard, who thrives on human interaction, was purring with delight. He was sat at the noblest of dining tables, a solid, worn and weathered centrepiece which was set off by a roaring fire and a bottomless teapot. He revelled in the companionship of kitchen conversation. We wanted to stay longer.

A scurry down the main road to Sedbergh was halted in town at the weekly artisan market. All local handmade stuff where marmalade and chutney brushed up against paintings and woodwork. Our foodie senses drew us to the authentic and traditional, epitomised by the handmade samosa stall, proper Yorkshire indeed. We scoffed as we stood, and we stored as best we could, procuring ample delights for the day ahead. From here though our bikes, laden with luggage, would require pushing up into the Howgills.

Our first top was Winder, a mere 473 m. I suspected generations of well-off sporty youths from the nearby public school got to know this hill well as they dashed up and down it in shorts and vests. On this day, there were flags out marking routes. We guessed at variations for under 12's, under 14's and under 16's. I prefer not see such waymarking in the hills, but I suspected it was the work of Sedbergh School. I also suspected that they would have a better relationship with the farmer of this hillside than I ever would. We passed by quietly and enjoyed good tracks across Brant Fell to the Calf the highest point in the Howgills at 676m. These are rounded, grassy, sheep-denuded hills, carved out of shales, grits and mudstones from a period of geology which preceded that of most of the rocky limestone Dales. The smooth slopes are appealing to the mountain biker and a quick glance at the OS map suggested bridleways of interest for a return visit. It was a fine day, quiet on the tops and the going was good, leading us on to the famous single track into Bowderdale.

I took a photograph looking down into the valley, both to celebrate the fantastic bike ride here but also to illustrate what our hills look like when they are subjected to a monoculture of sheep grazing. It's a bald landscape with little biodiversity. There is, however, a slightly amorous pleasure to be found when admiring the voluptuous curves of these rounded peaks. I was thrilled to find one starry saxifrage (a globally infrequent Arctic-alpine flower), and one small cranberry plant (an infrequent plant of acidic upland bogs), hiding wayside as I took my time in the lonely valley bottom. Above me though, it was crows and ravens with only a scattering of meadow pipits. In so many ways the Howgills are unremarkable hills, though it's a good place to travel through by mountain bike.

Our long Bowderdale downhill terminated abruptly at a major east-west trunk road, but we were pleased to be able to slink underneath it on a minor lane. Shortly, we dashed across the A685 to a garden centre café, recommended by Graham and enthused over by our gardening chum Richard. Tea and cake were a fine snack, given we hadn't eaten for nearly an hour! Back over the road we dropped on to a fantastic disused railway cycle track. It's a cycleway that hadn't made it to my map, so it was fortunate that Graham had chanced upon it on a previous visit, guided by the proprietor of the Garden Centre Café. It's a lovely route. It took us up Smardale and over Scandal Beck on an impressive viaduct. There were clusters of water avens in the damp banks, a plant I don't see a lot of where I live and work. The track led us close to Kirby Stephen and quiet lanes completed the link. It started to rain which naturally encouraged a pub stop. The Taggy Man was a friendly pub with fine food and beer. It was a hard place to leave. They accommodated our bikes around the back and didn't flinch as we wetted the floor whilst stripping off sodden outer layers. We huddled around the fire and, given the three of us enjoy our food and our beer so much, the die for the trip was cast.

A small copse out east gave us some shelter through a wet night before we headed across from Wrenside above Woofergill, through Potter Sike, and onto a minor road that took us up to the Tan Hill Inn. Winton Fell and Kaber Fell were bustling with Lapwings, locally known as peewits. Lovely to see, but conservation is a tricky and controversial business here, driven as it is by shooting interests.

The Tan Hill Inn provided a large, filling lunch and a couple of fine beers, enough to see us flow with gravity down fast tracks into Swaledale. This upper part of Swaledale around Kisdon Hill is one of the loveliest corners of the Dales and it was a thrill to re-visit. In 1976 I'd walked through here as a boy, undertaking the Pennine Way. I still have photographic images from that day imprinted on my memory. On a later, more adventurous trip, with good friends of the day, we played on the cliffs above Kisdon Force, a crag that never really caught on. I've no idea what we climbed and nothing in the current guidebook is recognisable. We had fun though.

My current team paused in Keld. We passed the Yorkshire Shepherd's husband off the tele, sat on a bench with his eldest son. We admired the limestone barns and drystone walls, all such an integral part of this landscape.

Richard and I were pushing again, up the road towards the Buttertubs Pass. We blamed the lunch for weighing us down as we hustled our bikes up the road. It was a tad embarrassing when a 'roady' zoomed past us with a cursory greeting and a smirk on his face. Nige on the other hand, was long gone, waiting at the top, drying his tarp/hammock combo whilst we made stuttering progress. I spent a little while reacquainting with the Buttertubs, open-topped roadside potholes, rather pit like in appearance. They seemed to be gradually filling up with wind-blown black plastic and jetsam from unthinking motorists passing close by. Peering down into them was less attractive than it used to be. I could also hear the haunting cry of a Golden Plover, somewhere on the moor above.

Then it was down again. Down to the next pub. Never mind afternoon tea in the Dale, it'd be rude to ignore an afternoon pint in the Green Dragon Inn in Hardraw. We declined to make the short stroll to the spectacular Hardraw Force on this occasion. Nige had two beers. Richard and I lagged again.

That late afternoon was hard. We were tired, and the way ahead was steep. Some off-road riding was avoided to get a jump on time. There's a fantastic bridleway section here though, part of the Pennine Bridleway. The underlaying rock is carboniferous limestone and the clues are littered across the map. We rode past a line of shake holes, then through an area of shake holes, to another line of shake holes. This was followed by some shake holes which preceded some more shake holes. This area has a lot of shake holes, unless the map makers were beginning to take the piss.

We found a small, hidden camp spot above Hell Gill and below Sour Hill, names that didn't really encourage one to linger! It hadn't been easy finding suitable camp spots this trip though. The reason for that was that Nige needed trees. He was experimenting with a tarp topped hammock. It needed slinging between two trees at a certain height. The tarp looked fantastic and provided great opportunities for sheltered faff. I was less impressed however, with its lack of wind protection and the hanging sheet of nylon upon which he made his bed. But Nige loved it, being a man who relishes discomfort and thrives upon such challenge. Who needs a good night's sleep anyway?

On the next day we rode past lots of holes, through some coves and past a ford, then another ford, then another ford then another, and another; those map makers were at it again. By Boggle Green I had a bike problem. There was a rattle and something needed tightening and adjusting, I've no idea what (consciously incompetent) and therefore I didn't have the right tool for the job. Nige sorted me out by making a repair that 'put me on'. We managed to cruise down to the valley below where we sent Richard forth to knock on doors. We'd spied an impressive shed, which had the air of being tool laden and we wondered if anyone there might be able to help. How lucky: it was the home of a cyclist, and the gent had just the right tool (and knowledge) to sort me out and put me on my way.

Once again, we were plodding up hill, no thought of riding this one. Richard and I ambled amiably, whilst Nige ran on ahead. I was impressed to see acres of tree planting on the slopes of Wild Boar Fell. I hope they have good survival rate, baked in their plastic guards. A horse and rider past us before the bridleway got really steep. It was impressive watching the horse plod up the steeper slopes ahead, even if the rider did dismount to lead the way. Once again, we were surrounded by fantastic names: Lordburn Close led to Little World and the summit was labelled as High Dolphinsty.

We raced down to Street the end of the Pennine Bridleway, pretty much in the middle of nowhere. Very strange. Heading south we passed Cold Keld on the way to Fell End. Lovely off-road riding along the River

Rawthey then led us back to Sedbergh, more food and beer and a relaxed cruise to our cars and our aforementioned farmhouse tea.

The Howgills and the Dales had given us some steep up and fun downs. This had been a grand arena for bikepacking, but it had been a delicate balance between needing more fitness and enjoying more beer. We'd drunk plenty beer as we drank in the Howgills, and fitness would stumble along in its own good time.

Across the Howgills

4: The Outer Cairngorm Loop

I couldn't help but hum the theme tune from Last of the Summer Wine as the three of us pedalled east from Glenmore Lodge. Both Graham and Richard were in their seventies, and I had just turned sixty. Fortunately, the going commenced with easy tracks and gentle climbs allowing us to warm up nicely on the way to Ryvoan bothy.

It was the last day of September, and the day had started early for me. I'd driven across to Cheshire from north Wales to collect my friends and head north. We'd had breakfast at Tebay and, through some friendly work contacts, I'd managed to arrange some overnight parking. The aim was to complete the Outer Cairngorm Loop. Graham, as ever, knew the area well and he was our guide. I was still riding my full-suspension mountain bike with a large saddle pack and a dry bag strapped to my handlebars. My set up was fine, but I knew it wasn't quite right yet. This trip would help me to understand better how I wanted to load my bike and what I actually needed to carry. Graham and I were carrying tents, whilst Richard, who had 'got away' with using a bivy bag on our Howgills trip, was now, belatedly, joining the tarp experiment. We had food for three days, plenty of warm clothes and lots of smiles. Graham was using a traditional map to find the way.

We passed through lush native forest under a grey and forbidding sky. It was good to be on the trail after our long car journey and we were just seeing how far we could get before dark. I don't think it rained much in the night, but Graham and I were pleased that we had learnt our tarp v. tent lesson, whilst Richard paraded around at first light trying to dry his sleeping bag after an uncomfortably wet night. By our next trip he'd be in a tent, meanwhile he was now looking at three nights in a wet sleeping bag. Good job he's hard as nails.

To start the day, we paddled through Dorback Burn. I've done lots of mountain leader training over the years and at no point did I ever tell anyone to take off their shoes and socks and paddle. You're taught to work as a team using poles and huddles and navigate carefully across any threatening waterways. The reality is, typically, you either don't cross because it's too dangerous or you do, as we did then, paddle across in your bare feet. Later on, in my bikepacking experience I learned that carrying a pair of flip flops was very useful for crossing streams as well as having some alternative footwear for the evenings.

We crossed low moors on good tracks, as an osprey passed over head, we arrived at a poor section of pushing and jumping along the banks of the Burn of Brown. This proved to be one of the very few awkward bits of trail on the entire journey. We reached Tomintoul just before midday and decided to lunch in a pub. This would give us some drying out time as well as a good feed. We shopped for afternoon snacks then cruised along by the River Avon to Glen Builg, passing banks of alpine lady's mantle and yellow saxifrage, plants not seen at home in north Wales. It was easy, chatty riding.

The going got tough passing Loch Builg as the track deteriorated, though we were soon back on good, fast tracks heading south towards Braemar. Unfortunately, the heavens had opened. Harsh cold front borne hail stones and heavy rain smashed onto to us as we descended at speed. The storm woke us up and all of us thrived on the challenge, glasses protected our eyes, hoods were pulled over helmets and big gloves were donned. We flowed down the double tracks, momentum helping us over the bumps. It was a bleak landscape, not the prettiest nor the most spectacular part of the Cairngorms. We passed a grand shooting lodge, sadly but wisely, locked and bolted.

Decision time as darkness beckoned. We wondered whether we should camp before Braemar or push on and camp beyond. Then common sense kicked in; why not stay in Braemar? We found the bunkhouse, conveniently attached to a pub and hosting a superb drying room. Kit was dried, beer was drunk, and chips were eaten. All in all, a very good call which set us up nicely for the next day. The next day didn't commence immediately though as a full breakfast in Braemar pleasantly delayed our departure.

Riding west from Braemar was straightforward on sound gravel tracks. We were dry and comfortable after our luxurious night, and all was well with the world. It was the second day of October, and we'd had no rain, and none was forecast; a perfect day for a Cairngorm passage. The route from Braemar took us west on a lovely little road, past Mar Lodge to the Linn of Dee. From there we were off-road for the rest of the day. It was a gorgeous ride with some native woodland on either side of the valley; this did peter out though as we got further into the Cairngorms. Looking north, towards Ben Macdui, we could see the first of the winter snows settling on the tops. I'd love to have had time for a walk deeper and higher into the mountains. As I climber I've had many winter adventures in the Cairngorms over the years, but I hadn't been to the central part in summer.

The track turned south and lessened in quality, there was a scrappy bit of woodland, the Red House bothy (subsequently renovated, but dilapidated as we passed) and a couple of ruins, the grandest of which provided adequate shelter for a lunch and cud-chewing break.

To say the Cairngorms are a spectacular mountain range would be misleading. There is a grandeur in their bulk and across the 1000m high plateau arctic-alpine plants can be found. The range contains five of the six highest mountains in the UK, with only the highest, Ben Nevis, being away from here on the west coast of Scotland. Ptarmigan, snow bunting and golden eagle are special but not common sights. But, sitting in the pass between Glen Moy and Glen Tilt, I could have been in the Dark Peak. The rounded hills stretched away in all directions and only the aforementioned snow gave any impression of great height. To our east we could see the patchwork quilt of burnt and regrown heather strips typical of moorlands managed for driven grouse shooting. No birds came close, no wild animals could be seen, and the flowers were finished. I know I need to explore the summer Cairngorm in more depth (and height), but sitting there, that day, there was little to pull me back. Only the openness, the peace and the knowledge that these mountains do open up to resolute explorers would drag me back, and then not soon.

We remounted our bikes for the afternoon and headed south on deteriorating tracks. We crossed some wide shallow fords. One came with otter scat and that proved to be our best wildlife spot of the day.

There was some excellent mountain biking at the head of Glen Tilt. We steered our way cautiously over narrow, steep and undulating singletrack. The valley was a little more featured, though trees remained rare, and sheep predominated. The Falls of Tarf were an interesting diversion and the good bridge there was very welcome. Fast and brilliant riding took us down to Blair Atholl and whilst the area is quite denuded of nature, the mountain bike riding is brilliant.

Once again, we found ourselves in a settlement. Not wanting to leave we figured the best overnight option would be the campsite. It was large and none too friendly for the small tent camper. However, it did have pods and pods were much more in keeping. Unfortunately, there wasn't a three-berth pod, but a pair of doubles were available. I graciously let the two older party members share: I figured their night-time noises deserved each other. I slept like a log.

Staying in Blair Atholl did mean that we were able to have another pub meal. Jolly civilised bikepacking this was. And again, in the morning, breakfast was cooked for us in a wonderful café. A café that not only baked its own bread but milled its own flour to do so. We certainly needed it: the team were tired, and we had a long day ahead to get as near to Glenmore as we could and allow maximum time for Friday's drive home.

The penultimate day started with some bike faff, of the deflating tyre sort, which Graham managed admirably without my help. I delegated myself to buying coffee. It's a long climb from Blair Atholl, heading north on a cycle track besides the A9. Most of the time you aren't particularly aware of the road nearby and it feels nicely rural. There is a warning sign here:

> "Weather conditions deteriorate without warning and can be severe even in summer. No food or shelter for 30km. No snow clearance or gritting on cycle track".

Exactly how we rough and tumble bikepackers like it! There is a parallel railway line however, meaning an escape could be made to a station without too much difficulty. So not that remote really.

The easy cycleway riding didn't last for ever. We needed to turn due north through Dalnacardoch Wood. We were looking forward to leaving the A9 and heading back into the mountains, we weren't however, looking forward to crossing it. We definitely felt like we were taking our life into our hands. We waited for the biggest gaps we could and legged it across the busy road, hoping we hadn't caused any motorist to actually have to decelerate and add a few seconds on to their precious bloody journey. Peace came soon, lunch came soon, and the wilderness followed.

A good track gave quiet riding back into rounded, featureless hills. We met an old gentleman hanging out near Loch an Duin whose face was far more featured than the land. He had a smart tent, partly hidden with a camouflage tarp. He wandered over to chat, in an old coat secured with a string belt, and we paused to pass the time of day. He seemed like a nice enough fellow; you can't be too sure in these out of the way places. Though, to be fair, boring tends to be the worst trait I've chanced upon. As it happened Graham took a tumble down a bank whilst bringing up the rear of the party. We'd left him behind so knew nothing of his trauma. Catweazle had dashed across to see if he could help. That impressed us, and the hermit like figure receding into the landscape grew in our estimations. We put Graham back in front; he was the map reader after all.

We crossed bogs choked with tree carcasses. We pedalled on single-track, we pushed on single-track, we stumbled on single-track, we forded a river and Loch an Duin passed us by. From Loch Bhrodainn we were back on free-flowing double track. Time to saunter, time to chat, time to look around and see very little.

Things began to change in Glen Tromie. This area is part of a large, jointly owned rewilding programme known as Cairngorm Connect. Gnarled old junipers were being joined by saplings, there was birdlife again and the devil's bit scabious was scattered across rough pasture either side of the road. My mood lifted, the team chatted more, and we took loads of photographs. This was a lovely, smile-inducing place to be. The riding was easy, aided by a tailwind and tarmac, and that gave us chance to breathe in our rejuvenating surrounds.

The riding from here into the Rothiemurchus Forest was absolutely magical. Large scale native woodland is something that few of us are used to. We visit pockets of it here and there, but they are usually passed by all too quickly. This area of the great Caledonian Forest brought a decidedly congenial feeling to all of us. We felt at home; this was where we'd come from spiritually and evolutionarily. The tracks were sweet, soft and silent. Single track led us riverside and then across low wooded hills to the dazzling Loch an Eilein. Late afternoon sun softened our journey. Glacially deposited erratics littered the forest, some were granite, but others looked like a layered old sandstone. Scots pine stood tall and proud, commanding the woodland around. Some were old, contorted and more like an oak in shape than the regular straight and tall ones with which we are so familiar. Juniper clawed its way above bilberry, cowberry and heather, leaving bracken no way of achieving domination. Graham knew of the small Jack Drake bothy hidden in the woods. It was in good order and seemed like a great place to spend our fourth night. Meaning we'd camped, stayed in a bunkhouse, rented a pod and slept in a bothy. Not typical on these trips but it definitely eased the passage for three mature gents.

I'd also worked out what sort of bike I'd use next, what to carry and how to carry it. I was making progress as a bikepacker.

5: Pushing in the dark

The Forest of Ae

Anyone can ride a bike in the dark if you have sufficient cash. You can buy some ridiculously bright lights, and you can ride anywhere, anytime and on any surface. You can carry on as normal and it's as easy as mountain biking in broad daylight. But pushing in the dark is another matter. Especially when, as happened to us on one occasion, we were pushing in the dark with low cloud, zero visibility and slight drizzle. We were also having to follow a compass bearing.

It happened in the southern uplands during a trip centred on the Forest of Ae. The day was old. It had mulled along easily enough, but we had been, with hindsight, perhaps a little too laid back. Earlier we had cycled slowly along a minor country road, three abreast, chatting. I remember at the time thinking that we ought to make up some ground while were on such easy terrain. We didn't and later it came dark, it tends to do that most evenings. But in December it comes earlier than you expect, even when you're expecting it. At home you'd be tucked up in front of the telly and the onset of darkness, and the speed with which it comes, doesn't really register. We're much more used to a summertime slow onset of darkness. But when you're on a bikepacking trip, you're on a mission, especially on those short winter days and our mission was to get to a bothy.

The southern upland way should have taken us nicely over the pleasant sounding Sweetshae Brae. Except it didn't. There was a steep little push to begin with which was ominous. We expected that though, a little push here and there, that's normal, but we also expected that the Southern Upland Way would be a good track. A clear path that we could follow to the forest where we would pick up gravel tracks and cruise down to the Brattleburn bothy. Either the track is not well-trodden and doesn't show up on the ground, or we had wandered off it – it was dark to be fair. The cloud came down, the drizzle intensified, and the darkness settled. The only way to be sure that we were going the right way, because we did not want to stray downhill and have to come back up, was to follow a compass bearing. Now this is something I'm rather good at. I've taught people how to do it, summer and winter, for many years. I'm quite happy holding an ice axe in one hand, a compass in the other and wandering along in a white out, aiming for my destination. Putting a bike in one hand however, and holding the compass in the other hand as far from the big lump of metal as possible, proved to be rather awkward. Not only that, under foot was rough tussock grass which made it impossible to stay on a straight compass course. Improvisation was required. It wasn't quite the leap-frogging technique that you might have done early on in your compass following days. It was, look about a bit, spot a tussock, fix on it, walk a bit, check a lot and try not to overcompensate, or undercompensate, as we contoured across to the darker darkness of conifers. Predictably the forest didn't welcome us with open arms, and it was another long handrailing leg along the boundary before we found a way in. That dark, muted plod irritatingly included some unwelcome descent and corresponding ascent.

Tussock grass, a shit-lined sheep trod and avoidable soft rush, on we plod. Sheep's eyes tempt us off route, in contrast to Percy Shaw's cat's eyes which saw him home from the pub. I enjoy being in the pool of light; I enjoy the funereal plod, I feel strong with plenty in reserve, the excitement of the task keeps me alert. I am keen however to be in the bothy and I'm disappointed when the woodland misbehaves. I have to dig deep, refocus, adapt our route and summon a little more energy. I remain in my pool of light and plod on…

There's something soothing about living in the pool of light cast by a headtorch when all around is dark. It can be a little unsettling if the cloud is down as well and when you look up your precious light just bounces back. I like the pool of light though; it's my space. It reminds me of alpine mornings or Welsh winter evenings; it takes me back to training and assessing mountain leaders. I can hear the crunch of a crampon biting into crispy snow, the thud of an ice axe in compliant ice or the squelch of a foot finding an unseen bog. I can imagine a weak sun rising or a moon struggling to break through. I sense a group's frustration as their temporary leader wanders off course. It has all happened in the private world of my pool of light.

Finally, we reached a good forest track, which led to a tidy path. We double checked our maps and apps then rolled downhill towards the bothy. The bothy hid in the woods and made us circle it before it let on its whereabouts. Richard got his second wind. He collected wood, chopped wood and built a fire, a fire he kept going through the cold dark evening. Graham and I slumped bedraggled, on the magical plastic chairs of the Brattleburn bothy. We brewed, we ate, we warmed and drank a dram. Those plastic chairs were, once again, the comfiest easy chairs upon which to slumber.

I did pop out to the loo at one point. A woodcock froze in my pool of light. It remained hidden in full view whilst I took a photograph, then it lost its bottle and flew off.

Brattleburn had been our second bothy of the Forest of Ae round. Burleywhag had been reached the night before at dusk after driving north and parking in Ae. A smooth ride in had been cruelly interrupted on the last stretch by the Burley Bog. The bothy was in good order and well equipped as bothies go. The most remarkable thing though was a picture hanging on the wall that bore an uncanny resemblance to my two companions. Kettleton Byre had provided a lunch stop on day two. The bothies, fine tracks and distinctive circular sheep folds had provided interest in this dreary patch of the Southern Uplands. Our last day, day three, had a fine frosty start with a bright blue sky and air that felt too cold to inhale (but we did!) A fine home run back to Ae had helped us forgive the tedium of the vast plantation. We would return to Southern Scotland, to the home of the bothy, for our next winter trip as those tedious forest tracks did make for good progress in the damp winter months, those monotonous conifers gave good shelter from seasonal winds. Besides, we love bothy nights.

The Forest of Ae and its bothies had provided a good, accessible destination for a winter's round. This was also the first ride out for my posh new bike. I'd invested in a titanium-framed, hardtail with an internal, Pinion gear box. It would take me far this bike, but there were some teething problems. It was a bike returned by another customer and it didn't quite have the set up I required as my bikepacking progressed. My local shop was patient and supportive as they helped me chop and change parts as I broke my way through them. I was lucky to be able to use my old bike on one or two in-between trips whilst this one grew into its role. The other big change for me was switching to a Tailfin rear rack. It kept my luggage stable and happily accepted a strapped on dry bag. It was easy to load and there was no sway. This bike and rack would turn out to be faithful partners, though this trip had really been made possible by cheap lights and good headtorches.

Part Three
Consciously competent

6: A Covid county boundary challenge

Conwy County Borough

There was a wonderful period during the COVID lockdowns when we were confined to the county in which we lived. I say wonderful – it was wonderful for me because of the county in which I live. Conwy County is little known as it's a recently formed administrative area dating only from 1996. It was once part of Caernarfonshire, then at another time it was part of Clwyd. Today it's one of the smaller unitary authorities in Wales.

As an outdoor person, it's a dream county. You can take a cross section from the Great Orme and its limestone cliffs, through the beaches around Llandudno and Colwyn Bay, across the estuary with its famous castle, through native woodland into the Gwydyr forest, across the Welsh Lake District and on to the mountains of the Carneddau. The highest point in Conwy is Carnedd Llewellyn, which at 1064 metres is also the third highest mountain in Wales. There is a strange kink in the county boundary which means that the well-loved mountain Tryfan is in Conwy. Llanwrst, Penmachno, Dolwyddelan and Cerrigydrudion are all included in the county as well as the bigger coastal towns of Colwyn Bay, Llandudno and Conwy itself.

The County boundary is centred on the watershed of the Afon Conwy, though it includes much of the Elwy basin in the north east too. I think the idea of creating a bike ride around your county boundary started in Scotland where access for bikes is a bit freer than it is in Wales and England. For me to ride the county boundary of Conwy meant seeking out bridleways and minor lanes as close to the county boundary as possible. Now, if you observe that the county boundary is on the watershed of the river basin, and the bridleways are in a bit from that watershed, then there's an inevitability that a Conwy county boundary journey will comprise lots of ups and downs. It needs to cross the head waters of the tributaries of the Afon Conwy and that involves dropping into valleys and climbing out of them again all the way around the boundary. This became more of a challenge than a pleasant bikepacking journey around home turf. I didn't actually get it completed within the lockdown time frame of COVID, but it was something that was on the menu for as soon as I had a decent time slot. A three-day window in March popped open and I thought that might be just enough time to do the route. As it turned out for me, it was a day too short.

I had by now, done some short one and two-night trips on my own.

Ever worried about mechanicals I considered a more knowledgeable friend to be an essential requirement for bikepacking trips. Gaps in life's busy schedules do not, however, always coincide and I needed to learn to go it alone. Making sure the bike was in good order, purchasing bicycle breakdown recovery and carrying my Transport for Wales bus pass (just in case) I set forth, alone.

I can see the Afon Conwy from my house. This could only mean one thing, I needed to climb to gain the bridleways as close to the watershed as possible. Right from the beginning then, this was a tough route with a steep uphill heading for Llyn Cowlyd. The road from my village up to Cowlyd is quite famous amongst hill climbing cyclists and it's a tough way to start a bikepacking journey. The track alongside Llyn Cowlyd is well-known to mountain bikers and forms part of a wonderful circuit which has long been a favourite. Llyn Cowlyd is a massive, dammed lake and the steep slopes of Pen Llithrig y Wrach and Creigiau Gleision rise abruptly from each of its shores making it a grand, wild open *nant* with the feel of a Scottish Glen. I like the track along Cowlyd, though if I'm honest it's got better, and more rideable since I switched to 29-inch wheels. It's rarely easy. There are still one or two bits of pushing and dancing around puddles to punctuate the journey, but it gives satisfying mountain biking in grand surroundings.

Reaching the bwlch, which leads through to Nant y Benglog (often referred to as the Ogwen valley), was one of the first significant stages of this journey; it was the first summit I achieved – the first of many. From here I needed to pop down to the valley and cross the Afon Llugwy to access an old road while spending as little time as possible on the inhospitable A5. There's a leat here, a near level waterway, which once gave good access to the Fynnon Llugwy reservoir road, which runs down to the valley in a very efficient manner. Unfortunately, the fences along the leat had recently been renewed and the old styles that were easy to climb over with a loaded bike had been replaced with kissing gates which were much more troublesome. The fence either side had been raised as well so that lifting the bike over was, to say the least, a rather painful process. It annoyed me that such a great route had been destroyed by such ignorant, and needless, management techniques.

I dropped off the leat sooner that I had done in the past, to avoid a couple more of those obstacles, then followed a bridleway down to the A5. The going was good and fast, but it led to a very unpleasant mile along the trunk road. I got my head down and pedalled as fast as I could along the road. Fortunately, it was quiet so the torment was soon over.

Gwern Gof Isaf provides a good campsite, with pods and a bunkhouse, but I wasn't stopping there. I was on what is known as the old road which parallels the A5 hereabouts. It's a track that once hosted 4x4s and had been a bit of a disaster. Some forward and bold thinking by the National Park Authority removed the motor vehicles from this track and tidied up the surface. This now provides a brilliant traffic-free route along the valley for walkers and mountain bikers. Travelling north it's pretty much all downhill to the coast at Bangor. More like this please. I raced down to Capel Curig. At the time of writing, the village currently has little in the way of services. There may or may not be a cafe open, there may or may not be a pub open, so for me it was a push up the damaged Chapel Hill, off-road, towards Dolwyddelan.

From the top of the hill, it was good riding to Dolwyddelan along a fast plantation road to the village where a SPAR shop provided some lunch. From the village, I took the Sarn Helen Roman Road route through Cwm Penamnen. It's an unpopular section of that route. It's tough and can be quite demoralising for the Roman Road traveller. This isn't a straight well-surfaced road in stereotypical style. The fact that the actual course of the route remains open to debate would seem to suggest that whilst the Romans improved some bits to leave their mark, for the most part they simply followed the existing ways. It started off easily enough along forest tracks below Carreg Alltrem. I remember climbing here and not particularly enjoying the evergreen plantation domination. Fortunately, there had been some recent harvesting of timber which had opened up views across what has been a rather tiresome valley. There is important Welsh history in this valley; it's hard to see though. Some rather basic looking rectangular ruins are almost unseen alongside the dead-end single-track road in the valley bottom. Dating back to the early 15th century, Penamnen Houses are believed to have been the seat of Maredudd ap Ieuan, Head of the Royal House of Cunedda, a house that once ruled across northern England and Scotland as far north as Pictland as well as the northern two thirds of Wales. He moved into this residence, from Castell Dolwyddelan, with several women and his 20 children. Today any historical palimpsest has been heavily cloaked by the plantations.

To exit the valley, it's necessary to leave the neat forest roads and make a steep push up a bridleway. On my visit, forestry work had devastated the line of exit. Fallen limbs created a tough obstacle course and time slipped away all too quickly as I inched my way up the mountainside. The track eventually deposited me on a featureless moor and, though the angle had relented, there was little to celebrate. I now had to cycle (admittedly mainly push) avoiding bog after bog across barren land with its failed drains and isolated young conifers. It's a strange path for the Sarn Helen cycle route to take; most of that route is on good cyclable tracks and lanes. This bit must be really challenging for anyone wishing to take a bike along those *traws – Cymru* Roman footsteps. On the other hand, it made perfect sense as the Conwy County boundary route. I actually followed the boundary almost perfectly across the moor and was soon upon more interesting ground.

Some see the disused quarries as an eyesore, but I like the industrial archaeology of such places. This is history and people not only worked on this moor, they also lived here. I pushed across to the visible slate tips and the invisible quarry holes of Cwt-y-bugail Quarry, named after a shepherd's hut. It really is a spectacular place; there are some enormous excavations, some incredible inclines and piles of waste, but more interestingly there's an old school, an old chapel and deserted, now ruined, homes. This is what the Americans would call a ghost village. I once met, on another day, a gentleman whose father had lived and worked in this area. It was fascinating listening to somebody with a familial connection to this now disused and abandoned place. The Cwt-y-Bugail quarry was well-connected to Blaenau Ffestiniog by the Rhiw-bach tramway, part of which I cycled along. Slate was extracted, on and off over the years, right up to the early 1970s. The name Cwt-y-Bugail has now been adopted by the still working Manod Quarry which I both heard and glimpsed as I passed through. The slate quarry theme continued at Rhiw-bach mine and quarry which I accessed via a steep incline. It's hoped that the Traws Eryri will officially pass this way someday instead of unofficially as it does now. If it does become official, then I trust the gate to access the site will be unlocked. This is another place to linger and explore; a large chimney draws the eye as do the elongated cutting sheds. I glanced into big quarry holes. In one, young willows clamoured together in the bottom, whilst in another the non-native sitka spruce had the upper hand. In a further hole, the last one on the left, I could see the gated entrance to the mine that's popular with outdoor groups.

I rode down the track towards Cwm Penmachno. It's a fast steep ride, blocked by one locked gate which was kindly held open for me by the local shepherd. Easily beating him to the bottom of the hill, I was so far ahead I had to unceremoniously climb the gate at the bottom. This is a former quarry track, good to ride a bike on (but not classified as a bridleway) yet progress is hampered by the barriers of arbitrary officialdom. We really do need to do better with access in Wales, supposedly one of the 'homes' of mountain biking!

I was losing count of the hills I'd ascended on that day and the next one was another biggy. It's a well-graded minor road that leads quietly up Cwm Hafodyredwydd to Fynnon Eidda and slow and steady wheeling made the journey pass nicely. It's a lovely place to ride and the angle is just right for a steady ascent. I was tired, the day was drawing towards a close and I was starting to think about where to stop. Low cloud smothered damp hillsides, but nevertheless I thought that Llyn Conwy, the source of the Afon Conwy, might make an apt destination to end the first day of the Conwy County boundary challenge. A good track led me there. It's a grand and remote spot (if you're fond of bleak that is) taking me right back to the south Pennine reservoirs of home. Unfortunately, there is not a particularly good spot to camp. I'm not sure why there should be, but I sort of expected one on the shores of the llyn. It took a while of scraping around to find the most level bit of ground that was bearably dry to spend that misty night.

So far, I was quite pleased at how well I had been able to stick to the actual county boundary. I hadn't crossed over into Gwynedd at all and the tracks had kept me just on the right side of the border. There was no way that I'd be crossing over the Mignant though, a featureless, trackless blot of land if ever there was one. From Llyn Conwy therefore, it was a fast roll down the untroubled lane to Ysbyty Ifan. This can be quite a busy road at weekends but on that particular day I thankfully didn't see any vehicles at all. Ysbyty Ifan is a National Trust village, part of a large estate that was passed to the Trust in lieu of death duties. It's a pretty little spot but don't come here expecting to find a hospital (ysbyty is Welsh for hospital), in-fact there are no services at all! The name comes from long ago when the Knights of St. John set up a hospital and hostel for travelling pilgrims. It's a nice place to sit and look at the pretty cottages and flowing river. I rode across, past a field of curlew and rabbit, to the wonderfully named Cerrigellgwm Isaf, not to be confused with the nearby Cerrigellgwm Uchaf, which sits below Cefn Gerrigellgwm! I'd passed this way before, and I was pleased to be able to say hello to the farmer and pass the time of day. A fine track led south-east from here round the little summit of Foel Frech. It was great off-road riding, but a tough climb up a stoney track that defeated me on that day. *Pob lwc* to you if you give that one a go.

It's a fab fast descent into Cwm Penanner. This is a quiet, untravelled cwm with a remote feel, populated by an isolated and dispersed farming community. It feels like you are surrounded on all sides by hills. I couldn't help but feel like a spider trapped in a basin, with no clear exit. Strangely, the roads and tracks don't follow the water course, the Afon Ceirw, but instead they leap over hills either side. This is a good place to be on a bike though and I continued south right on the county border before turning east and cycling for, well, not very far at all. Soft mud, like soft sand had before, stopped me dead in my tracks. Although the ground was level, I couldn't pedal. The track to Llechwedd-Figyn is marked on the map as an 'other route with public access'. I'd come across these before, some are drivable, some are not passable, this one was barely walkable, so a long push ensued, disappointing and tiring. I was a bit down at this point and I think that's what led me to cheat. I blamed it on being tired after a damp, windy, cold night. I blamed the appalling state of some of the off-road travel I had encountered. I blamed the deserted valley that I'd left behind, but really it was just me, weak in the legs and lacking spirit. I cut the corner off my proposed route and headed straight to the shop in Cerrigydrudion. At the time I justified my decision thinking that I'd be back fitter and stronger to do the route again, what I didn't know then was that the route was so tough there was very little chance of me ever returning to it. I cast my glove for you.

I cycled like a mad thing along the awful B5105 feeling like a bird on an airport runway. I could have avoided this, but I hadn't, and it was my fault I was jousting with the local farming youth in their American style pick-ups.

I sheltered from the rain in the bus stop in Llanfihangel Glyn Myfyr; I love wooden bus shelters and I'd used similar before. As I ate some lunch, I stewed a little in my mood. I was relieved that I'd soon turn off into the Clocaenog Forest. Forest tracks, dreary conifers and towering wind turbines were much more appealing than the bloody B5105. Fresh from cutting a corner before lunch, deep in the forest I strayed into Denbighshire. I don't think anyone saw me, but I pursued the easy way rather than a pedantic down and back up just to stay in county. I had wanted to stick rigidly within Conwy County, but as close to the border as possible. I knew I would have to compromise somewhere but I was surprised how disappointed I was when I actually did. One regression was down to me being weak, the other to topography – the bloody minded would have tried harder.

My conscience was cleansed by a fine downhill run to the dam of Llyn Brenig (all within Conwy!). The dam itself is large and open to the elements, and on a windy day it feels even bigger that it obviously is. Llyn Brenig is a tremendous piece of water, populated by fishermen, sailing boats and the odd osprey. There's a decent café, but I felt I needed to keep moving. All ideas about how far it's possible to travel in a day when bikepacking were being destroyed. There were just too many hills. Easy going along Llyn Alwen and a neat bridleway took me across to Llyn Aled. I can't quite believe that this small, damned lake is as dangerous as the signage might suggest, but I refrained from *nofio, deifio* and *foddi*. There was no thin ice, dangerous objects remained submerged, and there was no evidence of blue/green – or any other colour of algae for that matter. I simply rode my bike into the oncoming path of any local good time Bo and Luke.

Actually, I didn't ride my bike for very long at all; I pushed it for 3 ½ kilometres past Moel Bengam. I was shrouded in low cloud again and it was tough going. Tussock grass and bog conspired under wheel and foot to snare me. I dithered between gorse, heather and bracken patches looking for a dry way through. I was pushing for nearly two hours. It was painful, but somehow, I settled into the adversity and daftness of it and actually quite enjoyed myself. It would, of course, be nice if you could look at a map, see a bridleway and know that you could go and ride your bike along it. Imagine looking at a map and seeing a road, but on getting there finding out that you had to push the car, or it was simply impassable. This is just another example of how we are letting walkers, cyclists and horse riders down.

Exit from the moor came by a remote scrapyard and a lonely lane. It was drawing close to dark now and I needed to find a camp. Something always turns up, but you need to be canny on occasions. I don't need much space for my little tent but finding a flat, dry, private spot was getting trickier and trickier. Finally, I had to sacrifice one of the three, or I'd have been into farmed and habited land. I managed to tuck in, away from cultivated fields, out of sight and out of the way. It was however, on wet ground.

East Conwy has much more fertile land than west Conwy and every scrap of it is farmed. This means that over the years any tracks have been tarmacked and claimed as roads; bridleways are, therefore, few and far between. I found one, but it was impassable. Interestingly I reported to the council how overgrown it was and just over a year later I received an email telling me it had been cleared. I will return but haven't quite got round to it yet.

They are good lanes though. Despite living not far away from here this was all new ground to me. I was able to stay within Conwy and follow barely used highways though pleasant countryside and past delightful houses. I was heading north now, to the coast. Mynedd y Gaer was pleasant, as was passing Plas-Uchaf reservoir whilst crossing the Afon Elwy was quite spectacular. A stubborn hill on the north bank of the river lifted me to within sight of the sea and before long I was in the pretty little seaside village of Towyn. Rows of homogenous concrete buildings lined the busy through road whilst tracksuit clad visitors filled the pavements. The place smelt of chips rather than fish, the murals were advertisements for pies or KFC, the amusement arcade jostled with cheap burger and hot dog venders. It might be the dream holiday destination for some, but for me it was a place to pass through quickly. A bacon butty did manage to detain me for a little while though.

I turned left and followed the traffic-free north Wales coast cycleway west to Llandudno. This is such a useful route and, given it ran along the very edge of my county, it was just the job on the day. I ignored its brutal architecture, its litter and dog poo. I ignored the ridiculous signs warning of the dangers of scrambling on the sea defences. I just rode my bike. I was tired and I had a plan.

Knackered as I was, I had come to realise that the route would not be completed in three days, as I'd originally hoped. Four would be required. It's about 145 miles all told, so it should be possible in three days, but my goodness it's a tough one. There are just so many hills to climb, always more hills to climb. I was out of time, out of energy and my desire was now outweighed by a *hiraeth*. I wanted to go home.

Fortunately, it was easy riding along the coast past Old Colwyn, Colwyn Bay and Rhos on Sea. There was a detour inland just after Rhos which took me over the Little Orme and down into Llandudno, still all on traffic free trails. I knew there was a train down the Conwy Valley to my home at half past three and it would be free for me with my older person's bus pass! I actually felt a little guilty arriving at the station early. I needn't have worried, the heavens opened, and some torrential, quite spectacular rain made me very pleased to be under the railway station roof.

The Conwy Valley line is a single-track line, and trains are infrequent. The trains themselves are lovely and new, but only have two bike spaces. To be fair the conductors seem pretty chilled if there are a couple of extra bikes, but it'd be tricky to book for a group. On several occasions, I've been the only person on the train and it's a handy way of leaving home and cycling back or cycling out on a one-way route then getting the train back. I have seen the train half-full on occasions and whilst it might get more use in the summer, I can't help thinking the line might get more use as a cycle track. Still, on this day, it was nice have an easy run down the valley to take me back home for a good meal and my lovely bed.

It was a month or so later when I managed to get a lift to Llandudno to recommence my Conwy County Boundary Challenge. From Llandudno it's tougher than you might think riding around the Great Orme, it always seems so to me anyway. It's tarmac and uphill. The views though, are pretty spectacular. The road is hemmed in by steep limestone cliffs below and above with far reaching sea views to the north. To the west are nearly two hundred wind turbines and to the east is Ynys Mon and the rest of the north coast.

I followed the north coast cycleway as far as Llanfairfechan where I climbed up to the old Roman road through Bwlch y Ddeufaen. It's an interesting route for many reasons. Whilst it follows the A55 trunk route it keeps itself apart quite nicely. Conwy is always worth a visit and there are big beach views all the way along to Penmaenmawr. There's a great bit where it follows the old road around the cliff edge, on the outside of the modern road tunnel: smart work. To exit Penmaenmawr the road builders have had to work hard to keep the cycle track separate and use the old route where possible They have invested significantly in concrete works, and I was led beautifully above the modern road on to the most peaceful old track. It's really quite good fun. You could also shelter under the road bridge if it was raining!

I wove my way through the village of Llanfairfechan to a steep, slick-rock track up on to the open hillside where grassy riding sped me forth towards the Roman road. It was grand riding on tracks of old, weaving through patches of gorse decorated with sheeps' wool. As I met the Roman road I spent some time, as I always do when I pass by here, looking for the Roman board game. Somewhere, on one of these stones, is one that's incised with the ancient Nine Man's Morris game. I've yet to find it, one day someone will lead me to it, but until then I keep looking, The Roman road is a fine gravel double track which led me on past cairns, standing stones and electricity pylons.

A high-speed dash took me down (though not without an uphill sting in the tail) to Pen y Gaer hill fort. From here the going got cheeky.

At first, I followed an 'other route with public access'. In practice, it's a double track gravel road, unfortunately blocked by a locked gate where the public right of way ceases. The track however continues with no change in its character. I climbed over the gate and continued down the track to a leat which feeds water into the Dolgarrog hydro power station. The leat makes for great cycling. It's well-surfaced and level. Unfortunately, it's punctuated with locked gates. Still, it passes amiably enough until a good track leads to a lane. Just below Coedty Reservoir is a gravel track which took me home. It's not on the map, but it leads through lovely country to Cowlyd Reservoir and back to where my route had started. I finished with a fast blast back down to Nant Conwy.

I'm sure others will complete the Conwy Country Boundary challenge in faster times, but for me it was a tough route. There was nearly 5,000 metres of climbing over 232 kilometres or 145 miles and over half of it off-road. I know that should make it a three-day route, but Welsh miles are hard and the constant up and down is pretty taxing. It does deliver a wonderful smorgasbord of scenery from high tops and moorland, native and planted woodland, to farmland and coast. Perhaps instead of thinking about how fast it could be done, I should slow down and take a week!

I should also mention that this was another solo undertaking. I'd got the hang of using maps on my phone and planning routes. My bike was on the way to being reliable. Although there were more adjustments and part exchanges ahead, I was beginning to trust it not to let me down.

Ysbyty Ifan

7: **Chylchdaith Rhinogydd**

The Rhinog Round

A ride around the Rhinogydd looked like an interesting thing to do and the following factors colluded to tempt me in the creation of a circuit,

- I'd never done the Pont Scethin mountain bike round.
- I'd spotted an interesting looking route between Rhobell Fawr and Dduallt.
- I fancied including the Bryn Cader Faner monument into a bikepacking route.
- There seemed to be a linking leat on the northern edge of Llyn Trawsfynydd.

Such is the way new routes come together, though to call them new is probably a bit presumptuous. I try to link bits of routes that I know have been done before and I know are cycleable. Sometimes however, you just have to go and have a look. This is how the classic bikepacking rounds are drawn together.

I left the Trawsfynydd Lakeside café on a grey dank March morning. It's a great café, when open, but like so many others they are struggling for staff and making ends meet is not easy. Poor opening hours lead to a declining clientele as you're never sure as to whether or not the cafe will be open. It precludes using it as a meet up point and, on this day, I didn't even rely on it for breakfast. I parked a little further down the lane. The place is pretty quiet, so I had no worries about leaving my car. Pretty quiet that is, apart from the ginormous nuclear power station that casts a long shadow over the northern end of Llyn Trawsfynydd.

I think our relationship with nuclear power is warming, if that's not a scary expression to use. But this is one of the original power stations built in the 1960s. It won awards for its architects due to its perceived resemblance to a traditional Welsh castle. I can vouch for this. I was out on a misty day in the Moelwynion once, leading a walking group, when a youngster in the group took my elbow and pointed. "Look", she said, "look at that beautiful big castle down there with the clouds around it." I didn't have the heart to tell her it was a nuclear power station. As you get closer to it though the concrete monstrosity reveals itself in its full defamation. It is an incredible feat of human ingenuity, but the construction is, audaciously, in the middle of a National Park. Looks can be deceiving though. The land around and adjacent to the power station has not been farmed since it was built. I followed the most delightful lakeside cycleway through native woodland. The place was alive with birds, the leaves on the trees were beginning to open and the odd spring bulb was poking through the ground below them. There's an informative visitor display in a shelter part way along the shore and from there I dropped down to an incredible dam. The lake has been dammed for longer than the nuclear power station has been here, as further downstream there is a hydroelectric power station. The outflow itself goes through some remarkably unspoilt native woodland which is actually temperate rainforest, known in these parts as Celtic rainforest. This northern end of Llyn Trawsfynydd is a wonderful spot for walking and cycling. I went past my turn off, discreet as it was, and had to stop and resist the allure of the lakeside cycleway. The leat took me west across the northern side of the Rhinogydd and was cycleable for most of the way, in a mountain bike sort of way. There was a boggy bit and a little bit of pushing but then I came upon the most gorgeous ruins. I don't think I took the best route here, but I could see where the better route might be, slightly to the north, for my next visit: I already knew this was a journey that I would be repeating.

It's unusual to come across old, apparently disused barns with their roofs mostly intact. Sadly, there were signs of disrespect in one of these and a litter pick would need to be organised for another day. Still, it was nice to linger here, out of the drizzle for a bit. The old farmhouse is called Nant Pasgan -Mawr. It's a grade 2 listed, 16th Century, cruck frame, stone- built dwelling for domestic purposes. As such it represents a time in history when construction shifted from wood to stone. It was also during this period when open halls were replaced with internal floors to create upper storeys. Whatever its architectural significance, it's a marvellous spot to sit and ponder this lovely quiet corner of the Rhinogydd.

I pushed my bike up a steep, rough, but evidently ancient bridleway. At the top, there was a ruin which gave a nice windbreak for lunchtime. The following year I was here again with Graham and Richard and as we sat in this very same spot a dash of white caught our eye. A stoat in full winter plumage was hunting just across the hill from where we sat. It stood out so clearly against the March greyness as it darted in and out of every crevice hunting for food, it seemed like a speeded-up life, a hint of desperation about its pace. We saw it, then it disappeared, this was repeated several times until it vanished for good, seemingly into thin air. I really enjoy little wildlife sightings like this, but they are all too infrequent.

A little further up the hill, as the track levelled out, I turned right. The bridleway itself carried on to the east where seemingly in the middle of nowhere, (but actually at a Parish boundary) it transforms into a footpath. The turn I took to the right is also marked on the map as a footpath. On the ground however it's clearly a well-established (if largely disused) double track, an old highway. I had no qualms about following it on my bike. The laws around rights of way are pretty vague and arbitrary. In 1949 each council was asked by Government to decide which routes within its parish should become a bridleway and which should become a footpath. The lack of oversight is well illustrated in this vicinity. The track I followed crosses the northern Rhinogydd linking old settlements and hut circles with my intended destination: Bryn Cader Faner. I refuse to believe this track, with such a long history, was not used regularly by horses at some time in the past. This is yet another example of a need to tidy up our rights of way and other access laws.

Bryn Cader Faner is a stone circle with a difference. All its stones lean outwards and that looks deliberate. It's described as a Bronze Age cairn-circle, and it has been excavated in its centre leaving a depression. This ancient monument was, incredibly with hindsight, used for artillery target practice during the Second World War. Somehow, it has survived the disrespect shown it and today we see a rather graceful monument. This is also a reminder that many ancient ways passed across higher ground as the valleys would have been boggy or densely wooded and unfavourable for travel. This track, passing Bryn Cader Fanner, was once the main thoroughfare hereabouts. I had no hesitation riding my bike this way.

The double track south, probably used by the military with vehicles in the Second World War (and certainly used by modern farming vehicles), is a joy to ride on a bike, despite remaining as a footpath on the map. I rode and pushed a bit to the south of Moel Goedog. At one point, screaming downhill, my front wheel sunk into a bog. I'd spotted it too late. As the momentum of my bike was abruptly halted, the momentum of my body continued and I soared over the handlebars for a fortunately soft landing in said bog. No harm done, except for a broken phone holder.

I was tempted to keep on footpaths to the south, but common sense prevailed, and good double tracks took me to a minor road. There was a long tarmac section now, but it was deserted and took me through some lovely places. Gerddi Bluog is a significant and quite lovely building. Once a farmhouse it was the home of Edward Prys who translated the psalms into Welsh. Later William Clough Ellis, of Portmeirion fame, extended and modernised the building, losing some of its original character, but adding his own distinctive imprint. At one time it nearly became a Youth Hostel, but today it sits looking rather forlorn and unloved. It's not a place for the cyclist to stop though. I was going too fast, and it was only a glance over the shoulder, followed by some harsh braking, which allowed me to notice it at all, such is the hill upon which it sits.

Coed Crafnant hosts remnant Celtic rainforest, and it's a place I've enjoyed several times since this visit. There's definitely a distinctive feel to the air here. It's one of those places that's actually best visited on a wet day, and this early spring day was perfect. Moss and lichen-topped walls lined the single-track lane down which I wheeled. Zero traffic allowed my head to rotate and take in the rainforest ambience through which I gently flowed.

Beyond Coed Crafnant I entered Cwmnantcol, then climbed up to a departure from the tarmacked lanes onto abused and rough tracks which led me towards Pont Scethin. It's a lovely, weathered, hump-backed, packhorse bridge built from local stone. The parapets widen either side to funnel animals in and across the surface setts. The bridge enhances the landscape hereabouts. It was built to support an old Drover's route from Harlech to London and I wondered why we don't hear more about Drovers. Cowboy images and the romance of their world are part and parcel of our modern media. Drovers in Britain were actually around longer and played important roles in the development of trade, banking and the opening up of highways. We should pay more attention to the history of droving.

Unfortunately, around the bridge is a rutted quagmire – the mess has been created by recreational motor vehicles. I arrived in damp weather and the whole area around the bridge was unrideable on a bike. I strutted from rut to rut, lugging my bike and cursing the ignorance and arrogance of engine-powered visitors to this once extraordinary spot. I could have camped here but I used my anger to propel me up the steep hill beyond the bridge. A good honest push to the ridge above.

Fortunately, my smile returned as I crested the hill and saw the way ahead. The descent of Braich is classic wild mountain biking and I loved it. There were decisions to make about which track to use, confidence was required about speed and momentum, and I had to keep looking ahead. This was not a trail centre manicured track, this was real mountain biking, and I couldn't be quite sure what lay ahead. The cloud was low so my view was restricted, but I could see far enough to make good progress. That is, until I came to a gate which I needed to pass through that happened to be occupied. A sheep had somehow got its head stuck between the gate post and the wall. In the manner of removing a stubborn climbing nut from a crack. I wrestled with the sheep's head, rotating it this way and that. The premise with climbing gear is that if it moves, it must come out; the rule should have been the same here, but I failed to release the sheep from its self-imposed imprisonment. Knowing that the nearest farm was past my anticipated right turn, I rolled on down the hill. I went further down that track than I really would have liked to report the stuck sheep. The farmer was grateful, but no more than that, and I had to turn and cycle uphill again to rejoin my route.

It was close to dark now and no idyllic campsite presented itself. I tucked in behind a wall on damp ground, glad to be out of the wind, and settled in for a long lie down.

In the morning, I rode on along flagged tracks, hemmed in by crumbling old drystone walls. As with the earlier tracks of the day before, this was probably the main route along this valley, before the bottoms were opened up. It connected ruins and isolated homesteads. The track was a good track and gave me a fast descent to Barmouth.

Stopping in Barmouth wasn't necessary as I didn't need supplies, but I did enjoy some shelter from the rain before crossing the Barmouth Bridge. This 820 metre long bridge, opened in 1867, is the longest wooden viaduct in use in Wales. It's a pretty spectacular construction that cuts off a massive detour inland. The bridge has a railway line over it and a cycle track alongside that's shared with pedestrians and, bizarrely, motorbikes! Recently renovated it's a highlight of this route. It's something special to experience and it makes the journey from Barmouth to the Fairbourne area quicker by bike than car and it isn't often you can say that.

The bridge led me on to the Mawddach trail. This is one of the oldest cycle paths built on a former rail bed. It is a well-known and rightly popular route from Barmouth to Dolgellau and that's where I was heading. The track is as good as level, lined with trees on one side and the tidal estuary on the other. It's a relaxing place to ride and the cyclist can take some time to look around and enjoy the place. As you ride, you are watched over by swans, oystercatchers, mallards and the odd little egret from the left; then on the right it'll be robins, blackbirds, wren and the odd crow keeping an eye out for you. I love this trail.

On a previous occasion Richard and I were passing this way on a round Cader Idris trip when we bumped into a chatty old bloke. He sticks in the mind for his obsession with the French. Brexit was all their fault! He really gave them a roasting about the way they treated the British and the evil plots they were up to. Richard and I countered a little, but we were on a hiding to nothing. We seem to live in a world where you can choose your own truth. As I write this a year or two on, the UK seems a poorer place, culturally and economically, for that misguided decision. I'm glad we can still escape to the Mawddach Trail.

Dolgellau was quiet. A band of pigeons patrolled the streets while a host of sparrows bickered in a hedge. A cat sat nearby waiting its chance whilst a dog owner picked up his pooch's poo in a plastic bag. The streets were pinched in by tall grey buildings that overshadowed me. The pavements were narrow, and this made it a tricky place for bikepackers. On previous visits I'd tried a couple of cafés and one, which had a garden that made it more accessible with the bike, was poor and was now closed anyway. Another one required an unsatisfactory pavement perch for the bike in order to lend them some trade. Disappointed, I went to the Co-op for lunch, unable to easily support a local business. At least the trolley park provided shelter whilst I ate. (On future visits I discovered that there are two excellent bakeries here).

From Dolgellau I steadily climbed, on quiet lanes, to Llanfachreth, where I picked up some lovely bridleways. One was marred by ladder styles (which naturally I later reported to the council), but this didn't detract from the enchanting natural regeneration that was taking place here, bushy bilberry, rambling roses and juvenile birch jostled for position on the uphill side of the track. Heading north now, I followed a steep lane – just steep enough to gain height nicely, but not too steep to justify getting off and walking! The lane was packed with interest and took me past interesting houses, flower filled verges, crows in trees, a disused quarry, a scruffy wood, some ace sheepfolds, a landslide and views across to the Arans. Finally, I arrived at the *bwlch* between Rhobell Fawr and Dduallt. Sadly, this spot is rather buried in a conifer plantation. I'd been here before on foot and knew that the way here from Dduallt required a jungle bash. This time I wouldn't leave the track. What I did do though, was slip down a bridleway towards the upper Mawddach and it was another smashing piece of original Welsh mountain biking. The valley I descended into was deserted. No one lives here now and few visit. A farmer in an old van stopped and got out. He needed a chat. He was a young farmer keen to promote his elsewhere campsite. We talked for a while about his van, how he came to farm this land, the future of farm payments and how it was sad to see such wonderful properties abandoned to the elements. (I didn't say it, but unloved properties, in a place like that would make fantastic holiday homes without impacting on local people adversely.)

I freewheeled down the valley and entered Coed y Brenin. This is a famous centre for mountain biking. It contains the UK's first purpose-built trails; a visionary project, which brought cash toting visitors to a forgotten corner of Eryri. It goes without saying that the trails are brilliant. Overall though, the woods remain quiet, and I snuck in the back way near the utilitarian architecture of a community centre with no obvious community. Some forest tracks and a dirty bridleway took me past a renovation project down to the riverbank. A gorgeous, wooded trail slipped through the wood to an ungainly meeting with trail centre waymarkers. It felt odd to have arrived on the manicured trials. Unforgivably they didn't go the right way for me, but we did share a couple of bridges, firstly a stone one, then one cast in metal. Captivating gorges, admirable pools and boisterous waterfalls all clamoured for attention. A disused and secured gold mine was close by whilst other industrial relics provided haunts for bats, but also disagreeable firepits and plastic waste. Such is the human imprint of today.

I had a big hill to climb and needed to find a place to camp. There's something about the National Cycle Network (NCN) routes that makes me imagine they'll be easy to pedal along. The NCN route 82 seemed like the best way ahead. I suppose it was, but it was a flipping big hill to climb at the end of the day. There was little promise of a flat, discreet camping spot and before I knew I was back on a tarmac road.

Luckily, I managed to sneak into some woods by a ruined *hafod* where a decent bit of grass gave me a fine, flat and clandestine campsite. And really, that was it. One downhill, one uphill and one more downhill led me back to my car near the power station.

This is a good route to do over three days: a tough route to do over two.

The following year I returned, as I said earlier, with Graham and Richard. It seemed further with the two old blokes in tow, and conversational rests were required frequently. We enjoyed hotel bargains in Llanbedr and Dolgellau though, making the Rhinog Round or Cylchdaith Rhinogydd a circuit for all seasons and for all ages. I was pleased that my route prospecting had worked out so well.

8: The Highland Trail 550 – Part one, northbound

The ground beneath my feet is wet, with every other step I slip backwards. I look for stones to stand on to increase my purchase. The muddy track rises before me and reaches up into the cloud. Horizontal rain is whipping me from behind while the wind tears at my hood and buffets my thighs. The bike feels heavy as its large tyres stick in the gloop below. All I can do is plod on, there is no incentive to stop, nothing to even pause for. I push on, upwards, deeper into the clouds…

My relationship with Scotland has changed. I used to love visiting in the winter to go climbing. I roamed far and wide, the remoter the better, though always returning to 'the Ben' (Ben Nevis). I enjoyed moving on snow, ice and frozen turf. I relished the winter hot aches, camaraderie, long walks and dark mornings. Some of my best days in the hills were those Scottish winter days. Rock climbing was harder. The necessity to commit to a time and then travel a long way restricted flexibility. A few good days would get the pulse racing then it'd all be terminated by rain or, probably worse, midges. The climbs I 'won' in Scotland will be savoured for a long time.

I then tried sea kayaking and this really opened up Scotland in summer. A breeze to keep the midges away, well-behaved tides and reliably sheltered lochs and bays gave me, and still does, some great expeditioning around the islands and the west coast. If you like wild camping, then sea kayaking is the way to go. Pull up on a remote beach, search around for driftwood and you can have a low-impact fire below the high tide mark. In a sea kayak weight is less of a problem than on a bike so all sorts of real food and alcoholic goodies can be carried. A good day's paddling, then a campfire on a beach, watching the suns set with a 'wee dram' is a fine way to spend a day.

And then I went bikepacking in Scotland. The rain was unimportant, the access unrestricted and a right to camp responsibly have made Scotland a mecca for bikepacking. In the May between my two rounds of the Welsh 550 I decided to undertake the Highland Trail 550. Whilst Sally, my wife, was working hard I nipped off for a bit of a 'boys-own' adventure; she's very understanding.

The Highland Trail 550 is famous as a challenging race through the wilder parts of Scotland. Bikepacking race routes can provide good routes for more genteel bikepackers such as me, at times other than when the race is running. The route was mapped by Alan Goldsmith who also organises the race. Alan gladly sent me the latest GPX files in return for a donation to the John Muir Trust.

It's fair to confess that neither this trail nor the Welsh 550 trail are exactly 550 miles long, both being *about* 550 miles long, but 550 rolls off the tongue rather nicely, even if most people think you mean the NC 500 (of which the least said the better). I had three weeks put aside to make the journey and I'd need most of that if I were to complete the entire route, especially as I was starting in Glasgow rather than Tyndrum.

Thankfully, with a little help from Sally, I caught the train from Warrington to Glasgow. It was a funny feeling heading north, staring out of the window and too excited to read my book. I was apprehensive about what lay ahead. Changing trains in Carlisle was as ever, a bit stressful. I followed the crowds, all the time seeking confirmation from digital display boards above. I was pushing a heavily laden extra-large bike, so it would have been unseemly to dodge in and out of the crowds. I tried to stroll like a seasoned traveller, but inside I was churning, trying to quash the irrational fear that the train would leave without me. I embarked by a door with a picture of a bike above it, not really looking any further than the door. I was in a hurry and looked around the crowded carriage for a hook for my bike. Full. They were all full. I started to panic, but another cyclist calmly pointed to the next carriage which had the required hooks and space on them. I had boarded the same carriage as a cycling group, whilst the next cycle-friendly carriage was almost empty! I disembarked, hoping the train wouldn't scurry away while I swapped carriages, then boarded again. I had hooks to choose from, which was just as well as my bike is significantly larger than a typical road bike and needs a bit of extra space to accommodate its girth.

I knew the train from Glasgow to Tyndrum (and the start of the Highland 550), was not running due to engineering works. I didn't mind really because I'd quite fancied doing another trail. The An Turas Mor, now part of Cycling UK's Great North Trail, heads north from Glasgow up the centre of Scotland heading for Cape Wrath (it covers similar ground to another famous bikepacking route The Badger Divide). I thought this would make a good start to my Scottish exploration as it joined the Highland 550 near Loch Lyon.

Arrival in Glasgow was all a bit overwhelming.

Everyone else seems to know where they are going. I battle with my bike, off hooks, through narrow doors and into the speedy platform crowd. I enter the sprawling concourse but fail to exit the station. Hundreds, nay thousands, of people mill around each and every one of them knowing this patch better than me. Finally, I latch on to an exit sign and leave the station behind. I have no idea where I am or which way to turn. I pull my phone out, just to see whether it's left or right. I push my bike along crowded pavements heading to the riverside cycleway. I'm too scared to ride on the road. I find peace on the banks of the Clyde.

National Cycle Network trail 756 led me, via quiet backstreets, to Kelvingrove Park. The park required careful, slow, bell-ringing riding. I had to weave around scores of pedestrians out enjoying this green heart of Glasgow. Here began the An Turas Trail (The Long Journey when translated from Gaelic), a bikepacking route that has been worked out from Glasgow to Cape Wrath. The Highland 550 shares much ground with it as it heads north. The occasional pink ATM sticker showed me the way to go along the delightfully tree-lined, bluebell-adorned, Kelvinside Greenway. A surprisingly lovely manner in which to be leaving this large urban conurbation. People were friendly. If I paused for just a second to check the way ahead, somebody would say hello and ask where I was from, where I was going and did I need any help. The pedestrians of Glasgow welcomed me to Scotland.

Further north on the edge of the city the pleasant greenway, now bordered by fields, was rudely interrupted by a road; the A879. My information suggested that I should follow this road north to avoid an overgrown section of the riverbank trail. Well, overgrown comes and goes. As soon as I encountered this road, I knew pushing through riverside undergrowth would be better than cycling along its unwelcoming tarmac. The road was fast, narrow and busy with blind bends either side of my crossing point. To avoid it, I needed to cross.

Each car appears as if from nowhere at speed. Each driver's eyes are fixed straight ahead. Not one car slows as the road narrows for the bridge over the river. Each driver is in their own space, the car an extension of their homely castle, the ground beneath it theirs as they pass over. A family huddle on the far side of the road, their visibility no better than mine. We wait patiently for a half gap then leg it at speed across the road in opposite directions. We have no chance to chat and share our stories. We dive into bushes at the side of the road and exchange glances of relief.

I was rewarded by my way ahead not being overgrown at all and the riverside track was more than agreeable all the way to Milngavie.

In Milngavie there are all kinds of seductive services: bakers, takeaways and supermarkets. The place smells of food. There are benches to sit on and this is a place that wants you to linger. However, I needed to keep going north. Having arrived in Glasgow on the train at 3:00 pm I wanted to put as much distance between me and the city as I could. So, at Milngavie, I jumped onto the West Highland Way and pedalled north. There were of course, walkers, both local dog walkers, and visitors from afar along the West Highland Way. I was pleased to have a bell on my handlebars. I passed a few, then, just out of sight of any of them, I took my first fall of the trip. A gate stubbornly resisted my attempt to push it open and, with my bike in one hand the unyielding gate in the other, my balance faltered and over I went. Fortunately, no harm was done, and I managed to recover before the quickest of walkers could catch up and see me.

The way ahead was on a modern, multi-use track and I made haste north towards Drymen. As I rode through the meadows by Craigallain Loch, I passed couples wandering along, hand in hand, as if the height of summer were already upon us. Then, passing the spectacularly round hill of Dumgoyach, the scrub land around my highway opened up to allow me the first tempting views north towards the Highlands. The view was encouraging and gave me a little teaser of what lay ahead. I stuck with the West Highland Way; it took me along the valley of Blane Water where a rail bed multi-use track hastened my progress even further. From Drymen, where the eponymous Inn afforded me a fine dinner and a lovely pint (or two), I took the Rob Roy Way north, along which I was able to find a neat little campsite. It was out of sight of habitation, but on tidy sheep-cropped grass near some sort of waterworks feature. This was my first night in Scotland and I was happy to follow the Scottish Access Code and exercise my right to camp respectfully. On the morning of day two, plantation riding took me to Aberfoyle.

There's a brilliant bike shop in Aberfoyle. Not only is the owner friendly and helpful, but he also sells great coffee and bacon sandwiches. The proprietor kindly took a little time to fiddle with my brakes which had been catching and were slowing me down a little. Meanwhile, I munched casually on my second breakfast having no idea how to adjust the brakes myself.

The Queen Elizabeth Forest Park, in which Aberfoyle sits, is popular cycling country and that tends to mean that the trails are good and well-marked. I passed Loch Drunkie (and couldn't help a little chuckle at its name), then followed forest tracks down to Loch Venacher. The road alongside Loch Venacher had the most wonderful signpost suggesting that this was a 'walking and cycling friendly road'. A fast cycleway along a disused rail bed sped me north to Killin then spilled me out into the deer filled Glen Lochay. I was on my way. After another legal wild camp along the Allt Lairig nan Lunn, I joined the actual Highland 550 at Loch Lyon. To celebrate, I waited an hour for the Bridge of Balgie café to open. I was determined not to be in a rush, and it was raining so the shelter was welcome. Café time came and went, as did freshly baked scones and the small bit of cash I was carrying. Then I struck out north again.

I was pushing my bike up the hill in the Lairig Ghallabhaich when I heard a very pleasant and gentle English accent bidding me, "Good morning". A young bikepacker slowed down and cycled alongside me, passing the time of day in a well-mannered fashion. It was very pleasant to chat with someone else, someone doing the Highland 550. Hettie's plan, along with her friend who was following, was to do the route in nine days. We wished each other good luck and she pedalled away from me, up the hill, making it look very easy. I continued to walk. Her friend now caught up. With prior knowledge of her name, it was nice to be able to greet Katie as though I already knew her. She too, chatted pleasantly then cycled on, up the hill, as though it were flat. I knew my place and I carried on walking. I actually quite like to walk a bit now and then. Honest!

It was a pleasant surprise when I caught up with them a little later having some lunch and adjusting their bikes. In the lee of trees, they'd grabbed some shelter from the inclement weather to attend to their chores. We exchanged greetings again, but I didn't hang around as they clearly had more mechanical skills than I could offer and I continued on my way, safe in the knowledge they would pass me again quite soon. They did; and I watched them ease over the horizon pedalling effortlessly.

Scotland is the home of hunting, shooting and fishing and there are hotels all over the glens. Often fading in their glory, but still there trying to make a living, trying to attract a few fishermen or stalkers and teasing bikepackers with their wares. It's actually possible to do the 'rufty-tufty' Highland Trail 550 and stay in some sort of accommodation every single night, if there isn't a hotel there'll be a bothy, and I slept in both on my Highland 550 journey. I did have to resist making enquiries about a bed in the Bridge of Gaur Guesthouse on the shores of Loch Rannoch though. Despite the rain, it was far too soon into my journey to be looking for such hospitality and I knew that a bothy, Ben Alder Cottage, was within reach.

It was nice to revisit the Ben Alder trails, traversed on my second bikepacking journey a few years prior with Graham, Nige and Matt. This time, from the ugly shooting lodge on the shore of Loch Ericht – with its bizarre metal deer-shaped target – I stuck on the shore side and followed the good track to the Ben Alder bothy. It was a good plan, but what I didn't know was that the track runs out before the bothy is reached. There was a proper mud-fest, bog push over the last kilometre or so to the bothy. It was all a bit yuk.

Ben Alder bothy provided a fine shelter for the night. It was already occupied by two young lads, Dan and Will, who were following The Badger Divide, from Inverness to Glasgow. We admired each other's bikes, compared notes on bikepacking bags and studied our various GPS gadgets. The lads were heading south. I warned them about the bog and we settled down for a long and peaceful night.

Cycling around Ben Alder, first north-west then north-east, is probably one of the highlights of the entire Highland 550. It really is good, single-track mountain biking, fast and flowy in a nicely remote setting. Since my previous visit, the drainage ditches had shrunk; now that I was on larger wheels I rode them easily.

I glance right to a patch of snow then look straight ahead at the single-track descent before me. I raise my backside and weight the pedals, light hands -heavy feet, and let the bike roll. It's not long before I'm feathering the brakes. The track is fast, firm and flowing. I cross a stream or two with care. I weave around boulders trying to disrupt the path. Barely a pedal stroke is required before I arrive, smiling at the Culra bothy.

The Culra bothy was closed due to asbestos in the roofing, but I did take a quick peek before wheeling across to Loch Pattack. Heading north, quiet tracks, muddy at first then coarsely gravelled, took me past a recently enlarged hydro-dam and then down to the mountain bike centre of Laggan Wolftracks. Disappointingly, the café was closed due to staff shortages, so I carried on past the Spey Dam Reservoir into the upper course of the river Spey by way of General Wade's Military Road. This is the General Wade referred to in the sixth verse of the UK national anthem. The verse acknowledges the General's road building works, centred on Ruthven Barracks near Kingussie, and his role in 'crushing the rebellious Scots'. This verse is rarely sung these days, particularly in Scotland!

Heading towards the Melgarve bothy I was hampered by horizontal rain and wind. I dashed from plantation to plantation and fell into the bothy. This is an ugly valley. Conifers in straight lines are separated by bare overgrazed rough pasture and it's all topped off with a set of pylons, bringing the electricity we all need from somewhere in the north to the sockets in our walls. Not in the bothy though. It was raining heavily, and the old building provided a welcome shelter. I like staying in bothies, but bothies need fires. A bothy without a fire is a slightly damp, dark and lifeless place, despite the shelter it offers. Retracing my journey I went to fetch wood from the nearest plantation where I scrabbled about collecting as much dry wood as I could find. Despite the heavy rain squalls that had accompanied me through the valley, the denseness of the forest had kept enough wood dry for me to gather. I returned to my spartan abode and lit a fire. It wasn't a big fire, and it wouldn't last long, but it changed the atmosphere completely. It was now a happy place to be. Two Badger Divide travellers, Sam and Angus, stepped in long enough to warm their cockles then, as the evening brightened, continued on their way. I settled in for the night and relaxed, saving my energy for tackling the notorious Correyairack pass in the morning.

The Correyairack Pass wasn't actually so bad. It was certainly a lot easier than its reputation as a tough climb had led me to believe. I cycled most of the way, (I know people who could cycle all the way). I was pleased that I only had to push, and it's a good track, for about fifteen minutes on the steepest bit. The summit came quite soon and I was riding again, passing an odd, old electricity board building and over the bealach. The track lay ahead like a golden carpet stretching away, inviting me to race down to Fort Augustus. I was only slowed by flooded streams across my path and a fifteen-minute diversion to inspect the Blackburn of Corrieyairck bothy. General Wade's finely graded military road gave me a lovely long and lenient descent. I flowed down at quite some pace, down, and down some more to the tourist hotspot at the foot of Loch Ness formerly known as Kiliwhimin. I'd always planned to take a rest day in Fort Augustus which actually turned into a rest afternoon and a rest day! I think it was needed but it felt a bit luxurious especially when you consider the Highland Trail racers aim to be here from Tyndrum in a day! The small town gave me fresh food and a wonderful bed and breakfast at Morag's Hostel. I also took on the haggis, neeps and tatties challenge. It was a meal fit for the end of a very long hill day, it was piled high and spilling off the plate; served by iron ladle rather than silver spoon! It might have been Morag herself who did my laundry, chatted pleasantly and understood my need to hog one of her best sofas for a day. I had a shopping list too:

- Plasters
- Bike bag
- Luggage strap
- Water bottle

- Malt loaf
- Lunch

I replaced the bag that sits below my crossbar (the zip had broken); I replaced a lost water bottle and a broken luggage strap. I pigged out on fresh fruit and lamented Scotland's lack of malt loaf. I sat for the rest of the day and read my downloaded book. It was a little lap of luxury amidst the general frugality of my Highland excursion, crowned by an excellent pizza in the Beaufort House that evening. Refreshed and restocked I continued north.

Forest tracks by Loch Ness took me to a comforting stop in the Glenrowan café near Invermoriston, where a freshly baked, melt-in-the-mouth white chocolate cookie was washed down with tasty cappuccino. I scooted down the A887, as quickly as possible, before struggling to squeeze around a locked gate which gave access to the Levishie Forest. Above the forest I entered a moorland zone that was a stale brown colour. It felt barren, dark and lifeless. I passed a windfarm; the repetitive, baritone-whoops of the turning turbines sounded extraterrestrial as I laboured past. On the shore of Loch ma Stac however, the landscape sprouted sudden life. Here there were common sandpiper, ringed plover and, as I lunched on a malt loaf (rare in Scotland), a wheatear sat down, right next to me. But best of all, I saw an otter. I'm used to seeing otters when sea kayaking, but inland sightings are much rarer for me, so its unmistakable size and shape really lit up my mood. It appeared from a heather-topped grough and sloped across the track a mere 40 or 50 metres ahead of me, then melted silently into the loch. I didn't see it again, but I know that that's the way with otters. The track actually runs out as you arrive at the loch and I had to cycle/push along its shore. Then, as you approach the other end of the loch, a three-storey ruin with rusty scaffolding appears. It's a very a strange place, a former shooting lodge I think, but what's going on with the rusty scaffolding is a mystery, for renovation has not progressed at all.

The descent to the impressive 4,000-year-old Corrimony Cairn was fast and easy. I spotted beautiful wood anemones blowing in the wind and the much rarer (especially in flower) cloudberry, a berry of the arctic. An abandoned 4x4 distracted me briefly too.

I arrived at the campsite in Cannich on Fish and Chip Friday. The fresh cooked traditional feast was served with joviality and was just what I needed. I camped by a picnic table, used the drying room and engaged in shallow conversations. A shower was nice too. In the morning after a longer-than-was-comfortable wait for a cooked breakfast, I cycled northeast on a quiet lane to Struy. I'm not sure why I feel the need to say quiet, the whole route had been quiet. From Glasgow to here, I'd met six other cyclists – the tracks, the glens and the hills were pretty much empty.

This was all the more poignant a couple of years after my passage when someone set fire to a large area of land above Corrimony. The so-called Corrimony wildfire devastated thousands of acres of rewilding land on an RSPB estate. I say so-called because fire in the British uplands does not start naturally, it is always down to human causes. Indeed, this fire did not start on the RSPB's Corrimony estate, but spread there from a nearby moor. In the succeeding years there have been no announcements on how the fire started or who started it. Yet, those who promote the burning of moorland vegetation for the sport of driven grouse shooting crow on about the need to manage wildfires by controlled burning, completely missing the point that if the moor was left to its own devices it would return to native, broad-leaved woodland. And wet, temperate woodlands do not burn. They do however have space for nature.

North of Struy is the 'track of a thousand puddles' to Orrin Reservoir and it certainly lived up to its colloquial moniker on my traverse. Always another puddle to pass through. If you were racing along the Highland Trail 550 then I guess you'd just plough through everything, you' be tough and rely on skin being waterproof. If like me, you are on holiday then getting wet is something to avoid. I either passed slowly through the puddles or tiptoed carefully around them I noticed a tempting ruin, below the track, called Tighachrochadair. It was apparently occupied into the 1990s despite never having piped water electricity or drains. Cooking was done on an open fire; I presume fuelled by peat. It might make a rough bothy today, but I suspect most, like me, will pass by on the way to the Orrin Dam, searching out drier ground.

The Orrin Dam is a large, slightly spooky, concrete edifice. It was made all the spookier by cronking ravens enjoying the sound of their own echo. On the northern side though, is a bit of ungrazed scrub and suddenly there were birds. For a few minutes I watched a whole family of stonechats, then from nowhere, a cuckoo appeared, landed on a telegraph wire, called its name a few times, then flew. You don't see them very often.

After a fine descent from the Orrin Dam, there's a rotten bit of main road to Contin. The A835 is a busy fast road with no space for rambling bikepackers. I got my head down and pedalled as fast as I could. I veered into laybys and chose the verge where it was rideable. Contin shop was a welcome stop and then lovely forest tracks led me to Loch Garve keeping this slow two-wheeled rambler well away from the fast, twisty main road. As I approached the A835 from Longart Forest ready to sprint across it, I chanced upon a rather unruly scene. Sleeping bags, tents and clothes were spread out on signs, on posts and on bushes. There were two bikes and, as it turned out, two people in a reclined pose. It was the bikepackers who'd passed me with such ease on ascent from the Bridge of Balgie. I didn't expect to see them here. Whilst I'd been resting, chatting and pootling along in my own good time, they'd done the whole of the northern section of the Highland 550. Sadly though, they were now waiting for a train (several trains actually) to take them back to their car in Tyndrum, a broken bike and a poorly foot had terminated their challenging ride.

It was beyond Loch Vaich, in as remote as place as you can be, when I met Clare Alldritt. Clare was out 'horsepacking' or dobineering as she calls it, with two horses. Both horses were chestnut, one taller than the other; the smaller one had a tremendous white blaze on its face, whilst the other sported an off-white star. The larger horse carried more load and Clare walked between them in a high vis vest wearing a Go-pro topped helmet. It was lovely to see and there really should be much more of this type of travel going on. We had a good chat and I marvelled at the research she has to do. No track can be taken 'on sight'. It's bad enough wrestling with kissing gates in deer fences when you are travelling by bike, but with two horses any locked gate, awkward gate or other impediment means you basically have to turn around and go back the way you came. I admired her spirit and wished her well. Look out for her book – From East to West by Saddle is Best – a fine tale of adventuring on horseback across Scotland.

Through a low pass and beyond Deanich Lodge, I arrived on the Alladale estate. This was a place I'd been looking forward to visiting. Alladale is one of the biggest, high profile rewilding projects in Scotland. It had made the news for good and bad reasons. Fears of limiting access, wild wolves and a land ruled by incomers had frightened some observers. As I neared the estate it became obvious that different forces were at play in this glen. The closer I got to the heart of the estate, once bland bald glens started to feature trees, bushes and scrub. Passing through a gate in a robust and well-kept deer fence was like passing into a different world. A world where sheep and deer numbers are strictly controlled. A world with woodland, scrub land and rough pasture. A world with a range of habitats, all inhabited by wildlife. As soon as you chance upon a tree in the hills, you chance upon a bird. Here that sensation was multiplied.

On the Alladale estate, tall mature Scots pine trees tower over an understorey of heather and bilberry. Mobs of youthful birch sprout freely all around, alive with wren, chaffinch and a range of tits. The arising of the ancient Caledonian forest, of fresh growth recovery and the promise of wildflowers gave a worthy and authentic preamble to the mountains of Easter Ross, whilst the birdsong provided an accomplished soundtrack. Alladale had a wonderful feel to it, and I would like to see more of our glens managed like this. I'm sure there are ways. Quite when we'll be ready for wolves though, I'm not sure.

The next glen, Strath Cuileannach, contrasted in a rather jarring way. Here there were conifers, herds of deer grazing in the valley bottom and pastures were over-populated with scruffy mountain sheep. A tiny bit of wilder countryside, dominated by birch and heather, stood out in the bare landscape. It fought to present itself within a fenced enclosure, barbed wire its defence against the grazing herds and flocks. This is the landscape that support payments have bought across our uplands, a balance that needs tilting back towards a more natural state of affairs. There was also an Ivor Williams trailer; always nice to see a bit of Wales when you're away!

The Oykel Bridge Hotel is a significant landmark on the Highland 550. It's the start and finish of the northern loop. I wanted to stay, but it was Sunday, and the hotel was closed. Instead I pressed on to the Achness Hotel in Rosehall which could not have been more welcoming. A barn for my bike, a bar to myself and a sound meal led me to a comfortable bed and a welcome shower. Breakfast was taken with fishermen waiting for their ghillie guides. Elderly, tweed-clad men gathered around a jovial and well-spoken leader. Rods, bait and pegs were keenly discussed. Looking around the hotel at breakfast time it was easy to observe that bikepacking visitors maybe a little more youthful and were therefore a better future bet for remote hostelries such as this.

Rosehall sits at the entrance to Glenn Cassley. Whilst famous for salmon fishing Glen Cassley also provides a long and easy cycleway. There is little, however, to detain the eye. An unusual white violet with bold purple veins on its lower petal proved to be the odd exception, as it was one that I hadn't noticed before. The internet told me it was a native of America and not found in the British Isles. The internet however, is not always correct. Common sense would suggest it was a Marsh Violet, just a white one rather than the typical light blue.

I passed into Mackay Country by Loch Shin and then on past Loch Merkland. Excellent phone reception surprised me here as I really did feel in the middle of nowhere. I crouched for lunch and to gather important social media updates in the lochside heather. I was perched on a rough boulder away from the road to avoid the racing Telecom vans who seemed to have commandeered the quiet road and claimed it as their own. Easy off-road riding led me north to Gobernuisgach Lodge. The afternoon drew in, the rain strengthened, and a cold easterly wind found its voice.

I descended into the wonderfully remote Glen Golly, rather like a wee 'lost valley'. The wind assisted rain was hammering on my back. I was pretty wet by now and heading into the remotest part of the trail. Should I camp? Or just keep going? It was a great example of decision making in the outdoors. Armed with three modern forecasts which all predicted the rain would stop at around 7.00pm I carried on, using the wind to push me, seeing it as a help rather than a hinderance. It was walking though, walking into clouds as I began the plod to Lochan Sgeireach.

The cloud thins slightly as I descend, I mount the bike and roll for about 50 metres, then it sinks into the bog below me. I disembark and push, pushing downhill is not my favourite activity. The way ahead is not clear. I arrive at the top of a peat precipice. I look left and right to find the best way down. I think I find it, but I'll never really know. I manage to keep relatively clean then a boulder, a big boulder blocks the way. I try to go to its right, but a deep puddle bars the way. I go left and dance across a bog instead. My bike doubles as a vault to cross this slice of Kinder Scout lost in the remoteness of the Scottish highlands.

The sun pierced the clouds and shifted the rain as I arrived at the outflow of An Dubh Loch and a perfect campsite lay before me. The mood-changing rays even helped me to dry some of my gear, soaked by the afternoon storm. I was in a different world as the cold front had now passed over and the corrie was lit by bright, strong sunbeams. This is a magnificent place. It's the sort of place you might not get to as a walker. There are no Munros nearby and the neighbouring peak of Meall Horn is little known and barely makes a height to which walkers aspire. It was places like this I'd come for, off the beaten track: wild, beautiful and lonely. I loved that night camping in such a remote location. I was also about to hit the northern most point of the Highland 550 trail.

9: The Highland Trail 550 (train stress in the Highlands) – Part two, southbound

I'm loath to leave camp. I take my time. I rinse my body in the fresh waters. I pack methodically; the way ahead is clear. It starts with a bit more peat, then I pick up an old stalker's trod, clearly disused and now unmaintained. It's an honest push though, what you see is what you get. I have no chance of riding this, so I settle in and aim for the third hairpin wondering if Zimmer make bikes…

The third hairpin is a point of great significance. It's the most northerly point of the Highland 550, so from there I was heading south. A big smile crept across my face, even as I continued to push my bike up to the Bealach Horn. What a marvellous place it was to be. Gladly, the weather was much better than the day before and majestic views opened out in front of me. I gazed across the white quartzite of Foinaven and Arkle, hills I'd always wanted to visit, hills to which I'd return. My bike leant on a rock, striking a natural pose for a photo and I could have stayed longer, but it was cold and the descent in front of me looked fantastic. A descent of 460 metres, over six kilometres took me south to Loch Stack. I still had my big smile.

A party of school kids from London were departing Lone bothy on the shore of Loch Stack, bound for an adventure climbing Ben Stack. I loved seeing them here and thanked their teachers for putting in the hours to give these kids a chance to explore so far from home, both in distance but also in contrast. A contrast enhanced by track-side grazing red deer. I carried on over another hill, with a good descent to the shores of Loch Glendhu. Loch Glendhu and Loch Glencoul present an exceptional landscape to explore, but I needed to keep moving.

Tourist pressure on the North Coast 500 and labour shortages, meant there was no lunch for passers-by at the Kylesku Inn. Ordinary food and extraordinary views in The Rock Stop put me on. The multiple roller-coaster ups and downs of the coastal route were trying. Patient motorists bided their time while I barely made ground up the short stubborn rises, but if I'd have stopped, I'd never have got going again, and so I lurched from passing place to passing place. The Drumbeg Stores saved the day, always a lovely place to stop and chat.

I actually really enjoyed the road to Alltan Abradhan. From here I turned off on to tracks which would take me past the stunning Achmelivich beach, Loch Roe and over a rough track to Lochinver. The sea was to my right and inland, on my left, was an intriguing, undulating knock and lochan landscape. At one point I saw a post box closed for bird nesting and in another place mountain everlasting (an uncommon arctic-alpine plant) growing in the roadside verge.

A tasty meal in Delilah's of Lochinver sent me on my way to the Suileag bothy. It had been a long day, but nicely interspersed with interest and very satisfying to complete. The bothy was occupied. This was good as it meant the home fires were burning. There was space for me, and I chatted amiably with the southern English family and the lone Scottish Nationalist. Unfortunately, their *entente cordiale* did not last the entire evening and baseless tabloid headlines were traded to sour the atmosphere.

There are some big pushes on the Highland 550 Trail. One of them is above Glen Golly but you do get swallowed up into the magnificence of the landscape. There's a big push just past Shenaval bothy (still to come at this stage), that was very hard work, but again in a fantastic remote place. For me, pushing is part of bikepacking, I'm not averse to it. As long as it's uphill.

There is one section of the Highland 550 that cannot be forgiven and that's the push from Suileg bothy to Ledmore bridge. It's the worst kind of push because it's not even uphill. It started with bog and evolved into a disruptive, spiky-stoned unruly path. The headwind was irrelevant. From time to time, I threw my leg over the bike and gave it a go only to find it was a waste of time and a waste of energy. I might as well have just pushed for the three or four hours it took me to travel that way. It was quite nice arriving at Cam Loch. I was still pushing though, but the views over my shoulder back to Suilven will always be special. That was, for me, a really miserable section of trail. When I got to the end of it and met the road at Ledmore Bridge, I stuck two fingers up at the innocuous, inanimate sign saying Lochinvar 19k. The road from Ledmore gave me a smooth, quick and quiet passage, back to Oykel Bridge. But this was a destroyed valley, dashing under pylons between over-worked ground, from plantation to plantation. It brought no solace.

Feeling a bit down about this stretch of the route, I was pleased to make good progress, but was looking forward to better riding, which the next section to Ullapool would give in abundance. I needed a pick-me-up in the Oykel Bridge Hotel; a bed for the night and a fine bar meal was very welcome. Excellent breakfast too.

In the bar I met Tony, Darren and Glen. I'm not sure they really wanted to talk to me, but sometimes when you're travelling on your own, Billyno-mates as it were, it's nice to chat to someone, even if they are from Lancashire. They were doing the middle loop of the Highland 550 having done the southern loop the previous year. They picked my brains about the northern loop and were surprised it went in three days (to be fair, so was I!)

I was heading to Ullapool for lunch and the way ahead held much of interest. First up came the Schoolhouse bothy which I just had to explore. It was hard to imagine enough people living in these glens to support a school, but that was the case up until World War Two. It was whilst I was inside playing teacher that the Lancashire Lads cruised on past. I was a little sad as I thought that'd be the last I would see of them, but oh no.

Beyond the Schoolhouse bothy I missed a right turn, distracted by a fish, albeit one carved from wood. It drew my eye to the wrong side of the track. I plodded on upwards, on a good surface until I started to get a bit bored of the slow uphill cycling and was looking for an excuse to stop when a large patch of bright red, round-leaved sundew caught my eye. The tiny insectivorous plant was growing profusely along with butterwort and lousewort in one those little bogs formed by roadside drainage. I dropped the bike and lay down to take pictures of the little insectivorous gem. It was whilst down on the ground I checked my map and realised I'd come the wrong way. Bother.

Grumpily I rolled back down the hill then took a lovely grassy track, with one stream paddle, to Knockdamph bothy above Loch an Daimh. This bothy was in less good order than the previous ones I'd visited and apart from sheltering out of the wind, it provided little encouragement to hang around. I continued on interesting tracks, not too fast, not too technical, though rarely easy, past Lochan Daimh to Glen Achall.

I pulled up by East Rhiorroach Lodge to chat to a group who'd cycled up Glen Achhall for a day out. We chatted over butties and I admired their ancient bikes and one Brompton. Sitting comfortably enjoying some sun and amiable conversation, some more cyclists appeared from out of the hills. It was the three lads from Lancashire. I'd passed them somewhere but for the life of us we couldn't figure out where. I thought it must have been where I'd gone wrong, but it turned out that they had gone that way too and stayed going that way riding down Strath Mulzie before pushing their bikes for a handful of kilometres back to Glen Achall. As it turned out we were following different routes and as I'd gone past Loch an Daimh as they'd gone up Strath Mulzie (being from Lancashire they'd been too tight to make a charitable contribution to the John Muir Trust and get the latest GPX files!) I doubted I'd see them again as they sped off down the glen towards Ullapool but, as it turned out, that thought was premature.

In Ullapool, I met a friend from home. We lunched and chatted before I then headed down Loch Broom towards the Coffin Road, a notorious section about which I'd been warned by more than one source. When I arrived at the bottom, a local whose attention I'd caught through the open door of his kitchen, helped me out with water. As I stood there gazing up the steep hill, I noticed three figures pushing bikes in a laboured manner, all carrying black puddings. They were slowly, very slowly, gaining height. I chose to stay in the valley bottom and followed good tracks to Gleann Mor where I had to make a death defying, bike in one hand, Harrison Ford style bridge crossing over the Abhainn Cuileig. It was a rather silly thing to do especially as on the other side a tree was filling the space inside the kissing gate, I figured not many people come this way, but how was I to know!

The road section that followed gave me the only golden eagle sighting of the trip. Then I was at Dundonnell, and guess who was there, fixing one of their bikes, no less than Tony, Darren and Glen! Ah well, I'll just scoot on past if you don't mind. The Shenaval bothy was too far for me though, I camped along the way and enjoyed the descent to the bothy first thing in the morning. As I arrived at the bothy, the three Lancies were just about to leave. I watched where they crossed the river to see where was deep and where was shallow, then followed their lead. As with pushing, river crossings are all part and parcel of this game. I took off my boots and socks, popped on my flip-flops and set foot in the bitingly cold water. It didn't reach above my knees, but my goodness it was blooming cold!

This is a very good section of the Highland 550. Elsewhere I've heard Dundonnell to Poolewe referred to as the best day's mountain biking in Scotland. I'm not sure about that, but it was very good, despite the amount of pushing (and the cold water). The surrounding mountains of An Teallach, Beinn Dearg Mor and Sguur Ban tower above the over-deepened and widened glacial valleys. Each water course has remnants of native woodland illustrated by a lonely alder, a clutch of low growing eared-willow and flowers such as milkwort, lousewort and tormentil. In a puddle I saw a common newt, above were ravens, alongside were meadow pipits and a lonely willow warbler sang its distinctive descending song. If any day puts the 'highland' into the Highland Trail 550 it's this one. On a wet day it'd be hard work passing through here, but I was lucky with the weather and fully got to appreciate the grandeur of the Fisherfield Forest.

I caught up with the Lancashire lads again at Poolewe where we raided the fine little shop for tasty snacks. We cycled together on the road towards Gairloch, where I would spend a very lazy rest day, whilst the lads carried on to Kinlochewe. That was (this time) the last I saw of them. A whole day lying down is a wonderful thing. A whole day lying down when you've earned it, by riding off-road for eight consecutive days, is a sublime thing. But next morning it was another long road flog from Gairloch to Kinlochewe. I suppose some riders like making up a bit of time on these hard-top sections. The road was fairly quiet that morning, but I'd still prefer to avoid roads if possible. I was hoping for a second breakfast in the village hall café, but once again I was too early. Unlike when I arrived at the Bridge of Balgie Café I now had the bit between my teeth. I wanted to keep going, to finish. The fly wheel motion in my legs was unstoppable. I couldn't wait for the café to open and made do with scraps from the depleted shelves of the village shop.

Torridon came next and what should have been a route highlight was spoiled by the weather. It was raining hard as I passed through. I sheltered briefly in the tiny Tea House bothy, then stumbled my way down the hill to Achnashellach battling with rain, wind and a steep, rocky and loose downhill (which on a dry day, with an unladen bike, would have been brilliant). Fortunately, my only fall was at low speed, but it turned out that I had damaged my front brake as from here on it became progressively useless. I passed through Strathcarron, my damp clothes sticking uncomfortably to my skin, then ascended Attadale where I spent a damp night hidden in a hilltop wood before the descent to Glen Ling.

The downhill into the glen started well and was full of promise, but the level bit took me back to the Ledmore crossing. I pushed through bogs and tussocks for a couple of kilometres, in wet shoes, with wet legs and a rather damp spirit. There was a deer gate that wasn't big enough to get a bike through; I had to dismantle some of it to be able to pass, then reassemble it afterwards. I swore a lot on that struggly bit to Dornie (it was still raining too). On the plus side, a large bacon butty at the tourist hotspot of Eilean Donan cheered me up no end. It also stopped raining and I began to dry out.

My mood had completely changed by the time I was cruising up Gleann Lichd. The sun, the track, the surrounding mountains brought a smile to my face once more. The excellent track sped me onwards. I even enjoyed the walk up to Camban bothy and the descent down to Glen Affric was fast and beautiful. Just before the Youth Hostel I encountered three rather bedraggled walkers. They too had suffered from the overnight rain and were struggling to dry out. We chatted awhile and it turned out they'd travelled from America to walk the Glen Affric trail. A fine journey through some of the most scenic of the highland glens. I took pleasure in the Affric Caledonian Forest, but essential needs required attention. I was looking forward to a good drying out session. Not just for me and my clothes, but for my tent and bags too. The Tomich Hotel came to my rescue. It's lovely staying in these old hotels. They are always friendly, the evening meals are good, but the breakfasts are very good. I can wash my 'smalls' and dry them overnight. I carry a lightweight pack towel which works well, but not as good as a proper fresh and rough hotel towel. Then it was over past Loch na Beinne Baine to Glen Moriston. Beside this track, my eye was caught by a flower that I didn't recognise. I'd come across a little patch of the wonderfully American named 'arctic star flower', or the boringly English named chickweed-wintergreen. Whatever you want to call it, this was the first time I'd spotted this lovely little flower of northern woodlands.

Another early finish in Fort Augustus at the wonderful Morag's Hostel came next, then it was on to the Great Glen Way.

I definitely felt I was on the home run now. Despite heavy rain, the canal tow path and forest tracks passed quickly. I stopped for coffee in Banavie by the Neptune's Staircase, Britain's longest canal staircase lock system. It comprises eight locks, each gate weighing 22 tons, and it takes boats an hour and half to get through. I flew into Fort William. I'd been in touch by phone with the bike shops there as my front brake was not working at all. Nevis Cycles were able to replace my malfunctioning front brake and set me on the way again. A massive thanks to them for helping me out at fairly short notice.

One more, and probably the best B&B night, at Brevin's Guest House, accompanied by a fine Indian Meal in Fort William preceded what was now, undoubtedly, the final leg. I set off the next day down the West Highland Way, facing the oncoming thousands of walkers. It flows pretty quickly to Tyndrum (quickly on a bike being a relative concept, especially when cycling off road!). It was a squally day, but good tracks took me down to Kinlochleven and, well-rested and now quite fit, the climb to the top of the Devil's Staircase was easy. I wished the Devil's Staircase descent was longer, but it put me on good tracks all the way to the finish of the Highland 550 and even as the squalls got together to form continuous rain, it didn't slow me down.

I arrived in Tyndrum quite late. Actually, I didn't think I'd get that far but the weather was so poor it just seemed wiser to keep going. I'd managed to phone ahead and book a bed at the By the Way Hostel. At the hostel, the first of the riders were arriving, some from abroad, for that year's Highland 550 race. They took one look at me and clearly decided I had no information to share. I'd shaved in Fort William, eaten a grand curry, spent the night in a wonderful B&B and had arrived in Tyndrum looking quite fresh, not like someone who'd just raced around the Highland 550. I'd taken 14 days to cycle the route and had two rest days. To be fair I did start in Glasgow, and (unbeknown to me at this point) I'd be finishing in Glasgow too. But for now, wallowing in the bliss of ignorance, I was a pretty happy boy. I'd done the Highland Trail 550 and first thing in the morning I'd be on the train back to Glasgow where I'd get my pre-booked connection back to North Wales. That was the plan anyway.

I arrived at the station next to the hostel. The digital display board said the train was cancelled. It was hard to believe. It was not what I expected or wanted. I'd relaxed, I thought I was going home. I went back to the hostel because there's no reception on the platform. I double checked online to see if the train had indeed been cancelled. It had. There was another train due in the early afternoon that I could try, but I'd miss my north Wales connection, so in the meantime I tried the bus. You can take a bike on the bus, but only if it's in a bag. Surely, I'm not the only one to have cycled the Highland 550 without a bike bag! "More than me job's worth to let you on with an unwrapped bike" the driver said, "far too dangerous."

Back to the station for the afternoon train. I guess I should have thought this one through a bit more but given the morning train was cancelled it shouldn't have been a great surprise to find the afternoon train completely full. When I say full, I mean full. There was no room for me never mind me and my bike. The Guard was apologetic but there was nothing he could do. The train was full. I definitely felt a tear in my eye as the disappointment bit. I wouldn't be home that evening. There were no more trains that day and even if there were, what would be the point of arriving in Glasgow late in the evening with a bike?

I sat and felt sorry for myself, but slowly came round to the one and only option. I had a bike. The West Highland Way continues south to Glasgow (well Milngavie actually, but that's just daft!) from Tyndrum. I jumped on the bike and set off south (again, jumped is a relative term by this stage in the proceedings).

It wasn't quite as easy as I'd hoped.

The West Highland Way from Tyndrum to Loch Lomond isn't a very fast trail. For most of the way it's rather up and down, as like elsewhere the main road takes the easy way through the valley. The West Highland Way criss-crosses the main road heading up and down the side of the valley like a giant half pipe. Heading towards Loch Lomond I was well aware that many people had told me not to cycle along the East Coast of Loch Lomond: "it's a nightmare". It's one of those really bad bits of track with ups and downs, crags and boulders, tree roots and narrow gaps. It's slippery terrain and no one says it's not as bad as everybody says. Everybody says, it is as bad as everybody says. As if that wasn't playing on my mind sufficiently, more than one person walking the other way said words to the effect of, "Good luck with that mate!"

When I got to Loch Lomond, I'd already decided that I wouldn't stick to the West Highland Way. The ferry to Ardlui was due, it still took an hour to come, but I was on it. I was zipped across to the other side of the loch and then I scurried down the road, going the right way for a Friday evening as most traffic was heading north, and got to Tarbet in pretty good time. In Tarbet there's a nice surprise for the unassuming cyclist; an off-road cycle route leads all the way to central Glasgow.

As I approached the southern end of Loch Lomond, I came across two plucky youngsters who'd adventured here, on their bikes, all the way from Dumbarton. One had a broken chain. Fortunately, I had the required chain splitting tool and was able to help them on their way. With my low level of mechanical prowess that was very satisfying, though I was worried about what time they would get home and insisted they call to let their folks know where they were. I purchased the last portion of chips in Balloch then made a sneaky camp, well-hidden in some ex-industrial land, on the edge of town. I was nicely placed to roll into Glasgow and catch a train back to Wales on the Sunday morning.

However, another story was yet to unfold at Glasgow Central Station.

I'd missed my train. It went the day before. It wasn't my fault, Scotrail had cancelled my connection. But I hadn't booked a through connection, I'd booked the trains separately because I didn't know when I'd arrive. There were no bike reservations for trains to north Wales on this particular day. I could be transferred but my bike couldn't. I transferred my ticket and stood on the platform and watched. I watched people walking through the unstaffed barrier and on to the train. They were just walking down the platform with seemingly no checks. Well, I thought, it's worth a go. So, I strolled as confidently as I could towards the platform, bike in one hand, pretending it was small, not really there and hardly worth bothering with. I whistled innocently (very quietly mindst). Who'd be interested in me? I didn't stand out from the crowd, did I?

"Excuse me Sir," a polite lady requested, "can I see your bike reservation please?" I could have broken down in tears again. I had to confess immediately that I didn't have one, I was trying to scam the system, fraud the company, pull one over on my fellow people, I was a sinner, please forgive me. She was lovely, but there was no way I was getting on that train with my bike because 'rules is rules' y'know...

She explained that there were four places for bikes on this train and they were all booked. If someone did not show then she could squeeze me on, as a favour like. You can imagine how tense the wait was. You're in Glasgow, you probably won't be in Wales. It's a Sunday. You've got a ticket for the train yourself, but you haven't got a ticket for your bike. I had 40 minutes to wait for a 'no show'. I kept smiling, hoping it would help. I tried hard not to fall out with this very powerful lady, just doing her job.

Time ticked away.

Fifteen minutes to go.

Surely if you were catching a train with your bike you'd be here fifteen minutes in advance? Surely if you were catching a train with your bike you'd be here with ten minutes to spare? Surely you wouldn't leave it until five minutes before the trains departs to turn up and expect to get your bike on the right part of the train?

My hopes were beginning to rise when two men appeared in the station atrium pushing bikes. My heart sank. I kept smiling, willing them away, smiling at the nice lady, turmoil retained within. I really didn't want to be turned away from another train, have to book a hotel and try again the next day. Then the men veered, stopped, and looked at the digital display boards showing train departures. They turned away and went elsewhere. My eyes, working hard like those of a hungry dog, now implored the lady to let me on. Two minutes to go. "Let's go" the lady said, "come on, we'll get you on".

I was on the train and heading home.

I'd completed a Highland 725 (like the Highland 550 really needs extra miles!)

10: Midsummer Teifi time

Rhayader, Claerwen and the Monks' Trod

Our mid-summer trips kept me away from mid-Wales for the next few years, but in 2022 there was a drought. I wanted to take full advantage and cross the Monks' Trod. The Monks' Trod is a tough trail which heads west to east just north of Claerwen Reservoir. It would have been used by the monks from Strata Florida travelling to and from another Cistercian Monastery at Cwm-Hir, near Llandrindod Wells. This highway over the hills would have provided a good route avoiding the densely vegetated and boggy valley bottoms. Today, the hill is the boggy bit and the whole area is pretty much monogenetic. Only an occasional hawthorn casts above the ubiquitous *Molinia caerulea* or purple moor grass. The trail has been abused in different ways over the years. It has been neglected, intensively grazed and has, more recently (though currently banned) been subject to overuse by recreational motor traffic. Much of it today is in a poor state and is difficult to pass along, except of course when there's a drought.

I met Matt and John, two longstanding friends and occasional bikepacking chums, in Rhayader. They'd travelled from Cheshire whilst I'd enjoyed the amiable drive from the north of Wales. I was the map reader for this trip, Graham's substitute. I had made a plan which I hoped would work. An unwelcome shower on the Friday evening led us to shelter, eat and have a couple of pints in the friendly Triangle Inn. But, with darkness beckoning, we needed to be on our way. Fortunately, there's a handy bus shelter near the pub where we changed and strapped the bags onto our bikes.

The way out of Rhayader is really good. A purpose-built trail, it heads towards the 'Welsh Lake District': the Elan valley. There are four big reservoirs here and several smaller llyns in the surrounding hills. The reservoirs were built between 1893 and 1952 to provide reliable drinking water for Birmingham. The development here affected few people. There were protestations of course, but only from the handful of farmers who worked the land. (This development pre-dated the more recalcitrant flooding of Capel Celyn in the 1960's. In 1965 the Afon Tryweryn was dammed near Bala to create a reservoir to supply water to Liverpool. The scheme was opposed by most of Wales and has become a landmark event in the creation of a modern Welsh identity. It brought the north and south together and fed into the developing nationalistic mood. *Cofiwch Dryweryn* adorns many a wall across Wales and whilst it's the flooding of Capel Celyn that is remembered, the message means more. It tells of a people who felt forgotten, their culture bulldozed and it's a reminder that Cymru is not a mere region of England.)

There are pleasant woods, aqua vistas and superb off-road bike trails to discover in this area. I was pleased to finally be here on my bike. If there is one place that's synonymous with bikepacking, particularly in Wales, then it is this valley. Of course, it has its devotees in the off-roading groups as well, but it's usually quiet. There seems to be a lot of space to spread out. Trails have been developed for riding bikes and there are some old bridleways that keep me coming back time after time.

We had to make a rather subtle camp that night, having spent a little more time in the pub than perhaps was wise. Though, 'You should never ride past a pub' is not a bad 'golden' rule for the bikepacker! We found ourselves looking for a flat, sheltered place to pitch three small tents in the dark. In addition, we needed to avoid a wind that had gradually worsened through the afternoon. I can't tell you where we stayed as it was a bit cheeky, but I can give you a clue. All night there was a banging. I thought it was the lid of a nearby grit bin being lifted and dropped by the wind. But no, it was a sheep. A sheep was licking the salt in the bin. It would lift the lid, lick the salt, remove its head and drop the lid. It was a head banging night with *bin halen*, but the sheep had no rhythm.

The track alongside the Claerwen Reservoir is a classic and popular bit of gravel through the Cambrian mountains. It does see some traffic from motor bikes and 4x4s, but it's in good enough repair to cope and having travelled it several times now, I haven't seen it too busy. This though, was my first time here. These are not mountains in the international sense. I think the moniker 'Cambrian Mountains' represented the whole of western Wales, but as other parts have developed their own, more popular names, it resides here. Maybe as Snowdonia becomes better known as Eryri and the Brecon Beacons by the poetic Bannau Brycheiniog this region of Cymru will push its own local name of Elenydd a tad more.

On that Saturday morning, the Claerwen track flowed well and fast. There is space here and we appreciated it. Lunch was taken at the Claerddu bothy and that was followed by the excellent descent to Strata Florida, a route I had done before but was only too pleased to repeat. We arrived early in Ffair-Rhos where we battled with the wind to camp on the little campsite before retiring to the welcoming Teifi Inn for a long luxurious evening of fine beer, good food and amiable chat.

Sunday dawned fine and it was full steam ahead for the Monks' Trod. I wasn't sure where best to join the trail, so I headed for a junction at its western end which was clearly marked on the map. I knew where the junction was; it looks like a major turning, and it's enhanced by a sign prohibiting motor vehicles. The track started well and looked encouraging but disintegrated very quickly. We searched high and low for the best route: we paddled, we leapt across bogs, we used our bikes as vaulting poles. We got wet feet. Once across the Afon Claerwen however, the track improves and by the top of the hill the mood changes for the better. (I later learnt that there is a better approach up Esgair Cywion.) We cruised across the top of the *byd*. Not a soul, not a sheep, not a flower, nothing for miles. On the one hand, it's magnificent: big skies, long horizons and lashings of air to fill the lungs. On the other hand, it's a bit sad. Whilst I find myself drawn to these places, I do see why some people find them bleak, lifeless and without character. At least on the bike it's passed through with an element of fun. It'd be a long plod if walking.

The final descent to the Rhayader golf course provided a fitting final endorphin fix. It's a well-known mountain bike descent and conversations were dashed as we soaked up the fine curves, friendly bumps and smooth rock section. We all finished with a smile. It had been a lovely weekend with Matt and John, though John did suggest it might have been handy to have been able to throw a ball or a stick for Matt: he seemed to double back and cycle most of the route twice like an energetic dog checking on its flock. John was calm, a good listener with sage advice, and he was enjoying some time away from looking after his young son. But I have to admit, for me there was more to this trip than spending time with close friends. This trip was also a reconnaissance. The idea of the Cylchdaith Cymru was forming and I know knew it needed to take the Claerwen reservoir track rather than the Strata Florida descent. I also knew I'd be unlikely to catch the Monks' Trod in such an amenable mood again.

11: The Welsh 550/Cylchdaith Cymru 550

Day One – Llandudno to Penmachno

"Evening."
"Alright."
"Aiyaa."

It was close of play on day one. Dusk. The young man and his partner paused. They were turning right on their local trail, near where I was camped. I did recognise him, we'd met before, he was a friend of a friend, but I couldn't quite grasp his name. I was settling down, ready for sleep and I'd eaten my dinner (home prepared spicey couscous with herbs, vegetables, nuts and apricots, simply left to sit in boiling water for a few minutes). I was camping barely a handful of miles from home but had spent the entire day pedalling south down Nant Conwy from Llandudno on day one of my Cylchdaith Cymru mark 2. This was a strategic camp, a few miles on from the commercial campsite, but preceding the fast flowy downhills of the trail ahead (they'd be best tackled in the morning). I'd snuck in trailside and found some softer ground, as forest tracks can be challenging for tent pegs. I had a view; I could see no homes and I was out of sight. It was an unplanned, impromptu camp. It wasn't terribly late and I opened my book to read before going to sleep. Sam, whose name I remembered later, was out for an evening ride with his partner. Little did I know at the time that they'd be the last people I'd speak to for at least a couple of days (except for one bad driver and those I was paying for goods and services). Wales, between its coastlines, is very quiet.

The previous September, I'd cycled version one of my Cylchdaith Cymru. I'd been inspired by the Highland Trail 550 in Scotland and thought there was scope for a good Welsh Trail 550. In Welsh that'd be Cylchdaith (circular) Cymru (Wales). It was a superb route, but there were some sections on which I thought I could improve. I'd mostly grabbed parts of other routes and linked them as best I could with bridleways and the National Cycle Network routes on the map. In the intervening year I'd revisited one or two sections to help improve the route. I was now embarking on version two of my Cylchdaith Cymru. This time of year, when the main summer holidays are over, is quiet in Wales. It's a good time to ride.

Initially I had meant to cycle north coast to south coast. Traversing

Wales from north to south has always been a must do for bikepackers. There are several routes. Some taking in trail centres, some taking in the summits of Yr Wyddfa and Cader Idris. Some are gravel, forest track and road-based such as the Sarn Helen (though this trail has some out-of-character hard bits too). Even before today's trail centres were developed, Wales was considered an excellent place for mountain biking. Wales, being mostly rural, is thatched with quiet tracks, quiet bridleways, and quiet lanes. It's an ideal place for the bikepacker.

Most people tackle the Welsh 'coast to coast' one way, but the thought of sitting in Swansea, waiting for a train back to north Wales, which I'd be unable to pre-book, was just too much to bear. Due to the topography of the land, railways in Wales head east into England and then back into Wales so the journeys are not straightforward. If you can use the Heart of Wales line, or the Conwy valley line and stay within Wales, then it's hunky dory, but to travel the length of the country by rail with a big, loaded bike is not straightforward. I decided I might as well cycle back and make it a round trip; a Welsh 550. My rough outline was to head south from the Great Orme on the north coast, down the mountainous west of Wales, to Worm's Head on the south coast. Once there I'd head back north up the East of Wales, visiting Offa's Dyke and using the north Wales coastal cycleway to return to the Great Orme.

I've forgotten all the details of how I pieced the initial route together, but it definitely joins up other people's ideas. I came across a route by Nath Manning which went from the north coast to the south coast, I tweaked that a bit with ideas from Tom Hutton's Welsh Mountain Biking and with some local knowledge. To create the return route, I used some bits of a Welsh Triangle route, some bits of a Barebones Bikepacking route, then some national cycleways to link things. I sought advice from Graham Cole, a man who's done more bikepacking than most, and a route evolved. The first version did anyway. Now I was on mark two, an improved Cylchdaith Cymru.

Starting in Llandudno meant that I rounded the Great Orme first thing. This was a smart move to make. The route around the Great Orme is surprisingly uphill. I imagined finishing, having ridden around Wales, by cycling around the Great Orme, it wouldn't be anywhere near as nice as it was on that first morning. In-fact, it'd be a bit of a chore. As I slowly ground my way around on my laden steed, I was passed by morning joggers and morning cyclists all doing their rounds before breakfast. They had no idea that I was setting off with the full intention of cycling around

Wales and back. They had no idea who I was and where I was going. I got the odd pleasant "Good morning" or a neat "Bore da", but that was all. Starting with the Orme was a great way to start my Chylchdaith Cymru, finishing with it would have been a right pain.

It's a blue-sky morning, there is no wind, I have the Marine Drive to myself. I'm riding between glistening white cliffs, below and above me. These are cliffs on which I've had a lot of fun over the years as a climber, but no one is out on 'Pen Trwyn Patrol' this morning. Cackling gulls are circling over the tideline beneath me. I glimpse an eagle-eyed peregrine effortlessly drifting on the updraft and a chatter of choughs strafe the grass below Solid Gold (E3 6a). It's September so the red valerian is past its best and the cowslips and bluebells are long gone, nevertheless, the goat-cropped grass still sparkles with tormentil and harebells. I can't resist a stop before rounding the corner to the northern side of the Orme.

I remembered 1982 when Pen Trwyn had just been 'discovered'. I survived a hair-raising drive to the crag in John's car, Dave said "he was just showing off". We scooted about the walls, determining nothing in particular. Banter was rife, but climbing was absent. I remember wandering down to Pigeon Cave and ogling at the roof. Within two years this crag would be the crag of the day, with many climbers crimping tiny holds. The climbs, all longer than they look celebrate wonderfully featured limestone. Each has a lower off and given the weather it was as good a place as any to climb. There were tales of fly tippers being dobbed in, a police raid on the Milk Bar and dozens of climbers dossing in the caves. For Thatcher's vertically minded outcasts it was a golden time. For me, I scraped up a new route or two behind Dave and managed to leapfrog him on another, but it was never quite my kind of climbing, plus when the wind blows and the sun goes, the Orme is a cold place for small flat finger holds.

I turn and look back across the pier to Llandudno, sunlight dancing on the incoming waves. The town presents a grand Victorian frontage, a classical promenade, both sandy and stony beaches with the mountains of Eryri as a backdrop. It is the Queen of resorts: a good place to start my journey.

The remoteness on the far side of the Great Orme is always surprising, and the first traffic-free cycleway of the journey took me through Deganwy and into Conwy. If you ever head this way, then Conwy is well worth a look around. You can traverse the walls for free and enjoy some independent shopping. It's also a good place to make sure you've got provisions for the day because after here services are sparse.

I nearly managed to ride the whole way up Mountain Road from Conwy. It's a good bridleway and I left the town behind, mostly pedalling but with a little push here and there. It was the first proper climb of the route. As the track began to level out, I was greeted by the vivid purples and yellows of flowering heather and gorse. A confetti of meadow pipits lifted off and I could hear a round of applause from a solo, late season, wren. Crossing the Sychant Pass and climbing further required a little more pushing, but tremendous views opened up across to Ynys Mon, back to the Orme and into the Carneddau Mountains. I was on my way; this is Wales, and I was about to bikepack the length of the nation.

Conwy Mountain and over towards Tal y Fan is great mountain biking country. I stuck to the line of bridleways, but there's freedom up there to mix and match your tracks as you please. I passed ancient standing stones, went close to Meini Hirion, a neolithic circle, and I wasn't far from Graig Lwyd an axe factory from the same period. You could get very distracted up there. On this occasion I stayed with the line of some fine old dry-stone walls. Under wheel was firm sheep-cropped turf giving an amiable riding surface and I pedalled freely, with a smile on my face. I knew this hill well and never tired of seeking out its best passages and its secret shelters.

In some ways, Nant Conwy is one of the fiddlier bits of my Cylchdaith Cymru. I live locally and have ridden various routes up and down the valley. The best route stays to the west side. Unfortunately, it requires the scaling of rather too many locked gates. It follows reservoir leats and stays high above the busy B5106 road in the valley bottom which is an unpleasant road for the slow moving, solo bikepacker to travel along. The locals, as they do in so many places, often drive too fast, tearing along the dotted central line of this twisting country lane. This meant that the best route for this particular journey was to cross the valley to its eastern side. So, I headed down towards Llangelynen.

I've passed the little old 12th Century church at Llangelynen several times before, but I couldn't resist another look. I popped inside the gate and leant my bike against the porch. I took a glance at the eponymous well and wondered about the mounds that were once the footings of an inn. Drovers were welcome to the church; they even had their own section in which to pray, and the story suggests there was a cock fighting pit at the inn too. Maybe the church cashed in on those seeking forgiveness! I entered the church and stood below a wooden bier that was once used to carry coffins across the hill. For a moment I imagined being there, having arrived on foot for a service, stood quietly below the ancient beams, surrounded by people who'd never travelled beyond their valley, a priest who knew it all and hymns sung proudly in Cymraeg. I've little time for the idea of God these days, but the buildings built for his worship always impress and move me somewhat.

The route drops down the steepest of lines to the valley bottom. Before that, however, it enjoys the most perfect of green lanes. The thoroughfare lies between well-maintained, habitat-rich and gently curving dry stone walls. This pilgrimage route to Llangelynen is steeped in history so spare a thought for those who've passed this way before. Through a gate, the route steepens, gets rocky, and care is needed. This ancient path has been damaged by the passage of time and water, but is just on the right side of hard to be fun on a mountain bike. Perhaps not fast though! On a gravel bike you'll be walking.

I crossed the valley to Eglwysbach. This is a village which portents many to come. I noticed the twitch of a curtain, but as seems usual, neither the pub nor the shop was open. There was no one on the street, no one working in the fields and not even a gardener pottering about their beds. This village slept quietly waiting for its residents to return later. Eglwysbach was the first of many places like this. A house called Hen Popty (Old Bakery) told its own story, as did the vroom of a supermarket delivery van further up the valley.

The route climbed steadily from Eglwysbach to Pennant from where a by-way, dogged by invasive laurel, first dropped down then climbed up to post me on small lanes heading towards Llanddoged. A ruined house (also first of many) stood apologetically on the junction of by-way and tarmacked lane. In Scotland, good sections of mountain biking are often linked by either busy main roads or single-track roads with passing places; haunted by locals racing from one passing place to the next, they can be quite unpleasant on a push bike. The lanes encountered on the Cylchdaith Cymru are generally quiet and pleasant, often with wildflower verges, guardian trees and habitat rich bushes. Sometimes they share open views, but at other times they are dark and mysterious. Rarely is there much space to pass. Fortunately, few travel these routes and sometimes it seems a shame that so many of them were ever tarmacked. On this eastern side of Nant Conwy, I linked small lanes with the odd off-road section to keep me well away from the busy valley bottom roads. There were wonderful views across to the high peaks of Eryri as I passed the sleepy village of Llanddoged. Nant Bwlch-y-gwynt gave a taste of the terrain ahead. A bridleway was missing by Ty'n-y-bryn, no one was home in Capel Garmon and there was a lovely section of bridleway, reminiscent of the riding in the south Lake District, past Dinas Mawr.

I passed the campsite at Penrhyddion which would make a good end to day one, but the trouble with a journey like this is you never quite know how long anything will take, how you'll feel and what the surfaces will be like. In the bat of an eyelid, you can find yourself spending several hours pushing the bike up a hill or across rough terrain. One of the advantages of being a solo rider, complete with overnight camping gear, is the ability to be able to stop almost anywhere discreetly, slip into your dark green tent and spend the night, which brings us back to our evening nod to Sam and his girlfriend. They went their way, and I went to bed.

Day Two – Penmachno to Arthog

The trails flow beautifully. Quiet, manicured, fast-flowing, undulating, finely-surfaced and well-designed. I'm riding the closing sections of the Penmachno mountain bike trails which have been purpose-built for mountain bikes. It really does come fast. I can only glimpse briefly at the views, and I quickly lose any sense of where I am and which way I'm going. It's mountain bike country and it's fun. I've got the trail to myself, no one to keep up with and no one hassling me from behind. I've missed out the hard sloggy bits and jumped onto the fun closing sections. I ride a long way, down and then down again. A forest track climb is an interlude that is not unwelcome, particularly as it opens up more fantastic single track down to the finish of the built trails. One minute I'm looking down on Cwm Penmachno, and the next I'm high up and on a track, back to Penmachno village, knowing I have to complete a road ride to return almost all the way to Cwm Penmachno.

As I climbed to Ffynnon Eidda on the minor road from Carrog, I had my only adverse encounter with a motor car of the whole trip. An Audi came down the hill at speed as I was chugging up it, slowly but surely. I hoped he'd slow down... he must slow down at some point... he didn't slow down, passing me with no more than a metre to spare at a speed that felt far too fast. I stumbled off the road into the verge, turned, cursed him and threw a 'V' sign. He stopped further down the road, got out and shouted abuse at me for being on the road, then got back in and drove away at speed down the single-track road. I hate cycling on the road; I don't know why people do it.

This section is one of the longest road sections on the entire route. Fortunately, apart from Audi man, it's actually very quiet and it would be unusual to pass more than a handful of cars at all. It's mostly downhill too (after Ffynon Eidda that is) so it's fast and before long I was looking for the Roman Amphitheatre by Castell Tomen y Mur. I'd been here before so knew not to expect a grand structure, but still the fact that it's a mere, slightly circular, embankment remained a disappointment.

The route from here headed through history. There was a Norman motte, the Roman Amphitheatre, some Roman practice works (whatever they are) and, almost more interesting, there was a still-working slate quarry. It's a low-key affair; there seems to be one man, a digger and a quarry. He's churning out slate though, presumably to order. It was good to be passing the quarry. It's industrial, working and real, this is Wales after all. This journey passes countless contrasting landscapes and travels through many different land uses. It's totally appropriate that slate quarrying is one of those. Beyond the quarry the track was good. Yes, there was a little push here and there, but it was fun off-road mountain biking, wild country all the way to Trawsfynydd. The Cross Foxes in Trawsfynydd made a good lunch stop.

I could have pressed on to Coed y Brenin, but I didn't really want to rest there. I'd stopped there on version one of my Cylchdaith Cymru, and it had been a bit of a shock to the system. Far from being the conquering hero arriving to a hero's reception, I seemed to be the only one there with a big loaded bike, attempting to cycle the length of Wales. No one cheered me, no one knew about me, no one knew what I was doing, and no one cared. I wasn't the 'cool' one here. An anonymous face in a crowd with a big ugly bike that has stuff strapped to it. Weird. This was one of the few crowded places on this journey. My visit here on my version one trip had really put me off. I'd felt uncomfortable; I was clearly a bit different from everyone else. Though I swear I was mountain biking, I was not on the now ubiquitous electric mountain bike, I wasn't loud and I wasn't wearing lycra. On version two of my Cylchdaith Cymru I carried straight on and didn't even pause. I hopped straight on to the Minotaur trail (I wasn't going to miss that). I love it. It rides really well on a loaded bike, it's blue, it's flowy, it's fun. It sort of feels a bit naughty leaving the trail centre. Trail Centres have become the place to go mountain biking and when I'm near one, I almost feel as though I am penned in. It's like I've paid an admission fee, even if I haven't, and I'm not supposed to leave the arena and if I do there's no stamp on my wrist to let me back in. I was glad to leave the arena, even if it did mean a slog and push climb up the hill from Ganllwyd.

It's a hot day. I've ridden part of the Penmachno trail, some quick on road stuff, climbed a couple of big hills and gobbled up the flowy blue at Coed y Brenin. This is another hill to climb, and I am hot. When bikepacking you need to take your washes where you can. I duck under the bridge and strip off. The water is cold and it takes me a while to immerse myself, but my sweaty body enjoys every minute of it. Hot legs. Hot shoulders. I tip my head and hair under the water. It's pure joy. This is a good wash, a good cool wash, in a beautiful place.

Then I heard motorbikes. I dislike the noise and smell of motorbikes when off the beaten track. It just seems wrong that they should be allowed to accelerate the erosion of these wild places and to diminish the experience of peace and quiet in the countryside. I stayed in the water and let them go past. It really isn't worth doing anything else other than just avoid the intrusion. It's soon over. I dried myself on my pack towel then scrambled back up to the forest track I'd been following. That's when I heard another motorbike. Two had gone past and a third one arrived on the scene just as I reappeared. "Have you seen my two friends?" the German rider asked. I truthfully said I had not seen them, but I declined to say I'd heard them and suggest which way they had actually gone. He went the wrong way. I felt mean, but it was a slight meanness given that with their engines they'd soon regroup, which inevitably they did. I passed them later coming in the opposite direction. It turned out that as soon as they had regrouped, they realised they were all going the wrong way. They needed to turn around. These weren't the only motorbikes I saw on this journey. Indeed, on the very next day I encountered three more, also German. I pondered and stressed as to whether there might be promotion of off-road riding in Wales by someone in Germany, encouraging visitors of this intrusive persuasion to come and destroy the very places that make this land so special. Bog off.

I followed a good chunk of the Mawddach trail next. To reach it I crossed the lovely old wooden toll bridge. I actually didn't have the 30p required for the toll and I had to pay more to pay by phone, but that was OK. It's a grand old bridge that needs looking after. Across the bridge is the George III pub. It's difficult passing the pub, it's just so inviting, and, as ever, I failed to do so on this occasion. A drink and some crisps were in order, purely for salt replacement and rehydration purposes you understand. It's annoying how the clock speeds up when you stop and close to an hour had passed, seemingly in no time at all, before I was ready to depart. I followed the trail, completely level now as it followed the old line of a railway, winding its way along the estuary bank. It's almost perfectly flat, beautifully wooded and great for bird watching. It's serene and welcoming to cyclists and walkers who share the trail amicably. I did, however, need to find somewhere to stay.

Camp that night was a sneaky one. I won't tell you where because it was definitely in the garden of a holiday home. Well, when I say garden, I mean a field really. I wasn't in somebody's garden on their lawn and the only two properties visible were empty holiday homes. I generally like to be out of sight of any property, but these were most definitely empty, so I didn't feel too bad. It was a late night to bed and an early morning up. A 'dusk to dawn' wild camp.

I'm really organised with my camping now. I pick a spot, I remove two bags from my bike, one from the handlebars and one from the rear rack. The one on the handlebars contains my tent and sleeping kit. I pull out the tent which is always packed last, so it comes out first and, pretty quickly, the tent is up and pitched. It only needs one pole threading and two pegs in to look like a tent. It's served me well. I slide some 4 mm closed cell foam pad underneath the tent, this is better than an official tent footprint. I roll out my sleeping mat and pull out my sleeping bag. Everything has its place; my rucksack goes in the porch along with my stove and food. My clothes bags and spare clothes go in the tent along with my recharging bag and my reading glasses. I check to see if there's anything else I need on the bike and then roll into the tent stripping off my outer layer as I enter. Once I'm in I'm staying in. I lie on my side and cook dinner. When I'm in the tent, dinner is simply a matter of rehydrating some food that I have pre-prepared. I drink tea, black tea because carrying milk is a pain. I might have some sweets or chocolate for pudding. I usually read some pages of a book which I carry on my phone. I lie down with my head on the pillow that I've made from a dry bag encased in a T-shirt and stuffed with spare clothes plus the clothes I'm wearing. With my eyes shut I can put my hand on anything I need, torch, phone, electronics, water, even my blindfold and ear plugs should they be required. Everything has its place; it might not look tidy but it's organised.

I'm not sure that I actually like camping really, but it's a means to an end. It opens up incredible journeys and you get to some nice places. Camping makes these journeys possible. There is little option in central Wales other than to camp 'wild' as there are few people, fewer places and very few accommodation options (not without leaving the route anyway). But this type of camping is potentially a civil offence in the same manner as trespass. With the growth of roadside, vehicle-based so-called 'wild camping,' (it isn't 'wild' camping it's free camping, more akin to fly tipping, so it's often referred to as fly camping) it's becoming increasingly difficult for landowners and managers to look the other way.

In my lifetime, tinkers and travellers have slept in 'wild' camps. Before the motor car became ubiquitous, and especially before the railways, people walked for work, walked to see family, walked to find another life. This is how most people travelled across the British Isles. A few wealthier ones may have ridden horses, but most people walked. The drovers walked across this land to the south and the east of England with herds of cattle, sheep and geese. They didn't do it in a day, they didn't stay in the 'The

Drover's Arms' every night. They must have 'wild' camped. Wild camping is in our blood, it's our heritage. It should be our right.

Wild camping is lightweight, remote camping, and is typically a dusk till dawn scenario. It should not cause problems for local people or following travellers. It should not take place in obviously worked fields, with crops or livestock. It should be out of sight of dwellings and roads. All litter should be removed, and no pollution caused. No trace of passing is left. Roadside, vehicle-based camping is not really wild, and fires are not a normal part of this type of camping.

The Scottish Land Reform Act (2003) gives people the right to camp in this manner in Scotland, whereas in England and Wales you technically need the landowner's permission to do it. There's no way of knowing who the landowner is though, so take it as read, you're welcome to stay, as long as you are clean and tidy, unless there are signs to the contrary.

Day Three – Arthog to Bwlchystyllen

I knew this next section quite well as I'd ridden it before in both directions. It starts off with a beautiful green lane, past a bonnie old clapper bridge, past old houses with long stories and then there is a big ascent. On the map it's marked as Fordd Ddu, the black road.

Looking east, I can see the Cader edges, standing proud and seemingly impenetrable. There is a small, rocky hill which towers above Llynnau Cregennen giving a bite-size mountain that offers hope for aging walkers and youthful beginners. To the north-west is Barmouth bridge, arrow straight. It's the start of the Mawddach Trail and it's a shame to miss it on this journey. I make a note to return soon. Barmouth looks lovely in its strategic position where estuary meets sea. It's the home of the original national three peaks challenge, a challenge that linked Yr Wyddfa, Scafell Pike and Ben Nevis by sailing boat. I keep walking, it's not far now and the riding will be good. The Ffordd Ddu soon becomes a fine bikepacking track reminiscent of some of the Scottish glens. The surrounding land copies the north too. As I pick up some speed by Rhydcriw, I hear the unmistakable call of the chough. Sure enough, as I slow down, there's a small group, four or five, picking their way along the ridge above me. Working in synchronisation, landing, foraging, taking off then landing again and foraging again, ever on the lookout for baddies. It's a rare bird and a rare sight, one that I'm lucky to chance upon today.

Bryncrug has a pub that at the right time of day can be very welcoming. Failing that, as was my want on this particular occasion, Rhyd-yr-onen station provides a grand picnic spot, complete with shelter. No trains passed me on this visit, but you might be lucky at another time to see a steam train plying its trade on the tourist-orientated narrow-gauge Tal-y-Llyn railway.

The station has no staff but do look out for the 'pas will be prosecuted' sign slowly being digested by its host tree.

Then it was more classic terrain heading up to a track that runs alongside Nant Braich-y-rhiw. This track is often erroneously referred to as 'Happy Valley'. It's anything but. The anglicised name is promoted by the columns of 4x4 drivers who have destroyed this track. This ancient road, probably more than any other, illustrates the devastation these fragile surfaces can suffer when abused by motor vehicles. It might be legal, but it's not right and it shouldn't be. I'm pretty sure some poor motorbike etiquette has also contributed to the damage as well, particularly along sections where they try to get around the puddles formed by the 4x4s. There's one area where the track is at least fifty metres wide and it's like the surface of the moon. In anything but the driest of conditions, cyclists have to dismount and push around the damaged areas. This really does not seem fair.

I heard the motorbikes coming before I saw them. I'd just gone through a gate and the last thing I wanted to do was hold it open for them. I did pull over a couple of hundred yards from the gate and put on my best scowl. Each and every biker slowed down, nodded to me, then very gently accelerated away, making as little noise as possible. They were politely doing their legal thing. I grimaced as they were nice to me. Am I the bad man? I've actually met quite a lot of very respectful motorcyclists off road in the hills. Don't get me wrong I've seen some idiots too, but many are good people having fun and wish others no harm. At least riding a bike off-road requires some skill unlike those 4x4's...

It's a fun, steep and rocky downhill to the Dovey valley but there aren't any services yet. Cwrt and Pennal are devoid of such things and it's back up into the woods before dropping into Machynlleth. As an aside the highest point in the British Isles lurks innocently in these woods. Take a careful look at your OS map and you'll find a hill that's 2700 m high!

I'm in town. It feels wrong. Cars, people, shops and noise. Some elderly people shuffle along like they've had a hard life and are simply waiting for it to end. Others have a spring in their step, dressed in colours. Proud to be grey, they are living the retirement dream and enjoying every minute of it. Male youths hang around on a street corner, wearing sliders with white socks, dressed in shapeless jogging bottoms and black hoodies; they eye the girls that walk by. The girls jostle in small chattering groups. With quick conversations, clutched phones and cappuccino elbows they pretend not to notice the boys. But they do.

Machynlleth is welcoming, but it jars that so many of the youth seem to desire to be urban dwellers, that's the lifestyle they seem to choose. They could be out paddling, climbing, biking or walking, but no, street corners are the favoured habitat of our nation's youth.

There are good services here. A hidden hardware shop, a quirky hostel, a ride-in café, the tiniest of bike shops and a charity shop where I once replaced my forgotten spoon. There are large and small supermarkets, countless cafés and places to stay. For me though, on this occasion, it was only a lunchtime stop before, all too quickly, I was heading up the hill south towards the Cambrian desert.

Despite the climbing, I enjoyed the ride south from Machynlleth. It was interesting and quite varied, leading you through open pastures and contrasting woodlands. The tracks are good and well signed. You might, as I did, meet someone for a chat. It always helps to put the world to rights when you're high above Machynlleth. I passed the time of day with a couple of walkers struggling along the severely undulating Glyndwr's Way and then had to take avoidance action as two young mountain bikers hammered down the trail towards me, a little on the rude side I thought and unhelpful in our quest for better access and more shared traffic trails.

I cross Bwlch Hyddgen, and the Cambrian desert opens out before me. I can see large conifer plantations on all sides, but ahead of me are miles and miles over-grazed, depopulated, desolate, sheep-wrecked upland. I find a small 'wadi' to cycle down. So dry has the summer been the 'green desert' is turning brown, but I know this won't last. There is no one else on these trails, this part of Wales has become the bikepacker's own. It's good for us, there are old and new routes, progress can be made, and discreet camping spots abound. There is only one other significant group of recreationalists who love mid Wales, and they are a lot noisier that we are.

The term green desert was first used by nineteenth-century English travellers to the region. It's been desolate and treeless for some time now. The Welsh name is from a different root, Elenydd, meaning along the banks of the Afon Elan. Elan meaning fawn or hind, but I saw no deer. The so-called Cambrian Mountains were once in the mix to become one of our national parks, vested interests probably put a kibosh on that plan. Today, some hope it will be recognised as at least, an area of Outstanding Natural Beauty. In the meantime, they choose to call it an area of 'astounding natural beauty'. It does have some pretty bits, but these are usually around the edges, deep-wooded valleys or manicured farmland with hedges, barns and quaint farmhouses. The bulk of it has been overworked, by miners, foresters and sheep farming. The industrial archaeology of the mines requires more than a passing glance and this region would have been every bit as busy, as populated and as important as the southern valleys of Wales or the slate mines and quarries of the north. Copper, gold, silver and lead were mined here for over 2000 years. The coniferous plantations are often home to windfarms and large machinery, their good roads help us along the way. It was George Monbiot who, in his 2014 work Feral, called this area a "dead zone, devoid of life". Monbiot put the blame fairly and squarely on intensive subsidised sheep farming of the 1970's and onwards. He coined the term 'sheepwrecked'.

There is a grandeur to the openness, but this is a landscape bereft of life and beauty as we know it. Climatically much of this area could be temperate rainforest. Instead, the early industrial revolution shift from cattle and small scale, mixed farming, to larger scale sheep ranching has denuded the biodiversity of this area to a state from which it will struggle to recover on its own. It's still abused, not just by off-roaders and foresters, but by idiots visiting the bothies. Go to any of the four fantastic bothies in these hills and you will find trees chopped down for firewood and part cut in a vain search for warmth. Once a upon a time everyone knew you couldn't burn green wood. When did people become so detached from the land and nature that they forgot this? These Cambrian Mountains are not mountains, they are not beautiful, but they are great, wild, lonely and empty places to ride your bike. You'll find your peace and solitude here and not much else, unless of course its rally day…

But first to camp. I passed the half empty Nant-y-moch Reservoir and followed rough tracks west. I passed some walkers heading east on a 24-hour cross Wales walk, looking very tired with many miles still to go. I tucked in beneath some ash trees, by a long-abandoned farmstead close to the track. On a previous visit, just up slope from this camp, I had come across mountain pansies. These are not common on my Eryri patch. To my west was an unappetising flat, wet landscape of soft rush. In the distance another grazed hill rose above Llyn Craigypistyll which I could just glimpse, and it seemed further away in real life than it looked to be on the map. I could see the edge of conifer plantations that would run down to tightly farmed fields hemmed in with barbed wire. Each field littered with sheep shit, empty sheep lick buckets and discarded fleece. A robin, a wren and the dying ash were all that made this spot a snug one.

I settled into my tent, shedding outer layers and boots. I popped on my warm jacket and enjoyed lying down. Dinner was my standard freeze-dried meal. Couscous or freeze-dried rice is made more appealing with spices, herbs, freeze dried onions, garlic, peppers and so on. Various combinations come together to make up Italian style, Moroccan style or Indian style. It does the job.

Day Four – Bwlchystyllen to Bwlch y Ddau Faen

The following morning, I followed a good level track from my discreet wild camp towards Llyn Syfydrin. The track was dry and it rode well. There was one ford, but I could squeeze across the adjacent footbridge. Two 4x4s passed me coming the other way. They were clearly in first gear just crawling along, the drivers barely holding the steering wheel, just making more dips for the rain to sit when it next comes along. I arrived at the Llyn under the gaze of a group of portly gentlemen also armed with 4x4s. They were here to marshal and watch a rally, that they couldn't believe I hadn't heard of. I asked them if they could keep the noise down, but they seemed to think I was joking! Their amused, yet jovial banter resonated in my ears as I cycled on. Sadly, I'd arrived on a day where motor sport was in the area. It was the weekend of the Rali Ceredigion. Remarkably in these days of climate change, a group of people are still burning fossil fuels for fun as well as disturbing the peace and quiet of the countryside in an act which can only be considered (by me anyway) as utter vandalism. I'd love to say each to their own, but really this should be winding down to a stop. Slightly further south and the *rali* forced me to detour (surely 'sail' should have right of way over power?)

At Nant y Arian I enjoyed a run down the trails. It's always nice to pop on to a deserted, purpose-built, flowy trail. It wasn't far, but it felt great and it always feels a little cheeky to cruise down trails like this when fully laden with bikepacking gear. The visitor centre and café was closed and deserted. The entrance from the road was blocked with high barriers and keep out signs were posted on the other side, not my side. I could only just squeeze past the end of the barriers. I would have loved to have stopped for coffee and a bacon butty, but thanks to the *rali* that was not an option on this day. I accelerated away, downhill on fast tarmac then off onto silent lanes, far from the smattering of rally fans. A dog with a scowl and a growl emerged to dissuade me from leaving the lane and taking the bridleway through her patch, but I committed, and she kept clear. Noisy, but not a biter. Phew. It was with slightly mixed feelings that I enjoyed the descent into the deep Vale of Rheidol. It was very good though. I crossed some fields on a sweet, grassy, curving line, then steeply down a wooded track – an ancient bridleway. In the valley bottom, on reaching the minor dead-end road, I breathed deeply for I knew that the only way out was a big push, having done exactly that on a previous visit. But I've said it before, it's all part of the game and after wiggling around the unobvious route over the bridge to avoid a ford, I commenced my climbing. This steep uphill push could be avoided by using the road and heading further west, but that's not what I was there for, so push it was. I was cycling in dry weather after a long dry period, but this was a wet push, through temperate rainforest. It's been wet every time that I have visited. It's a good track, but it's steep, very steep. I like it though. It's an important part of this journey and it gives time to look around, to listen and to contemplate the journey. Embrace the push. Rhiwfron Halt, complete with shelter, gave me a nice break point and a chance for some more trainspotting. This is the Vale of Rheidol Railway, built in the early 1900s to capitalise on the lead and timber trades operating in the upper part of the valley. It's an impressive line clinging on to a shelf high up on the valley side. Today it's a popular tourist line, which gave me an opportunity to wait for the next train and enjoy the passing of a steam locomotive whilst waving to strangers on the train.

There is some confusion about which way to go above Coed Tynycastell. The map shows a bridleway and a cycleway on separate lines. I'd tried to follow the bridleway previously and I'd followed the cycleway in the opposite direction. Neither route flowed well, and both have blockages. Both lead to a scruffy farm with copious junk. The story assembles itself.

On my Cylchdaith Cymru route small lanes lead from here to the little known (and unnamed on the Ordnance Survey maps) Llantrisant Church. This is a lovely, peaceful spot to shelter. Although the current church is 19th Century, there is evidence on the site that it has been a sacred place for many hundreds of years. It's got some great bridleways passing it too. But today, the approach lane was closed and I was forbidden to visit this quiet place. The *rali* had taken over. I passed by, close to Pontarfynach, then down an ace bridleway by Rhosyrhiw. It's a slippery, treelined, cobbled old route and care is required. Tree debris is ever present. Whilst that atmospheric old lane took me just where I needed to be, the bridleway to the west, past Craig y Fan, might be more agreeable to most people.

I have a fondness for Pont-rhyd-y-groes and I'm not quite sure why. There really isn't very much there. It's not a pretty village: it has no centre, no village green, no lovely old bridge and not even a tempting pub. There is a pub there, but it doesn't operate as a pub. It can be pre-booked for overnight accommodation, and it caters well for the bikepacker. There's a wonderful book swap in the bus stop, but the main feature is the cafe. This is an unusual café. If Sharon is there it's great: chatty, comforting and welcoming. If she's not there it works on an honesty basis, so you go in, make yourself a brew and leave the appropriate amount of money. What's on offer to eat can be variable. On my last visit the place was being rewired so hopefully it will become more amenable to those searching for a decent lunch. But Pont-rhyd-y-groes has an agreeable feel and I've always found it friendly and welcoming. From Pont-rhyd-y-groes however, it's back to climbing.

I was now entering the hallowed ground of mid-Wales bikepacking. I knew I couldn't go everywhere on this journey, so I decided I'd stick to the classic route along the Claerwen reservoir.

An alternative is to descend to Strata Florida. It's a brilliant track down to the ruined abbey which is well worth a visit. From there you climb through plantations to a good viewpoint. Then you drop down, then you climb up, then you wiggle your way through another plantation to the head of the Dothie valley. The descent here is long single track and it's very quiet. It's a classic of Welsh mountain biking. It's not perfect though as it's quite boggy and very wet in places. It doesn't flow quite as well as you might have been led to believe! It's also hampered by bracken when that gets going in the summer season and it's best enjoyed in a dry spell outwith the bracken season.

I'd chosen the fine gravel past the Claerddu bothy down to the Claerwen Dam as the best route for my Cylchdaith Cymru. If you are new to the area, it's a must do route. If you've been here before it may well have been coming the other way on the Trans Cambrian Route. Here you'll fully appreciate the wide-open spaces of the Cambrian desert. You might see sheep, you might see ponies, you might see motorbikes, or an ancient land-rover as I did. The driver of the Land Rover pulled over to say hello. He had a passenger and they both looked old enough to know better. It turned out they were on the way to rescue another old Land Rover which the passenger had, accidently and rather unfortunately, driven off the road the day before. These things happen in the 4x4 community and I'm usually uninterested, however, on this occasion the age of the Land Rover definitely caught my eye. I asked the driver about the vehicle. It was built in 1958, "It's older than me!" I exclaimed. He then told me that he was brought up near the Land Rover factory where it was built and actually went passed it every day on the bus to school. He reckons that as a seven year old he may well have been going past the factory when this particular Land Rover rolled off the production line 65 years ago! I suppose it just goes to show that even in the 4x4 community there are some interesting tales to be heard. As for the land around this gravelled road, it's pretty mournful, very quiet and if I'm totally honest, abused. This is no place for agoraphobics.

I arrive at the dam as the heavens open. One of those torrential downpours you get in a summer storm. I ride as fast as I can down the hill on a long zig and then a zag, to the public toilet below the dam. In minutes I'm soaked to the skin. There's an open porch and I dash in, out of the rain. It's only been ten minutes, but I'm cold and wet. It's a lonely place. Two sheep wander past, probably after the same shelter, but they look away, as aloof as sheep can muster. They walk on and pretend they are going to a better spot. It's an act, like when you've been ignored for too long in a shop or at bar. You pretend it's OK and you're not bothered, but inside you're properly pissed off. That's how the sheep looks, I can see it in her sideways glance. I'm lay down on the floor of the disabled loo, taking the chance to get horizontal, I've brought my bike in too. I've locked the door and I toy with the idea of staying here for the night. On the one hand it's dry and warm, on the other it's a toilet. I eventually decide it's too early to stop for the night.

The rain cleared – to be fair it was the first rain for a few weeks – and I knew the track on the other side of the valley is another one abused by the 4x4s. I'd rather get it over with in the evening than do it first thing in the morning. The track goes OK in this direction, heading east that is, and then it's a fair old climb up to Bwlch y Ddau Faen where I managed a discrete overnight camp.

There can be quite a lot of romanticism about the idea of wild camping. Yes, of course it can be wonderful. You might have enjoyed a swim in a remote lake, you might have shared your meal with friends, you may have lain back in the dark and watched shooting stars, or at least seen an amazing array of stars in the darkest of our skies. And one thing Elenydd does have is dark skies.

But typically, it's not like that. You wake earlier than you want to either because of the wind or the sun. Your tent will be flapping, and you can hear the next big gust of wind approaching before it hits you. It might have been a dry night, but you'll still be disappointed by how wet your tent is with dew and condensation. You thought you'd pitched it level, but you've woken to find yourself scrunched into the bottom end of the tent or rolled off to one side. Despite having done this several times before, things have disarrayed themselves in the night. You stare at your unseemly collection of litter which you're not quite sure how to manage. A half-used teabag that you want to use for breakfast, another bloody plastic bag and some of that foil off the chocolate. Which bin does that go in? You might be too hot or too cold in your sleeping bag. Once awake you probably won't sleep longer, you can try, but the daylight will win through and you're just wasting time.

In most tents, it looks sunny because of the bright colours used on the inner. When you do peep out of the door, it's cloudy. The forecast says dry, but you can feel, and even hear, moisture in the wind. You don't really want to strike a wet tent, but it's something you have to get used to. And then there's your body: your back aches and your legs are tired. Cramp is never far away. Lying down feels right, but you know you need to move. You are sweaty even though you've tried to wash with a mug of water and a little bit of sponge. Wouldn't a shower and a shave be great? You can't have it. You need to lie on your side and light the stove. You have to start your morning. Tea and porridge follow, then the dreaded packing. Get yourself on auto pilot. The weather is never as bad as it seems once you are out and in it. It all hurts your back a bit more, but this is the joy of wild camping. If you're a bike packer, it's a means to an end. It just goes with the terrain. Packing up, you reverse the order of events that took place the previous evening. You can get quicker and slicker with practice. I can do everything under my tent outer when the weather is foul, then emerge, nip that down, stuff it in the last dry bag, strap that on to my rear rack and jump (ha!) on the bike and pedal away. Once your legs are turning, you're in the place you belong. Enjoy riding for now, you'll soon be pushing again.

Day Five – Bwlch y Ddau Faen to Llanddeusant

The track up to Carnau is on the indistinct and featureless side of things. This is a monotonous moor, with very little going on apart from the odd sheep picking its way across the coarse grasses of the already overgrazed upland. If I were to describe the route to Carnau it's as follows: 'Push your bike along indistinct tracks, turn right at the rock and head for the summit of Carnau'. I know that sounds a little simplistic for a moorland journey of a couple of miles, but there does seem to be just the one rock up there amidst the endless tussocks of *Nardus stricta and Molinia Caerulea*. That one rock, which is angled into the ground as though placed there as a proud standing stone, is just where you turn right and if you can see it, head across to the cairned summit of Carnau. Summit might be a slightly misleading word. This is a slightly higher hummock atop a bit of a slope which happens to be where people have piled stones to make a cairn. Looking around I felt that there were other prominences, mounds and lumps that could equally have lay claim to the grandiose title of 'summit'. That these stones are marked, by the ordnance survey as a 'pre-roman antiquity' might seem a little far-fetched just now, but 2000 years ago this track may well have been a well-travelled route between Elan and Abergwesyn.

I undertook this Cambrian crossing on a clear day and attaining the so-called summit of Carnau presented few problems. On another day, low cloud might have meant a misty march on a compass bearing. The tracks, under wheel and foot, were not always clear on the ground having been scribbled over by countless sheep tracks. Carnau felt like the summit of my Cylchdaith Cymru route, but at a mere 537 metres above sea level there was actually higher to come on Y Mynydd Du. With its large cairn though it was a place to stop, take stock, and admire the views. It also had a halfway feel about it. It isn't geographically halfway, but psychologically, from '*by yere*' I was in *Cymru De*, south Wales, and *Cymru Gogledd* was far behind me. Continuing south it was downhill and this was a fine, long, very enjoyable descent. I rode carefully across the moor, avoiding tussocks, picking out sheep trails, but as the way down steepened my speed increased and a smile flickered across my face. I needed to concentrate. I was in a remote place with no phone reception, but this 'wild' riding is a large part of what it's all about. I soon entered a forest which wasn't quite as much fun, but the tracks were fast and clear leading all the way down into the very quiet Nant Bach-helyg.

I tried a bridleway heading south by Llethr Bach-helyg. I should have known better than to even try and open the gate!

Gates can be one of the most annoying aspects of bikepacking. There are too many gates. On my Cylchdaith Cymru, I counted the gates, there were more than 300 in total, but this was one of the worst ones. There really is no set procedure for passage through a gate. I look ahead and, on approach, try to gauge its geniality. I look for a sound hinge, the base clear of the ground and for the latch to be accessible. If the closure is of a clip style, I'll dismount my bike on the gate side and hold it clear of where the gate would open. Ideally the gate opens away from me, less helpful is when it opens towards me. It's a tad bothersome when the gate opens this way and I have to reverse the bike to open it enough to get through. Somehow, I constantly seem to be doing this. If there's a hedge, a fence or a post, it's easier just to lean the bike against that, then wrestle with the gate. It certainly will be a wrestle if it's a complex opening, a disintegrating gate or one that needs lifting to open.

Some gates are well-behaved and swing open with a gentle push. A graceful gate will gently return to me ready for closure, having stayed open for just the right amount of time to pass through. Some gates can't wait to get away and as I free the latch they fly to the other side of the track. Then I need somewhere to lean my bike whilst I go and fetch the gate. Gates without suitable bike leaning posts are to be treated with suspicion; it's rare they're well-behaved.

Next, the gate needs closing. If it's a nice clip it can swing back into place as good as gold, then I can be on my way. If it's a bolt that needs pulling back and inserting, then this can be hard to do whilst holding on to the bike. The worst gates are the ones that need lifting to ensure closure and fastening. Opening and closing gates is a bind, but it's a good reason to take a companion with you, especially a quick strong one, like a Nige or a Matt.

If travelling in a group, then there is one particular drawback to gates of which you need to be mindful. For some reason each member of the group likes to stop in the gate. I'm sure it's just a courtesy, just a pleasant passing of the time, just a human need to say thank you to the person holding the gate. I know one particular group where they have instigated a 10-metre rule. It's strictly enforced and can cause a slight mood to descend over the group should the 10-metre rule be disobeyed. The 10-metre rule means when passing through a gate which has been held open by another member of the team, thou shalt not stop within 10 metres of the gate. This ensures clear passage for everybody and no bottleneck in the gateway. It means that while the group have a little chat beyond the gate, the gatekeeper can complete his or her duties and ensure the gate is firmly back where it belongs.

Look out for bailer twine. If the gate is secured by bailer twine, that yukky-orange-nylon-frizzy stuff, it must be suspected of not playing ball. Sometimes it's a simple loop that can be slipped on and off the gate post. Sometimes, bailer twine can be knotted. Sometimes that knot will come undone easily. Sometimes that knot will not come undone. I admit I carry a knife, a pocket penknife, and I slice the bailer twine apart. Of course, afterwards, as best I can, I re-tie the gate closure. It can be a little frustrating when a gate closes perfectly well on its own and doesn't actually need the extra bailer twine. I can't help but feel someone's being a little awkward.

This particular gate, at the base of Llethr Bach-helyg, was one of those that fell open at an angle. It happens when one hinge is dysfunctional; it's a sign that the gate is rarely used. It's back-breaking work to open it, get your bike through and then close it behind you. I wrestled my way through to the other side and wedged the gate across the opening behind me. I was determined to use the mapped bridleway. I pushed my bike for about ten yards and looked up. It was a mistake coming this way: it was steep and overgrown. I couldn't face it. I turned around and resumed my gate combat in order to extricate myself. I took the road for a short distance, to pick up forest tracks around Bryn Mawr. I tend to try and avoid Bryn Mawrs, for it means big hill in Welsh. This track however, contoured around nicely and gained height in an orderly fashion. On this occasion the long way around had turned out to be the easy way around. Not only that, some fine riding took me through the Irfon forest and down to Llanwrtyd Wells.

Llanwrtyd Wells is a good place for services. It's a small place though. Indeed, it claims to be the smallest town in Wales. I found a cafe almost immediately and, although it was nearly midday, I fancied a proper cooked breakfast. It's tricky when the frontage of a cafe is onto the pavement, particularly a narrow one such as this, and there's nowhere satisfactory to leave a bike. Fortunately, this cafe had a tea garden round the back. I was very pleased to be able to take my bike into the garden and not only leave it safely there, but also be able to get my wet tent out from the night before. I draped it over the railings and brambles at the bottom of the space overlooking the Afon Irfon. The blackberries were nice too.

Llanwrtyd Wells was put on the map in 1732 when the Reverend Theophilus Evans spied a healthy-looking frog sitting in a spring-fed well. He thought that the water in which the frog was living would therefore hold qualities that might be beneficial to people. Quite soon this sulphuric spring was a destination for health tourists from all over Britain.

Taking the waters is not so much of a draw for tourists in the 21st Century so Llanwrtyd Wells has diversified and made a speciality of specialty, some might say daft or odd, events. Llanwrtyd Wells is home to the World Bog Snorkelling Championships, the World Championship Mountain Bike Chariots race, the Mari Lwyd (burning torches, procession and poetry on New Years' Eve), Welsh Open Stone Skimming, the Trailhead Beef Jerky Devil's Staircase Trail Race, an international horse v. man challenge, a Bogathlon (60 yard bog snorkel, 2 mile cross-country cycle, 1 mile cross-country run) and the rather tame sounding Real Ale Wobble (except that is undertaken on a cross country bike ride interspersed with drinking local ales). And that's not a comprehensive list. I get the idea that Llanwrtyd Wells is home to a few rather eccentric, but fun-loving people. It's either the maddest or the most fun place to live in Wales. I tried not to eat my lovely big breakfast in a competitive style for fear of starting a new event.

Non-descript forest riding led me to Halfway. That is, a place called 'Halfway' rather than halfway on the journey. Quite where Halfway is halfway between I have no idea. Trying to internet search 'where is Halfway halfway between' doesn't bring up any satisfactory results I'm afraid.

I had a miserable time on Mynydd Myddfai. I started cycling along the ridge and it was a good track. I'd really wanted to carry on along the summit ridge, but the inviting track took a left turn and it's the one marked on the map as a bridleway. It ran down to the edge of the forest above the Usk Reservoir where it turned southeast. It was well-marked on the map and I couldn't find any good reason not to follow the official route. The first bit looked excellent, and it was. I had a blast down to the edge of the forest, but there it ended. There was no track leading southeast. With hindsight I should have retraced my route back up to the ridgeline. When I pass this way again, I'll stay up there and carry on over the summit of Mynydd Myddfai. But no, I couldn't be bothered going back up, so I carried on pushing, pushing and pushing. It was by far the worst bit of my journey. It was at least three kilometres of pushing through mat grass, soft rush and general bog. To cap it all, right at the end, there was a wooded section where there was no track. I had to jungle bash downhill for another half kilometre before finally meeting, what turned out to be, a lovely track. It's actually the track that leads down from the top of Mynydd Myddfai, a well-surfaced track with new, easy-to-open, gates. It'll be a nicer ride next time.

Then it was that time of day when a place to rest overnight needed to be located. It was raining. I was wet and getting wetter. Dusk was fast approaching. Had Mynydd Myddfai gone better I might have camped up there or even made it further up on to Mynydd Du. The land was now farmed more intensively and offered little hope for a surreptitious overnight stay. I chatted to one old farmer and dropped hints about sleeping in a barn. He gave me water, but no offers of a roof were forthcoming. Perhaps I should learn to be a bit more direct.

I'm stood in the doorway dripping, unsure about entering. I struggle to find the confidence to do so. I can see the light at the window, and hear voices talking, it looks like someone's house. I hear knives and forks; I can tell its mealtime. It's a youth hostel; I know the accommodation is available for group bookings only, but it's raining and almost dark.

I'd arrived at the Youth Hostel below Y Mynydd Du. I thought perhaps it might be worth just asking if I could stay, particularly as I'd failed to be direct with the farmer a short while earlier.

Seeking the kindness of strangers, I opened the door and immediately felt bad. I was dripping from head to foot and soaking the threshold. It was a cosy scene; the group were enjoying a fine home-cooked meal. The warden (I presumed) was at the stove, working hard. Everyone stopped what they were doing and it went quiet. All heads turned in my direction. It wasn't quite American Werewolf in London, but it was awkward.

I managed to speak when looked at, as politely as I possibly could – overdoing it somewhat I'm sure, I wondered if there might be a bed available for a stranger in the night. It was only as I spoke that I realised what an awkward position I'd put the warden in. She'd have to check with the group. The group were now in the awkward position, and they were sat in front of me enjoying their evening meal.

No one would have had the heart say no to the polite but dripping stranger on the doorstep and fortunately for me, they didn't. Not only that, but they also cleared out of one of the dormitories, so I had a room to myself. That night under the roof with good company (a mature team who were walking the Brecon Way in chunks) some comfort and a shower was perfect for me before the ascent of Mynydd Du: the Black Mountain.

Day Six – Llanddeusant to Swansea

I'm stark naked in the furthest spot from the road that it's possible to get in southern Britain. I'm submerged in the shallow head waters of the Afon Twrch, sun beating down on one of the hottest days of the year. I feel like I've cooked myself as I pedalled and pushed to penetrate the vastness of Y Mynydd Du. The cooling effect of the water enveloping me is magical. I'm relaxed, legs soothing, my body content as the chilly waters flow gently over my body. Looking upstream it seems like I could reach out and touch the summit of Fan Brycheiniog, whilst downstream I can see a tiny area of native woodland hiding in a steep sided gorge, I wonder what lives in there. There's the odd meadow pipit on the endless grassland whilst a grey wagtail hunts waterborne insects just downstream. This is sheep country, there's little life on the beggared grassland which stretches to all my horizons. The odd greener section marks the higher ground, limestone country, but the sandstone soils are impoverished and the over-worked land is species deficient. It's quiet, nay silent, with not the slightest whisper of wind.

Refreshed, I stand up and dry myself. I get dressed. I want to linger longer in the mini oasis, but it's time to move on. I struggle my bike up the embankment away from the watercourse to be greeted by some cheery hellos. I gulp with relief at my fortuitous timing and welcome the burdened D of E youths to the middle of nowhere.

That was a close call, but it was great to see them out there, clearly on a mission and having an adventure. They were planning to camp on the shores of my pool. I think they'd earned the right to be there, carrying the heavy loads under the burning sun all day. It was nice to pass the time of day with their instructor, one of my own kind.

This memory had been my experience the previous year. On this circuit it was still a fine day, but less hot and I needed to keep going. I was excited about the contrast that this upland would make to what lay ahead. This journey has always been partly about seeing Wales, visiting different places, seeing contrasting land uses and unravelling its palimpsest landscapes. On this day I would journey from the remote uplands through the Swansea valley to the coast and to the city. But that lay ahead.

I'd left the hostel in good time and plunged into a walled lane that led me down and across a deep wooded river gorge. I love those lost fragments of our ancient woods which are found tucked away, hiding around and within our overworked landscape. But there was of course, a steep climb to exit the gorge. Some fields led to the edge of the open country. A steep tree-lined lane led me away from cultivation to the barren prairie of Y Mynydd Du. The trees provided some shade for the slow ascent. This was clearly an ancient way, a sunken lane, a drover's way. Although the lane was steep it meant that I gained height quickly. At the top of the lane the slopes relented, and I ventured on the grassy moor. I could ride my bike again, there would be pushing ahead, but there would also be descents and gentle climbs. From here, Y Mynydd Du is an undulating plateau to be crossed, all around 550 metres above sea level. It was good to be there on a dry clear day as the vague, intermittent yet somehow alluring tracks led me on.

There was a richness of views over the fertile lands of the Dyffryn Tywi. I could see towards Llandovery, Llandeilo and I could (just) pick out Castell Carreg Cennen, the original finish of the trans-Wales Dragons' Back Race. On foot, participants traverse the spine of the land from Conwy to Cardiff in around the same time as I was doing on my bike. The race is run over six days; it would also take me six days with the aid of a bike and excluding the highest tops, to cover Wales from coast to coast.

I like the openness of these uplands. It reminds of my youthful forays on the south Pennines. There are even some jagged edges of limestone above the acidic Twrch sandstone, the geological Welsh equivalent of the much-loved Millstone grit found in my Yorkshire homeland. The limestone has been worked. Depressions and mounds abound. For hundreds of years this was a working landscape with the limestone being quarried to use as fertiliser or in the early iron industry. It's hard to imagine teams of tweed-clad, leather-booted, flat-capped men chipping away at the ground, or leading ladened pack horses on this lonely, remote upland.

Today the Black Mountain is an empty quarter. Large sheep nibble the sweet grasses on the high limestone. I also saw a squirrel, far from the nearest trees. I don't know why it's called the Black Mountain though, there is nothing black here, except maybe the winter clouds.

I had to keep my wits about me to spot the track, but as I headed further east it became better marked. It wandered between sinkholes and visited circular pools full of legend. As the plateau was crossed near Cerreg Goch, the track became fast and the way towards to the Swansea Valley was free rolling. The verdant valley of Cwm Tawe came into view below the valley scarp, with little evidence of the urban conurbations that lay just around the corner. It's a steep, rocky descent down to Glyntawe. Glyntawe shows little sign of industry, past or present, as the village lies just beyond the south Wales coalfield. It is home to the Dan-yr-Ogof show caves, a Shire Horse Centre and a friendly pub. Today it's passed through all too briefly by the motorist on the A4067, its attractions diverting few of them. I suspect it may be different at the weekend, but on this fine weekday, I had the place to myself.

I crossed the valley to find a lovely tree-lined bridleway of the highest order. There's a real feeling of history on this wooded way. It's good that it hasn't been tarmacked and the main road runs on the other side of the valley. Native woodland, caves, a nature reserve and the river Tawe peacefully led towards Penycae where I followed the main road briefly, but neatly to a handy shop, heading for the NCN 43.

National Cycle Route 43 is one of the Sustrans marked cycle routes of which there are now many miles across the south Wales' valleys. I wanted to incorporate some of these routes into my Cylchdaith Cymru for contrast. This one provided an exceptionally good traffic-free route into Swansea and on to the coast. The NCN routes generally provide good links between interesting bits of mountain biking and whilst the network is not perfect (there are many missing links) it's a brilliant step in the right direction. I'd love to see groups like Sustrans, the BMC, Cycling UK and the Ramblers working much more closely together lobbying Governments and councils to create traffic free foot and wheel ways.

I gained the NCN 43 up a steep hill in Abercraf and sped along the sylvan former railway line to Ystalyfera. It's an irritating trip through this small town. It might be handy if you need to stock up, but I confused my way through and back onto the 43 by the Ystalyfera Iron Works, which is now a supermarket offering part-time work to former steelworkers, shopkeepers, other ancillary trades people and their family members. Such is life in the valleys today. Still, they have got the NCN 43 to pass along and it really is very good. I continued southwest along the former rail bed barely noticing any built-up locations on either side.

What I did notice however, was the memorial to the Gleision Colliery disaster of 2011. That four men could go to work in the UK in the 21st

Century and not come home at the end of the day or indeed, ever again, is quite unfathomable. It would have been rude to whizz past the formal and homemade memorials here and not pause for a moment or two of reflection. How lucky I was to be here, cruising along on my bike with not a care in the world.

Further down the valley the NCN 43 switches from the old railway line to the Swansea canal towpath. Even as I headed into Swansea itself, with retail park, a new stadium and a plethora of modern roads overhead, the route was wonderful to cycle on. It gets a bit confusing in the redeveloped dockland area, but before you know it you've popped out on the Promenade at Swansea. Or should it be Abertawe, the mouth of the Tawe? Though in this case, it's possible the name Swansea, with its Viking origins, actually predates the Welsh name!

If you've never been to Swansea, then you might be surprised to discover that it really is a seaside city. Ok, the tide goes so far out that on some days you can't even see the sea. And, in line with contemporary urban planning fashions, the city is separated from the massive sandy beach by a dual carriageway. So, it isn't perfect, but on the bike it must be one of the easiest cities to pass through. The cycleway on the front runs all the way around the bay to Mumbles. You'll have flocks of sea birds on your left, a busy road, prison and university on your right and joggers heading straight for you.

I am lucky to have lovely friends in Swansea. It's always been a joy to spend time with Pete and Hilary. When I lived in Frome in Somerset, Pete came to knock on my door and welcomed me to the small town. He invited me on the weekly climbing evenings and the Wittocks Lane Ramblers monthly walks. It was a super place to live and being made so welcome was perfect. That Pete and Hilary had now relocated to Swansea was wonderful for me and gave a great opportunity to catch up.

It did make me think a little about the fallacy of the kindness of strangers. I've read so many travel books which feature impromptu meetings with people the author has never encountered before. I'm ever so jealous. Maybe it's because I'm an ageing man who's travelling solo and is self-sustained, maybe it's because I know where I'm going or maybe it's because I don't ingratiate myself enough with people, or maybe it's not true. On this journey one of the things that I had decided to do was to make sure I made myself talk to strangers. If a random bloke comes up to you who's rather smelly, got dirty legs and is pushing an oversized, overloaded filthy bike, don't be alarmed. It might be me. When did we stop talking to strangers?

I'm sure it's the reason we've become scared of catching the bus.

My plan was to ask people for water. I don't carry a water filter. The water I collect on the hills is fine to drink and I can usually find a tap somewhere to fill up. Maybe I refill in a pub, a cafe or a garage. Towards the end of every day, when I'm heading into camp, I do need water. If there is no tap available, I look for a person to ask. I will scan the gardens to see if there's anybody out and about. I will look at houses to see if they have an outside tap. I've even waved at people in the window (rather like a scary madman) to attract their attention to ask if I can have some water. It always works. "I wonder if it wouldn't be too much trouble if you could possibly let me fill up my water bottles, please?" Typically, people will enjoy being asked. They will appreciate being generous, they will even wash my water bottles and ask about my journey. We have a little chat that I think makes them feel better and it certainly lifts my day, so the kindness of strangers has to be sought and the way I seek it is by asking for water. For this evening however, I was in the company of good friends.

I went to stay with Peter and Hilary. Their water was lovely and plentiful.

Day Seven – The Gower Cylchdaith

The Gower peninsula became Britain's first area of outstanding natural beauty in 1956. There's no doubt the coastline is spectacular, but inland tends to be rather more agricultural and for the cyclist it can be all too easily dominated by the A4118. I found a couple of versions of a bikepacking Gower route to try. There is a saying that time spent in reconnaissance is never wasted and that proved the case here for me. On a work trip I'd checked out the Rhossili end of the trail and on my previous round I'd followed someone else's route in an anticlockwise direction; the one on bikepacking.com. This route was good but through Parkmill is slow on a bike and the busy road is unpleasantly narrow. I wondered if this could be avoided. I also thought it seemed a shame to be pushing my bike up the hill above Rhossili beach rather than enjoying the descent and the view. The other piece of track I found was the Cline Valley Cycle track and I wanted to incorporate that as well. I swotted up, studied the map and decided to reverse the direction of travel: I would go clockwise around the Gower.

I left the coastal cycleway at Black Pill and ascended to Cline Farm. It's an easy climb and it takes you onto some lovely grassy bridleways across a golf course towards the airport. A brief section of the A 4118 is level and wide, before turning left to Kittel with its independent family bakery. Something that struck me about purchasing food from the bakery in Kittle was that the delicious pastry and custard slice were served in paper bags. The coffee came in a cardboard cup, consequently the amount of litter produced therefore was pretty insignificant compared to a typical supermarket stop where you end up with plastic and cardboard galore and sometimes things that are not even recyclable.

One of the gems I discovered on this journey was crossing the golf course at Southgate. I know that sounds a bit bizarre but actually it was a really pleasant experience. Golf courses can be a little intimidating to the public rights of way user. You know where you should be (if you can read a map) and you don't want to spoil anybody's game, but you need to spy ahead to spot any waymarkers. Here, at Pennard Golf Club, a double line of boulders, painted white, marked the way ahead. It seemed too good to be true, but when I checked with a golfer, he was very welcoming and reassuring. He even suggested some useful details to look out for on the way, such as where to turn. It all adds to the rich variety of this route. I stayed off the road by using a bridleway past the campsite at Nott Hill and then it was the classic section of Gower bike packing up onto Cefn Bryn.

Cefn Bryn is a five-mile ridge of common land locally known as the backbone of Gower. The ridge has provided a viewpoint for people since at least Stone Age times. There is a neolithic monument called Arthur's Stone (apparently removed from his shoe whilst he was walking in the area), which is accompanied by three Bronze Age burial cairns. Today the ridge provides lovely riding with great views on all sides. I passed the usual dog walkers, sheep and a few ponies. It's the sort of place that makes you smile, and I really enjoyed it. My decision to go clockwise was paying off nicely. Oddly, there is a trig point at each end of the ridge and the second one marks an appealing descent to the aptly named Hillend Farm. From Llanddew I followed a handsome bridleway to the west.

It's an interesting quirk of history as to why some tracks are bridleways, some are footpaths, and some (an awful lot) have been tarmacked and turned into roads. It might come as a surprise to anyone driving a motor vehicle that the road along which they are driving was, in the vast majority of cases, once a footpath. In time some of those footpaths were travelled along by people using horses, either riding them or pulling carts. The growth of the motor vehicle was actually quite slow through the first part of the 20th Century and the push for smoother, tarmacked road surfaces actually came from cycling organisations. The push bike was the people's transport. Through the 20th Century unsurfaced tracks were lost to tarmac. Routes that had developed between places along the easiest lines to travel that were suitable for wheeled transport (carriages and bikes) usually became roads. It wasn't until the 1949 National Parks and Countryside Act that our rights of ways were formally recognised along the lines of footpaths, bridleways and by-ways (open to all traffic). The work to classify these routes was undertaken by County Councils who worked with Parish and District Councils. It would seem that the criteria used was not consistent and we can find examples of rights of way that stop at parish borders, or bridleways that change to footpaths as they cross a border, like the one I'd followed on the Cylchdaith Rhinogydd. There is no obligation to keep a bridleway cyclable and where those bridleways are cyclable, cyclists have got to give way to pedestrians and horses. It's therefore an accident of history as to whether a route became a road, a bridleway, a by-way or a footpath. You can imagine some heated conversations in local council meetings and I wonder who would have held the upper hand, walkers or horse riders? Intriguingly, we currently have the right to push a pram or wheelchair along a footpath. I suggest this means that it's perfectly reasonable to push a bike along one. If you were to mount that bike and ride it you would not be committing a criminal offence, but you would be committing a civil offence against the landowner. None of that would matter if all bridleways looked like bridleways and were ridable, and if all footpaths looked like footpaths and were more suited to travel on foot.

We also need to bear in mind that the 'easy' route between places was the one that developed into a road, so it's pretty much only luck that has given us any bridleways at all. The cyclist or horse rider will always need to use roads (or paths) to link their journeys and the 'art' of bikepacking is to stay off the road as much as possible. The bridleway from Llanddew to Middleton is therefore a very special routeway. Without someone (probably a farmer or a landowner) using a horse along its length it could today be a footpath. On the other hand, it's a quirk of fate that it never got tarmacked and turned into a road. Today it's clearly an old lane, lined with trees and hedges and is mostly ridable. It's quiet and I think it represents all that is good about bridleways. I sometimes wonder if more minor roads, those marked yellow on the Ordnance Survey map, should be retired and upgraded to bridleway status.

And then I was there. A slow ride from the café-dominated hamlet of Rhossili along serene grassy tracks weaving in and out of wandering tourists (you need a bell for this bit) led me to the Coastguard lookout overlooking the Worm's Head (and the intriguingly named Kitchen Corner.).

A strong, raindrop-laden westerly wind picked up as I left the tarmac behind. Walkers were being blown back abruptly to the car parks. Few people were heading into the wind, but I had no choice: this was an important moment for me. I'd cycled, as off-road as I possibly could, from the Great Orme to Worm's Head, from north coast to south coast. The journey had taken six and half days and on arrival at the cliff top above Worm's Head all I could do was seek shelter in the doorway of the Coastguard look out. The wind, now accompanied by a lashing rain, was hurrying my decision to turn around and ride back north. I was, however, somewhat pleased with myself.

I took lunch in one of the lovely cafes in Rhossili and the sun returned. Sitting in the café was a little odd. I was so pleased with myself and my accomplishment, but there was no one to share it with. I do like solo travel, it has many advantages, but at times like this it would have been agreeable to share a moment of satisfaction with someone else. Right then though, all I could do was drip on the café floor, overeat and smile to myself. The truth is no one else in there knew what I'd done or cared about what I'd done. This was my journey, for me.

One of the reasons I'd chosen to go clockwise around the Gower was for the next section. Previously I'd toiled uphill to the settlement of Rhossili from Llangennith in the north. This is one of the longest hills on the Gower *cylchdaith* and by arriving at its southern end I was able to cruise down and enjoy the scene. I didn't fly down: there were walkers, ruts and sheep all needing avoidance. Instead, I cruised down so that I could admire one of Wales's most spectacular beaches. A playground for surfers and paragliders; climbers lurked in hidden zawns and fishermen danced with waves. Rhossili is a wonderful 'golden mile' of the best sand below a classical moorland. It's accessible, but not too accessible. It's iconic, and the backdrop of the very distinctive shape of Worm's Head makes it even more so. You should visit Rhossili beach. It's great bit of downhill too.

The views and off-road riding soon returned after Llangennith as I contoured around Llanmadoc Hill to the pretty little villages of Llanmadoc and Cheriton. From Llanrhidian the tarmac continued but with an interesting twist. On a previous visit here, on a fine dry day, I'd been surprised to find the road full of large puddles with standing water to cycle through. It turns out that the road is tidal, not a common occurrence when travelling through Wales. I think it's only the high spring tides that cover the road, but perhaps I should have checked before committing. As it turned out the road was clear of salt water on this occasion but was closed for an excavation. As ever though, the closure didn't really mean bikes. I can't remember ever cycling past a road closed sign to find it impassable on a bike. It would be a little more reassuring however, if they could suggest this on their bossy road closed signs.

Arrival in Pen-Clawdd is met by the very welcoming Cwmbach Road. I paused by the sign for Station Road and admired the platform with its official 'Penclawdd' sign and the perfect lawn where the railway once lay. This was the famous cockle line, despite transporting more coal than cockles. It took shellfish delicacies to markets further east and as far away as London and Birmingham. Cockle pickers were typically women, with men working in the iron industry. To earn extra money the cockle picking ladies would sell door to door and pub to pub up the South Wales valleys. I can remember in my early drinking days the cockle seller coming into the pub in my West Riding town of Cleckheaton. The cockles complemented nicely the black pudding and cheese which the landlord of the Wickham Arms would leave on the bar for drinkers to nibble upon! Cockling has changed enormously today and the hard working, empowered women of Pen-clawdd have been replaced by smaller male-run, tractor toting businesses. Today the cockle harvest is much reduced due to contamination of our seas, industrial collection and unlicensed over-collection.

The cockle line cycleway kept me off the road to Gowerton where I picked up the aforementioned super cycleway down the Cline Valley. The NCN 4 speeds you back to Swansea Bay in no time at all.

Gowerton is a scruffy place these days. There are shops here, and there are takeaways if that's what you require, but I chose to pass through quite quickly. It was only afterwards I discovered that in times gone by the people of Gowerton were referred to as 'starch'. When steel processing was a major industry in this area, the steelworks' owners and managers tended to live in Gowerton hence the name 'starch' to represent their white collars. The manual workers who lived in Pen-clawdd were known as 'dunks'. Gowerton does not have a white-collar feel about it these days though.

The Clyne valley cycle path, once the Clyne valley railway is now part of a National Cycle Network route (NCN 4) from London to Fishguard. This section is also included as part of the Celtic Way Cycle Route. The route has had more success in this role. When it was a railway running from Llanelli to Swansea it was never very successful. As a cycleway, its gentle slope back down to the coast gives a fast finish to a wonderful and varied day, which is rather like Wales in miniature journey.

After my passage around the Gower and given that this was, geographically if not mathematically, the halfway point on my Cylchdaith Cymru journey, I treated myself to a hotel night. It was a good hotel with an accessible cellar area to store the bike. The room was the lap of luxury, the shower was heavenly, the food was gorgeous and, after a good night on a lovely bed, the breakfast set me up for the day ahead. When you're on these long journeys, you shouldn't ignore the opportunity for the odd hotel night if you can afford it.

All I had to do now was cycle back to Llandudno up the eastern side of Wales.

Day Eight – Swansea to Pontsticill

The following morning, after a fine breakfast, I rejoined the wonderful cycleway along the Swansea frontage. It really is a gem. The early morning trail was being picked over by a clattering of jackdaws, whilst on a nearby sandbank a stew of oystercatchers chatted amiably amongst themselves, ready to protest at the slightest incursion into their space. I passed freely along the city frontage on the excellent by-the-sea cycleway. Occasionally I crossed pads of blown sand as the track was framed by beachside scrub on one side and neatly mown grass on the other. In places, rideable single-track trails dallied onto the grass adding even more interest to what was already a compelling journey. I passed the large hospital, the university, the old cricket and rugby ground, the prison, some uninspiring modern flats, and then it was time to get lost in the redeveloped docklands again.

I wonder if this Swansea waterfront looks better than it did when it was derelict? There are modern concrete buildings, a hotel, the occasional restaurant, university departments, halls of residence and even some houses. I see nothing attractive about this place. It's a concrete jungle. There is no green apart from an odd, rather bizarre, sheet of artificial grass draped over someone's garden wall. There's not a tree in sight, never mind a patch of rough grass. The grey water does little to lift the spirits here and it's a reminder (to me at least) that it is in places like this that so many people live; it's no wonder they are often divorced from nature. Tucked in the middle of it all is an old, corrugated iron church. This is the Scandinavian Church, strangely relocated here from Newport in 1910, left over from the days when Norwegian sailors might need to seek forgiveness.

SA1 is an ugly place, too neat, too uniform, the worst of modern planning. It lacks life and colour. It's best exited as soon as possible in my mind. I headed for the modern tower of the *allan* bridge, frustratingly I missed the shortest route and unwillingly delayed my exit from this concrete and steel misery by going, literally, round the houses to get out.

The bridge, a fine expensive looking traffic-free route, crossed the main road and took me out to a forgotten part of Swansea.

Rows of terrace houses were squished in between a quarried hillside, a dual carriageway and the docklands. The houses themselves had more character than any on the dockland development but were clearly deemed to be of lesser class and seemed to be pending the next chapter in their history with a certain degree of resignation. The cycleway, NCN 4, led me past disused warehouses, derelict sites and abandoned railway sidings. These in turn, were superseded by enormous modern retail storage and distribution facilities which had sprung up on this cheaper land. One enormous warehouse which belongs to a large online retailer took 10 minutes to cycle past. To be fair, this was all traffic free and it's very much part of the contemporary Welsh landscape in which we live today. It was good to see the contrasts and the variety. The cycleway led me under the M4 (more concrete, but this time high above me) and then across the road bridge. This felt like an old bridge, but it isn't. It has tall concrete pillars and metal sides. There is space for an agreeably separate cycleway as it carries the busy A48 over the Afon Neath at Briton Ferry. Briton Ferry, once the site of a ferry, is now lorded over by the sweeping concrete line in the sky taken by the M4.

My trail swept around and back under the bridge and, in an instant, I was transported back in time. Beneath the Afon Neath viaduct is St. Mary's Church, looking rather like a lost soul itself, completely out of place and overtaken by the march of industry and highways in the air. It cowered below the fly over whilst being harried by a semi-circle of modern houses. A row of older terrace houses gave little comfort to the setting as they themselves were dominated, this time by a large abandoned industrial site.

I followed the Neath canal a long way north. It's a linear wildlife and nature haven through the Vale of Neath/Cwm Nedd. At this southern end, spearwort margins hosted dragonflies, a grey wagtail foraged on the far side, mute swans glided through water lilies and the opposite bank was crowded with woodland and its understorey of bilberry and heather. A look at the Ordnance Survey map shows a pretty built-up area here, but I just didn't see it as I wheeled along the canal side passing underneath Neath. I remember surfacing briefly to hear two local ladies chatting. Their parish accent was soft on my ears, I would have liked to stay and listen more, but I thought that might be a little rude. If you do pass through Neath, it's worth seeking out opportunities to simply listen: it's the heart of the lovely south Walian accent.

I carried on along the canal.

There was an anomalous bit of quiet road past Resolven, but it was wide and proved to be an exception. The wooded canal towpath, once regained, led me pretty much all the way to Glynneath where a big surprise awaited me.

There was a functioning coal mine. I honestly thought that coal mining was over. I knew there were still one or two open cast mines, but this is a traditional colliery. I could see the winding gear for the lifts that descend to the coal face, conveyer belts transporting the coal, much dust, dirt and big ugly lorries. It's quite a remarkable scene and one I hadn't cast eyes upon since my youth. We actually used to explore the surface buildings of a disused colliery not far from where I lived, we tobogganed down old pit hills on bread trays and dug out bike trails in the spoil. Aberpergwm Colliery has been operating since the 1800s. It was closed by the National Coal Board and reopened more recently to become the only coal mine in Western Europe producing high-grade anthracite coal. Whilst some of this coal still goes down to the Port Talbot steel works most of it is crushed to use in carbon filtering systems. As you can imagine this incongruous industrial activity is strongly opposed by many people and I can't imagine it staying here for much longer. Anyway, big picture, this is Wales and Wales, particularly these southern valleys, was for many years world famous for producing excellent coal. So, in the context of this journey having seen a slate quarry earlier, the industry of the north, it was only appropriate that I should pause and ponder at the gateway to a working coal mine in the south.

Glynneath is a small town with a long history of coal mining. Its housing stock is dominated by typical workers' terraces. Today it feels poor, its streets and back ways are litter strewn, and it has a very unkempt air about it. This is such a shame as every interaction I had with the locals was very pleasant and friendly. I suppose it's typical of so many of our ex-industrial towns which really have no reason for being in this day and age except, importantly, they are people's homes. Many Joneses, Davies and Evans call this home, this is where their roots are, as are those of one Max Boyce, singer and comedian. This is their *cynefin*, hence, despite industrial change, people remain in tight knit communities.

On my first visit here, I had taken the thoroughly unpleasant Rhigos hill on the NCN 48 out of Glynneath. It was a terrible bit of litter-lined road cycling up a long, slow hill with lots of fast traffic. Even the bus seemed to enjoy making a close pass. Once again, I marvelled at the bravery of road cyclists. I did ponder a route from Neath through the woods to Aberdare, but I couldn't pinpoint the best way to go from my map-based research in north Wales. When I did manage a reconnaissance visit, I stuck with the route through Glynneath. I wanted to include the town and its colliery on my journey through Wales, so I tried a bridleway heading north to Penderyn, famous for Welsh whisky.

The bridleway hugged native woodland along the banks of the Afon Neath. This was noticeably a well-cared for place and I saw interpretation signs and evidence of field study with children. It's worth a visit.

It had been raining on and off all morning. I'd purchased some food from the Co-op in Glynneath for my lunch and I just needed a nice place to sit. I found a dry spot, sheltered from the passing squalls under the umbrella flyover of the A465. (That road sheltered me on this lunchbreak, but it would, however, bite me on the bum later that day). It was a bizarre place to sit and shelter, not at all claustrophobic and incredibly dry. Native vegetation thrived, a robin sang and a wren hopped about nearby by whilst a few feet either side of me it was lashing down. The viaduct is concrete and ugly, but the shelter was real and appreciated. Such is the shape of our landscape today. In the Welsh valleys, nature, history, poverty and modern highways butt up against each other uneasily. The Heads of the Valleys road roared above as I sat and contemplated, again, just how much litter one supermarket lunch can create.

I really enjoyed passing through the Craig y Dinas Woods. There was some pushing, but it's such a lovely woodland to be in. The bridleway continued, steep and narrow, up to Moel Penderyn. On my reconnaissance I'd really enjoyed this section. On this passing though, the September bracken was shoulder high and sodden. Having dried out over lunch, I was soaked again. Such is the bikepacker's lot.

On the route to Penderyn I drew a mental image and expectation of the distillery. I could see it as an ancient building that had been there for many years, I thought of the distilleries that I'd encountered in Scotland, and wondered if the Penderyn distillery might have a similar appearance. It doesn't. It looks like any modern out-of-town retail warehouse. I'm sure the shop is brilliant and whilst it might have been lovely to call in, I was on a bikepacking tour and carrying a bottle of whisky was probably a little bit beyond my remit. So, on my Cylchdaith Cymru route, I decided not to bother with the little detour to pass it. There is a gorgeous church with a superb looking pub next to it from where I dropped down steeply to connect with a grand little cycle track into Hirwaun. Hirwaun, like every village I'd passed through, was quiet. There are few pedestrians out and about in our small towns and villages these days. The walkers you do meet tend to have a dog restrained with one hand and a little squidgy black plastic bag in the other. We have become a car borne people. So many of us only leave our homes to work, to school or to shop in motorcars – what have we done?

The next section from Hirwaun is blighted by traffic and road works on the aforementioned A465. I left the village along some tight (and to the cyclist) unfriendly minor roads followed by a short section of cycle track to a hilltop junction. Opposite was a security conscious Kingdom Hall of the Jehovah's Witnesses. This busy junction was as ungodly as it can get for a cyclist. The cycle lane stopped abruptly at the side of the busy B road which joined the A465. I was waved across and encouraged to hurry by a kind driver. But I wasn't sure where to go and things got worse as I crossed the road. There was no exit. The cycleway across the road was fenced off due to construction works. A couple of cars, zooming around the bend expecting a clear road, beeped at me before I managed to scramble onto the restricted grass verge and push my bike round the corner. I tried hard to get away from the road but the roadworks' associated ditch digging prohibited any such escape. I managed to stay behind the bollards and coasted down the busy road, facing the traffic, feeling like I was breaking some law or other. My escape from this little highway hell could not come soon enough. One day, I'm sure the cycle lane will be reinstated and all will be well. The lack of consideration during construction though was very apparent.

I entered the Gellideg estate and for the first time in a long time there were people on foot. Gellideg is typical of many estates on urban fringes and life has challenges for the people who live here. It's not an easy place from which to start becoming upwardly mobile. The iron bars on the shop window, the vandalised signposts and the youths hanging around shouting obscenities at each other did not encourage me to pause here.

Luckily, I found the unmarked cycle trail exiting the estate and within five minutes I was on a converted railway line crossing a fantastic stone-built viaduct across the Afon Taff. This river is thought to be the derivation of the 'Taffy' moniker. The Taff trail cycleway is a predominantly traffic free 55 mile route from Cardiff to Brecon. On this, I followed a short section as far as Pontsticill. It's welcome level riding on a good surface. With a nature reserve on one side and ignored woodland regeneration to the other, I was neatly hemmed in by healthy native trees. Birdsong followed me all the way to Pontsticill and the contrast with Gellideg could not be more stark. To reach Pontsticill I kept my height across the village's eponymous dam. The dam has a clay core and is stone faced. This downward face is grassed over and it holds back the Taf Fechan Reservoir. It's a grand spot. The dam will have its hundredth birthday in 2027.

Pontsticill seemed like a good place to end a wet, rainy day. My dampness gave me the excuse to look for accommodation. There was a hostel advertised in the village and I'd sort of set my heart on staying there. Unfortunately, it was closed. But a fine guest house offered me a bed for the evening and I was not going to refuse. A pub meal, a shower and a bed were a real treat after a damp day's bike packing.

Day Nine – Pontsticill to Painscastle

I left Pontsticill in good time the next morning and headed north alongside the reservoir and through some woodland. I wanted to take in the famous mountain bike route through The Gap; its proper name is Bwlch ar y Fan. It's a great way to go through Bannau Brycheiniog on a mountain bike because it's one that can be pedalled pretty much all the way. There was a stream in a loose rocky gully near the beginning that required some care and a little push out, but after that it was steady wheeling to the bwlch between Cribyn and Fan y Big. Down below to my left was the dry Upper Neuadds reservoir. It would appear that it's being taken out of use, as is the Lower Neuadds reservoir, which seems strange in this day and age. Its Victorian structures stand proud. The dam is solid old stone and it hosts an ornate tower just off centre. The whole edifice is sheltered by trees that tell us how this valley could look with lower grazing levels. To my right was a hillside of coarse grasses, interrupted only by the occasional water course. Sheep were spread out across the entire landscape.

As I steadily climbed towards the gap, zig zagging from smooth bit to smooth bit along the stoney track, I encountered a good number of runners coming the other way. They looked like local military personnel out for a training run. Some were cruising, but a few were flagging, and it didn't appear that they were all enjoying themselves!

The bwlch was a fine spot to reach by bike especially as it's a whopping 599 metres above sea level. It was one of the highest spots on the route. I didn't pause for long. I rolled my bike slightly down the northern side where I met a DofE tutor and the group she was tracking. I always like to have a little chat with the tutors and their groups, it's wonderful to see young people out having an adventure. As ever their rucksacks were large, but their spirits were high and on this fine day they were evidently having a positive experience. The way ahead was clear and alluring.

Cwm Cynwyn dropped away steeply to the north. It's a big wide bowl of a cwm which has been over- widened and deepened by ice. The stream within it now looks dwarfed by its surroundings, a true misfit stream. I wondered if the bwlch might have been a glacial overspill channel at some point, but for me the lure of the long descent could not be resisted a minute longer and glacial gazing time was over.

It was a surprisingly good track through the Gap, and it must have been travelled by people for a long time. It's the easiest way through the central part of these hills so will have long been used to travel north and south. As ever, it's lucky it never got turned into a road. The track started off on the rocky side, but very quickly I was flowing fast and free. I didn't hang about too long as I had an important lunch date with myself that I wanted to keep. As the track proceeded north it become grassy and it was sumptuous to ride. As soon as I arrived at the tarmac, I took a right turn down a bumpy, overgrown bridleway to Tir-ciw. It had a cobbled base and the overhanging hawthorn, interspersed with rose, banks of nettles and brambles either side, all conspired to slow me down somewhat. I was very pleased I was wearing long trousers that day.

Some quiet lanes led me to a by-way that descended to the northwest and down to Aberhonddu/Brecon which made a fantastic way to approach this ancient place. Unfortunately, the town was lost in thick cloud and heavy rain and wasn't quite as welcoming as I hoped it might be. I passed through without so much as a pause, but I knew where I was heading. I was heading to the famous 'Hills' at Bishop's Meadow Caravan and Camping Site for one of their celebrated burgers. This was my lunch date. I'd seen Hills vaunted in the national media and actually adjusted my route so that I could visit their appealing eatery. It helped that there was, seemingly, a series of good bridleways from here across to Talgarth. But first it was lunchtime. I arrived at midday in the rain. Sadly, my bike had to remain outside in the rain. I covered the saddle, entered and shook myself down. People were clearly making special visits here for special lunches. I sat on my own, as far away from the busy part as I could, given I was the only one in dirty wet biking gear. It was noisy and full of razzamatazz, a little much for me, but the service was great and the burger was excellent. Well worth a visit.

The bridleway beyond Bishop's Meadow started well. I was admirably fed, in good spirits and the rain had stopped. Pretty soon though I had to divert into a field so that I could navigate some bridleway blocking nettles. Next came one of those ridiculous obstructions where the local farmer had decided that the best place for his sheep pen was right across the bridleway. The only way to get around it was to actually go into a field of sheep. This required some bike pushing, but was much easier than going through, and opening and closing, the four hurdles that were blocking the way. The writing was on the wall. This was not going to be an afternoon without interruptions and the stuttering progress that I was already making began to contrast unfavourably with the flow of the morning.

Worse was still to come. Two bridleways sandwiched a quiet lane that took me down to the A470 where there was a house with its own scrap yard, guarded by a gate which hung at an unnaturally jaunty angle. It needed two hands and my legs to lift and open it. Needless to say, the procedure used to open the gate needed to be repeated for closure. This darn barrier also managed to draw blood from my forearm. Needing a moment when the task was complete, I looked around me. There were a surprising number of bikes in the scrap. I thought perhaps, best not to linger too long.

I went to the cross busy the road. For road read motorway. A super slick surface, with immaculate edge lines and a clear demarcation down the centre meant that road traffic was traveling well beyond any speed that might make sense on a rural two-lane highway. Given the state of those bridleways, it seemed to me, more so than ever, that our spending priorities are not quite right. Money needs shifting from tarmac to gravel. I lined myself up at 90° to the black belt, waited for a gap and scurried across the road on foot. I felt like a mouse in the open. I felt like an intruder in an alien world.

Surviving the ten-metre dash I followed a silent lane to Lower Tylecrwn. It looked from the map like bridleway or by-way most of the way to Talgarth now, so no more traffic to joust with. But the bridleway from here was terrible. I pushed my bike for the next two kilometres with little chance of riding. It was wet underfoot and wheel. The whole thing was overgrown, and it was back into that world of briars that snare, and nettles that bite. No one had been this way for some time, and it was, to say the least, disappointing. Not only that, but this was a byway rather than a bridleway so it should be possible in a motor vehicle. It's good that motor vehicles don't come this way and maybe that's why it's neglected, to dissuade them. But when you report the blockages and the poor state of repair to the local authority, you report it to the rights of way department and they tend, with glee, to point out that that is a by-way and therefore a road. "Different department mate, more than me job's worth to comment on that route."

A rather wet and tedious trod eventually brought me to Llanfilo. Llanfilo is a pretty village with a gorgeous old church and houses that suggest there is money in the area. It's a centre for horse riding so you'd expect the byways and bridleways to be in better condition. The by-way from here to Tredustan was totally impassable. I detoured around blockages, through fields (including a ploughed one), cursing, hoping to get caught, but all to no avail. If you come this way, take the lane.

Talgarth has a shop and a place to sit so it seemed like a good spot for afternoon tea. I sat in the lovely little community garden, drank tea and ate the cake that I'd purchased from the understaffed, rather cramped, village supermarket. There were people around, but as ever, no one spoke to me; the 'Wildman of the woods' perched alongside his oversized bike.

I was cycling well. I felt fit and strong despite the labours of that afternoon. It made the eastward leading hill feel easy and I knew there was a fine descent down to Felindre. It was just a shame I didn't have time to stop in Felindre and enjoy a pint in the smashing Three Horseshoes.

After passing Three Cocks, I crossed the Wye to Glasbury and headed for the Begwyns, an unknown little patch of hill in no-one's land. The Begwyns are used to horses and made for bikes. What a lovely little patch of land on which to cycle, rest and admire the view. There's a high point called The Roundabout, only just off route, but well worth a visit for the vista.

It was nearing the end of the day now and I was on the damp side, but the pub in Painscastle is small and there was little space. In a way that was a blessing. I was getting a bit soft (maybe it was all the rain) so I really didn't need a night in the Roast Ox, but I did vow to return to such a lovely little pub. Instead, I mooched around in the village looking for a barn or campsite but nothing showed up, so I carried on up the hill, heading north onto Open Access Land. There is no right to camp on open access land, in fact it's expressly excluded from the terms of the act, but once well away from the village I was able to make a secret wild camp amidst the bracken, the tall ferns giving me plenty of cover.

Bracken is a woodland understory plant. It's a pretty tenacious one as it spreads by underground rhizomes. The only way to effectively stop its spread, now that the sprays to kill it have been banned for health reasons, is to shade it out, and that means letting native trees grow. They will only develop if sheep are excluded by fencing. Bracken isn't nice. In the past it was managed by the many small farms that were dotted across the countryside. It would be cut and used as animal bedding in the winter, particularly for the horses that were working on every farm. That used bedding would then become fertiliser on the fields. Bracken would be trampled by cattle in the spring and then, for a few years, when there were fewer farmers and land was more intensively used, the bracken was sprayed with poison. It needs managing again, but whether this means the keeping out of sheep so shrubs and trees can out-compete it, or whether it means cropping it and using it to make compost, will depend on the lay of the land, individual farmers and the way their support payments work.

There's an old saying that under bracken there is gold, under gorse there is silver and under heather there is poverty. This means that the soil under bracken is good, fertile and deep. I've been told that if bracken grows there, oak trees will grow too. There are better ways to use the land than leaving it to the bracken. On this evening, the bracken made a dry comfortable bed for me, under bracken there may be comfort for the wild camper too.

Day Ten – Painscastle to Llanfair Waterdene

It was a steady climb from Paincastle up on to Llanbedr Hill. Llanbedr Hill is part of the Powys Moorland Partnership. This is a heavily managed landscape. It's a little like being in Scotland, or north Yorkshire, in that fantastic tracks which make for good cycling, lead across the tops of the hills. Across Glascwm Hill and onto Gwaunceste Hill, I followed well-maintained double tracks. But there is a ghost here. A ghost of nature. This moorland is heavily managed with the input of the Game and Wildlife Conservancy Trust. The key word being 'Game'. The Wildlife bit was added in 2007 as the organisation tried to shift the public eye away from its central purpose: that of shooting birds for fun.

We are learning that what is a good landscape for one species is not always a good landscape for another species. Our upland heather moors, rare in the world, are a totally artificial construct. Their purpose is to assist one wild bird, the red grouse, to have the most favourable conditions to increase its population. As a by-product of this management, birds such as curlew and lapwing can prosper too. I do, however, notice that this is not a uniform benefit. In Swaledale, Yorkshire, for example, these birds and Golden Plover are doing well on the south side, but not on the north.

In many ways, for me, crossing these moors was a bit like going home.

My hillwalking days started a long time ago on the Yorkshire moors and parties of tweed-clad, gun carrying, wealthy folk, followed by welly clad game keepers was not an unusual sight. We'd often be asked what we were doing on the moor, keeping a tradition going back to Victorian times, along the lines of 'Get orf my land". It was only the Countryside Rights of Way Act 2000 (CROW) that opened up access, as a right, to mapped open country, including moorlands such as these. That right does not unfortunately, stetch to riding a bike or overnight camps. You still, therefore, get a feeling of the 'good' old days if you bikepack across these lands. Woe betide you if you leave the bridleway.

We like the moors. We love the open spaces, we love the august colouring of the heather, and we love the ease with which we can cycle across them on good tracks, but as I said before they are far from natural. As I cycled across the moor I was struck by the freshness of some patches of heather. Square blocks are burnt off to facilitate new growth so the grouse can feast on fresh shoots. Older heather is left as cover for nesting. Occasionally there are mini dams, a sop to holding back some water on the hill. Left to its own devices, you see, this moor would be woodland. Heather, along with bilberry, is a woodland understorey plant. These shrubs are happy on the more acidic soil of these uplands, but so would birch, rowan and hawthorn. I suspect that moors are so much ingrained in us that we would not want to see these hills revert to their natural wooded state. Even if we could allow these woods to return, they would need management that mimicked that of the wild animals such as elk, aurochs and beavers, that once roamed free. There really isn't any going back to that on any sort of scale. I do believe however, that there is scope for more woodland in the deep valleys and smaller gullies that cut through this high ground and it would be interesting to see at least one of these hills let go and return to nature.

There is a dark side to the production of a surplus of grouse for shooting. Each grouse will lay between six and nine eggs, sometimes up to a dozen. Rather like the blue tits that nest in your garden, the survival strategy of the red grouse is to have a lot of young hoping enough will survive to become adults. Grouse are part of the food chain and foxes, weasels and stoats will all take their eggs. Then as the chicks appear they can be useful pickings for birds of prey such as peregrine and hen harrier. To ensure the survival of the red grouse families in sufficient numbers to shoot, a gamekeeper needs to 'manage' the predation levels. This is mostly, we are told, done by legal trapping, but there is little doubt that bird of prey numbers are low in areas that are managed for the shooting of grouse.

Today though I am merely passing through and contributing nothing to this landscape, just out for a bike ride. What right do I have to comment or intervene? I am a modern countryman, I make my living on the hill, and I spend all my time in the countryside, but in a very different way from those who work this land. Should I not have a say?

I passed a Shepherd's Hut seemingly in the middle of nowhere and cycled on by Black Yatt, Pentre Tump and Pool Redding; all fascinating names with stories to tell. At Pool Redding I played with a very bouncy dog. I'd stopped to admire some wonderful shaggy ink caps on the lawn, but this collie, like a thing on springs, thought I wanted to play. He tried to grab the shaggy ink caps I was admiring and in doing so, completely destroyed them. Ah well, they are ephemeral.

I was rather excited to get to New Radnor, once the County town of Radnorshire, a new settlement that would be thriving with people and services and would really look after me during my lunch hour. Except that's not where I arrived at all! I'd passed through New Radnor previously and seen no one. Zero, zilch, not a person. I'd failed to find the shop, but I had noticed the old bakery, the old school and the old *siop*. The village was asleep. On this visit things were marginally more interesting.

An overly ornate monument greeted me on arrival. I think I was slightly disappointed that it exists merely to commemorate local lawyer, MP and Government Minister Sir George Cornewall Lewis (1806-1863), of whom I was oblivious. Far more interesting to me, was that I chanced upon someone in their garden, and they were only too happy to let me have some water and direct me to the wonderful community shop. The shop has a surprisingly good supply of Indian snacks which (with my Bradford roots) I relished. I took my time in New Radnor: it's a lovely old place, though it is very much on the quiet side. There is a small school, but no pub. The Old Post Office is now a private home but stands out clearly flanked as it is by a letter box and old telephone box containing a defibrillator. The village, for that's what it is (despite having served as a County town in the past), was built in medieval times on a grid pattern. The history here is for the connoisseur rather than the bike packer. I left the village with the knowledge that just ahead of me was a very steep hill through Mutton Dingle.

It was gratifying to be able to cycle up Mutton Dingle hill. I find cycling up steep hills requires not just strong legs, but fortitude of spirit. All too often, I'm happy to step off the bike and push. In fact, I do like to push now and then, it means I get to see places at a different pace. On this occasion however, I wanted to make it. So, having set myself the challenge, I cycled up the hill. When you do something like that it is rewarding. I felt like a competent cyclist when I got to the gate, not just someone using a bike to make a journey. Through the gate however, a push was required, but that was OK: I felt fine and in a good mood for what came next.

Whenever cycling on the edge of a place where people, live the bikepacker will encounter dogs. Dog walkers are usually friendly and if they are friendly, their dog probably is too but…

Firstly, establish the dog is under control. Either it looks to be walking to heel, or it's on a lead. If it bounds towards you, stop. A dog is far more agile than you are, so wait and see what it does (should the need arise, you'll find it's surprisingly difficult to kick a dog). Rest assured however, most of them are simply looking for food. A standard joke with the owner is one that involves asking them if they feed it! The two dogs I met on that hill, and their owners, were lovely. Both were keen to wag, and the owners keen to chat. On some bike rides, the only people I meet are dog walkers.

The gate where I met the first two dog walkers took me into a firing range. There were dire death warnings to anyone who might be tempted to leave the path. Today wasn't a firing day and all was quiet. There is some lovely moorland here. It's rich in bilberry and cowberry. I got down and took photos of the lovely little pink cowberry flowers and tasted their disappointing red berries, before feasting on the gorgeous bilberries.

I'm lying on my stomach, flat on the ground, trying to get my camera focused on the pretty little pink flower (cowberry). I take a picture that most likely no one else will see. As I focus, I can hear chatting. Then I feel a wet nose. I'm in the dog's territory, nose down sniffing the ground. I hear a shout and the dog bounds, off. "Sorry!" the young couple shout as I remain prone. Have they any idea what I'm doing? They just accept me, call the dog, and walk on by, completely accepting the nutter on the ground.

A perfect track led me past the wonderful looking hill called Wimble. On another day, I'm sure it would have been well worth scrambling up this small, but perfectly formed mini mountain. At 599 metres high it just misses the list of Nuttalls as well as the list of Y Marilyns. It's neither over 2,000' feet (610 metres) or surrounded by a drop of more than 150 metres from the next hill. Such is the uselessness of such lists!

The track brought me to a fence. It's an interesting one and it's across a presumably, commonly used route. Where the track meets the fence, the barbed wire topping has been replaced by a wooden one. This, it would seem, was where you were expected to cross over. When you look closely at the map the bridleway doesn't actually enter the forested bit of the Radnor Forest, it skirts around it to the south. The wooden bit therefore seems to have been made to enable you to climb over the fence more easily and enter the forest. I might have preferred a gate myself, but at least crossing here was not being dissuaded and although it was painful to lift the bike over, I didn't feel as though I was doing wrong. The forest is a fairly monotonous coniferous affair, but as ever the tracks were good. There was the option of ascending Black Mixen, which at 650 metres does make the aforementioned lists. I declined to enter into such mindless list-ticking behaviour, but later regretted not having visited that summit. It's probably one of the highest that is easily accessible by bike, another reason for me to return and repeat this brilliant route.

The descent through the forest was great. I picked up some single-track sections and flew down to Monaughty. The beautiful house here dates back to the late 1500s and is one of the oldest stone buildings in Radnorshire. It was now a beautiful day. The views across the undulating countryside, carefully wrapped in ancient hedgerows and interspersed with copse, were of a comfortable old pastoral style. It was the sort of view that ends up on a tin of shortbread or a box of tea. I took a moment to sit on the edge of the byway through to Ganders Wood just to let it all soak in.

Then I heard the noise of motorbikes. As I sat, with my poker face on, about twenty of them came past. They were well-behaved and polite, giving me no reason to be grumpy about their perfectly legal presence. It's just that somehow, it doesn't seem right. Horses yes (and I saw precious few of these) but motorised vehicles of any sort, I'd prefer not. However, I did have a lovely sighting beyond the woods when I was back on the lanes. A gentlemen came along on a two person pony and trap. The pony trotted boldly, the man sat comfortably yet slightly inclined forwards, looking like he knew where he wanted to be. They were going quite fast, but still had time to nod hello. It was for traffic like this that our roads were built. Lovely.

I followed in the same direction and eventually the lanes took me to Knighton.

Knighton is an interesting little place. It's well served by take-aways and grocery shops, but it seems to lack a little in overnight options. There are a couple of lovely looking pubs and one odd looking hotel. I stayed above a real ale bar once and that was nice, but it's changed hands now. The campsite on the edge of town at Panpunton is well recommended though.

Knighton, Welsh name Tref y Clawdd which translates as 'town on the dyke', is located on the Welsh- English border. The dyke referred to in the town's name is Offa's Dyke. There has been a settlement here for a long time. The meadows by the river attracted farming and the dry, fairly gentle slope on the south side of the river was ideal for building. It has some pretty little corners and interesting old buildings, but this is no Ludlow. Knighton is, I'm sorry to say, a little down at heel. It shouldn't be, it should be thriving. As far as bikepackers are concerned though, it remains an important place. This is where the well-known and well-travelled Trans Cambrian trail commences. You can also get here by rail, and the Heart of Wales line can be a handy train line to hop on and off with your bike, far from the mind-numbing bike booking procedures on the main lines of Britain.

On this occasion, I passed through. I bought snacks in the shop. This is more challenging than you might think. The shop is on a hill and the pavement is narrow. It takes a minute or two to get the balance of your bike right, before you can trust it not to roll away whilst you then pop inside.

On the edge of Knighton, I crossed a bridge over the River Teme into England. I didn't mind that the Cylchdaith Cymru crossed into modern England here, I had little intention of straying over the Offa's Dyke into 'ye olde England'. Besides, the other route heading west out of town was taken by the Trans Cambrian route and that could be enjoyed on another day. After passing some houses where I managed to have my water bottles filled, I ascended up to the dyke itself.

Offa's Dyke, as an important ancient monument, is a little underwhelming I'm afraid. It's a ditch, a ditch full of nettles. I wondered if there was a wall or fence alongside it for the purposes of defence and that the ditch, sorry dyke, might have just been somewhere the soldiers went for a wee. I enjoyed cycling alongside the dyke, it's sheep country again, but it's a good track, the farms are tidy and, weather depending, the views are rather pleasant too.

On entering the parish of Llanfair Waterdene and, not far before Llanfair hill, I tucked in behind a hedge for an overnight camp. I had no qualms about camping here. Surely if one cannot camp on the patch of Lord Hunt of Llanfair Waterdene then where can one camp? Sir John Hunt, Lord of this Parish, led the successful 1953 Everest ascent expedition. He was a man who promoted the outdoors all his life. Sir John was the first Director of the Duke of Edinburgh's Award scheme and sat on the management committee of Plas y Brenin, the National Outdoor Centre. There could be no more appropriate manor for a surreptitious bit of quiet overnight camping. I knew John's spirit would be welcoming my adventurous spirit to his district.

Day eleven – Llanfair Waterdene to Llanfair Caereinion

The following morning, I cycled north along the Offa's Dyke on a route shared with the Jack Mytton Way. 'Mad' Jack Mytton does not sound like the sort of bloke with whom I would have got on. He was, apparently, an upper class hellraiser. Expelled from his private school he still made it to study at Oxford. He paid constituents £10 each to vote for him and elect him as a Tory in 1819. Once elected, he spent 30 minutes in the Houses of Parliament before getting bored. He was a fox hunting, gambling, racehorse owner who seemed to do no work, but instead spend his family money. Ending up penniless, he fled to France for two years, but on his return, he was imprisoned as a debtor and died whilst incarcerated. There are several ungracious stories about him. So, quite why he's bestowed the honour of a lovely bridleway way through Shropshire being named after him remains a mystery. Don't be like Jack.

I was enjoying well-surfaced, speedy bridleways across tidily farmed high ground alongside Offa's Dyke. It's a grand thoroughfare for bikepackers and the eastern side of Wales was shaping up to give a very enjoyable, interesting ride which complimented the wilder west rather neatly. Just beyond Llanfair Hill I crossed a minor road where a large 4x4 was parked, clearly having spent the night there. We got chatting and it turned out the team in the vehicle were doing a sponsored, across England and Wales, off-road adventure. He complained that there wasn't enough off-road to follow, but he was pleased that me, a mountain biker, had deigned to talk with him. He recognised that we typically are not keen on the 4x4 community and their activities. I can't imagine where he gets that idea from! I did feel rather two-faced though, but it was a pleasant chat and when cycling on your own, you don't actually get many of these. Besides, I do like to hear alternative viewpoints; it helps temper my views and can usefully inform them (though the odd 'breek' wearing 'Gun' on 'Peg' might want to disagree with that I'm sure!)

The Cylchdaith Cymru heads west now, and small lanes fed me into Felindre. On the map there is a pub marked, but I knew by now not to build my hopes up; this is another 'closed' village. I cycled north then west again heading for Kerry Hill. Here I had my first, and only, navigation error. I was crossing a moor known as Y Drain. That does seem like a rather apt name for a wet moorland, but apparently it translates as the thorn. I saw no gorse, but I did ride off course. The cloud was down low and visibility was down to a few metres. I picked the wrong track across the moor. I knew I should have checked, but I just blindly cycled on until I realised I was in the wrong place. Instead of retracing my steps, I stupidly decided to cut the corner and head across the moor to the proper track. That was a bit daft, and it took me quite a while of pushing through tussocks to get back on track. It's a lesson I'd learnt before, and now I'd learnt it again, always check your route at junctions.

The push brought me to the grandly named Radnorshire Gate. It's marked on the map, but there really is nothing special here. Well there is gate, but there's nothing significant about it. It's just a standard five-bar gate like any other: rusty, old and difficult to open. I believe it marks the edge of what was, until 1974, Radnorshire.

Beyond though, lay the Kerry or *Ceri* Ridgeway. I turned left, heading west, although I did have the feeling I was going the wrong way. The ridgeway stretched away east into Shropshire and this ancient well-surfaced and graded route looked very appealing. I vowed to return and ride the eastern end on another day, but now I was westward bound. It's a marvellous hilltop route with a long history and far-reaching views. This is a drover's road that has probably been established since the Bronze Age. Often the best routes to travel were not in the valley bottom due to dense vegetation, bogs and the risk of ambush, so the higher ground often held the best highways. Think of the Ridgeway in southern England, it's the same sort of thing. The Ceri Ridgeway runs at a height of just over 1000' for 15 miles east to west and gives excellent off-road cycling. I did bowl along a little quicker than I would have liked, to be fair, and I was grateful for the interruption of the Two Tumps shelter and viewpoint. The view here is quite astonishing and had it been a clear day, I could have picked out Cader Idris and the Rhinogydd on the horizon. Meaning that from here, you can see north Wales, which meant it couldn't be far to go! That 'not far' started with a belting downhill to an unloved, but quiet picnic spot.

I headed west towards Llandinam Windfarm past a wonderfully named hill: Glog. The wind farm is on access land so it's handy to be able to cycle through on the good tracks provided. Unfortunately, the gate to access the windfarm was locked. It was a pretty hefty gate so quite a big lift over for an ageing bikepacker with a big bike. The locked gate was all the more maddening given that this site is owned by Scottish Power, shame they don't apply Scottish Access Law here! I'm generally in favour of wind power, but when you get up close to a windfarm it's amazing the mess they create. The roads and turning circles are enormous. The turbines themselves are massive towers, really imposing when you're below them. The rhythmic 'whup, whup' of the spinning turbines fuels a rather spooky ambience. I just tell myself that they can easily be taken away after use. This one has sheep grazing between the turbines so all in all, it's a pretty desolate landscape. A few native trees might make it all a bit more palatable (and unlocked gates!)

Having passed the windfarm, and enjoyed the views, I was treated to one of the best downhills of the journey. It's a fantastic run on good tracks down to Cobblers Gate. There's a bit of a hidden gem from here too, as I turned north and cycled on cute little bridleways past Little London to where a metalled, but quiet lane, took me down to a supply stop in Caersws. I was a bit spoilt for choice of pitstops here. On another occasion, when arriving in the morning, I'd breakfasted at the Season's Café, a throwback to transport cafés of old. It's made from containers, sells pop made from girders and diamond breakfasts that fuel you up for the day ahead. Run by friendly, helpful staff, it's a handy place to go to the loo and fill up your water bottles as well. I'd recommend a stop here if it works for you. It's a bit of a scurry down the A470 to a narrow bridge which leads you into the village proper. The mature Welsh attitude to speed limits does help though, as the long straight road into the heart of the settlement is limited to 40 mph and once there it's down to 20 mph. I had been avoiding A roads on this journey, but this one was necessary to bridge the Afon Hafren and it was far easier to ride than I'd feared it might be. In the village there is a butcher, a well-stocked garage grocery store and a former borstal. It's all a bit overwhelming really. The first time I passed through here, someone was washing their motorbike and I managed to use the last of his money's worth to give my bike a rinse. All in all, Caersws is a handy place to pass through.

Despite still being a long three days' riding away, I felt like I was in the north now, and on the home straight. I did think about a couple of things I would like to do before journey's end. I was keen for a nice, slightly posh, pub meal and I wanted to sleep in a barn. I wondered if I'd achieve those arbitrary little goals as I cycled up the hill to Llyn Mawr.

This is one of those bits of Wales that nobody tells you about. It isn't designed for tourists, there's little for them to see and few places to stay. It really is a sort of no-one's land in the middle of other more well-known areas. But on a bike, especially off road, it's all rather wonderful. It's quiet, the views are good and the tracks flow nicely. I sauntered over Bryn Du on good gravel before picking up lanes to Llanfair Caereinion.

Tractors permitting, it's a fine off-road descent on a by-way down past Hengefn to Llanfair Caereinion. Now, here's a place that is right off the beaten track. Despite being the terminus for the little-known Welshpool and Llanfair Light Railway, there is not a lot going on here. Llanfair Caereinion is a very sleepy former market town, with little reason to exist in today's urban world. Thank goodness for the Goat Inn, but how long will that remain so? I'd stayed here before and was looking forward to revisiting. This is a proper old pub. There's a fire burning in the hearth, the beer is good, there are locals in the bar and others out for a family meal. The menu is small and simple but all cooked on the premises. This is a 17th Century coaching inn, and the coaches have long since stopped passing by. The owners have been here for over 30 years and are probably looking for a way out. Trouble is the building is old and any new owner would need to invest heavily with little guarantee of returns. It's a conundrum shared by many a rural pub. I like The Goat, yes, it's creaky, yes the plumbing is fading and the electric sockets are not really where you want them to be, but it really is welcoming. It's a proper homely place to rest, the ceilings are low, some of the furniture feels 17th century; it's what you might call authentic. And, before going any further, let me tell you that they serve one of the best breakfasts in Wales. Enjoy The Goat, they've a garage for your bike and a hose to rinse it too. I hung my tent to dry, put socks on the radiator and revelled in the creaky old double bed. Smashing place, besides it's the only one in town!

Day twelve – Llanfair Caereinion to Llanarmon Dyffryn Ceiriog

I crossed the intriguingly named 'Afon Banwy or Einion', the river which flows though Llanfair Caereinion to join the Vyrnwy and thence the Severn. These are crucial rivers which supply water to towns and cities across England and Wales. It's a great looking river and it passed under the bridge looking like it meant business. I marvelled briefly at my ignorance of Welsh rivers; there are so many '*afons*' across the country and I knew the names of a minority. What I did know though is that they flow in valleys and valleys have valley sides and some of those valley sides are steep valley sides; here we go again. I climbed steeply out of Llanfair Caereinion on yet another steep, but quiet lane. It's remarkable how quiet the lanes of Wales are. There's always a fear of meeting an agricultural youth, too familiar with the road, rounding a bend ahead of me a little too fast. But it never happened on this journey. Passing motorists were more likely to wait a while and say hello, than run me off the road.

Now, there is one thing you really do need to be aware of if you mountain bike across Wales. Not showing on contemporary geological maps is a layer of ovine faecal deposition. Wales is, quite literally, covered in sheep shit. I know you wouldn't expect anything else, but whereas you might get sticky mud on your bike on the chalk downs of southern England and up north in the limestone dales or you might experience excessive brake wear on the granite of the Cairngorm and the gritstone of Yorkshire, here you will be covered in sheep shit. It's not the worse shit to be covered in, but covered in it you will be. Your bike will soon be protected from the elements as effectively as an old wattle and daub wall protected the occupants of houses in days gone by. But here, above Llanfair Caereinion, there is a change.

I encountered my first dairy farm: Neuaddlwyd. Dairy farms are rare in the west; it's pretty much all sheep with a few beef cattle. Here, in the more fertile east of Wales are dairy farms. Cattle are brought in for milking twice a day. Dairy cattle are big and heavy, the land is soft and wet, cow shit flows like a leaking tap from the rump of a Friesian. The by-way, from here towards Pantyanhouse is a gloopy mess of cow shit porridge. I danced around it somewhat by diverting into fields, but the mess was unavoidable. I prefer sheep shit to cow shit. I was grumpy and then I had to get into the rather primordial green lane that would take me to Pantytanhouse. It was a full-on gate wrestle and bramble bash to a nettle-lined, cobble-bottomed, sunken lane. The romantic in me could see this was a special place; the cyclist in me cursed. I exited on to a perfectly tarmacked road that led to one house and one farm. Surely we could do better with our bridleways?

At the end of the house I spotted a hose. It was too good an opportunity to pass by, I needed to remove some cow shit from my bike to make space for the forthcoming sheep shit. I could see the front door of the house was open. Leaning my bike against the garden wall, I crossed the lawn in front of the house, carefully avoiding some dog shit (there seems to be theme running here) and knocked gently on the door. I could see a man in the kitchen. I didn't think I needed to knock hard, but he didn't hear me. I knocked again and coughed. "Excuse me please, I wonder if I might borrow your garden hose?" To say he was shocked was probably an understatement. He was clearly busy doing something, fully engrossed in the kitchen table task he had set himself. I think he was making jam. The man grunted and waved. I took this to mean something like, "Yeah go and use my hose, but just don't interrupt me right now."

Back in the garden, I was able to pull the hose over a little wall into the lane to avoid washing the cow shit into his garden to join his dog shit. That would not have been a nice way to show my gratitude.

The bike was clean, my shoes were clean, but for how long?

A lovely wood, some quiet lanes and bridleways across fields took me to Pontrobert. Pontrobert has, as the name suggests, a bridge. A nice old bridge. Pontrobert's remaining importance is as a bridging point over the Afon Efyrnwy. I was downstream of Llyn Efrynwy and today the settlement is no more than a few silent houses and one closed pub. I moved on to find the Ann Griffith walk.

Ann Griffith was a prolific Calvinist hymn writer of this parish. She passed away during childbirth at the tender age of 29 in 1805. Ann lived in Dolanog, which is not actually on the Ann Griffiths way, but I'm sure she would have travelled this route. Remember in those days most people walked everywhere. It really is a lovely bit of track. It's riverside, it's wooded and has open views across lovely countryside. I really enjoyed being here: it was peaceful, calm and very soothing. So, it's no surprise I took the opportunity to rest awhile and nibble on my snacks. As I ate, I could appreciate the rolling hills ebbing away to the west like an outgoing tide. This is one of those little gems of pastoral Wales that you miss if you concentrate on the mountainous ground further west. The eastern leg of this bike ride was proving rather special. I was made to feel even more special as a tree-lined old lane led me to a sign declaring a full prohibition on motorised vehicles passing this way. I smiled, opened the gate, and then had to avoid the hasty, motorised postie who chased me up the track! From the top of the track a wooded, gravel-topped, bridleway ushered me along to a wicked rocky descent to a place called Blaen-y-cwm.

Here the beauty ended.

This is pheasant country. I've always been aware of pheasant, but I didn't know anything about pheasant shooting. I've seen many a pheasant smeared across the road, and I'd watched pheasants running across fields until they remembered that they had wings and could fly. On this bike ride, I rode through a field of pheasants; I could have caught them with a kid's fishing net. From my vantage point I could see hundreds, possibly thousands, as they spread across the head of the valley and on my exit road. There were large cages in which the birds had been reared, and feeding stations regularly placed across the land. Pheasant is a non-native species. It's imported, with no licence requirements, in incredible numbers every year to be raised, released and then shot. When I say imported, the quoted numbers are disputed, but without doubt they run into millions.

Yes, millions. Numbers as large as 50 million are offered. Compare this with our most common wild bird, the wren, which has an estimated 11 million pairs. In fact, it's suggested that the population of pheasant has a greater biomass than all our other birds put together. The plot thickens further when the shooting organisation, The Game and Wildlife Conservation Trust, admit that 25% of the birds are predated, typically by fox, but also by buzzard and corvids. Fewer than 40 % of the released birds are actually shot and around 16% survive and live out to the following season. The unlicensed importation of these birds is even more bizarre when you brush up against the administration and hysteria surrounding the release of formerly native species such as beaver, white-tailed eagle and lynx. Or the simple relocation of a pine martin.

The shooting industry are quick to point out the benefits to other species (apart from fox, crow and buzzard) of the way they manage land. The land does look lovely with its patchwork quilt of open grazing, hedges and small patches of woodland. This landscape must provide habitat and food for many other species, but the science is not abundant. There are concerns about how pheasant rearing and release can impact soils, undergrowth, invertebrates and reptiles (they are, for example, accused of depleting our adder population).

One of the bizarre claims is that pheasant shooting is an old established traditional country pursuit. It didn't actually gain any real popularity until as recently as the 1870s, long after Ann Griffith's time, when Edward, Prince of Wales, the eldest son of Queen Victoria, purchased Sandringham Estate to develop his love of shooting. Soon after, this driven pheasant shooting became the leading field sport. Another oddity is that much of the 'bag', the enormous numbers of birds shot, is not eaten but is dumped. In fact, they contain high levels of lead shot (which they seem to be very slow to phase out) so I'd question how much of it you'd really want to eat anyway.

As I climbed slowly out of this valley I dodged pheasants galore, confused about what we are doing to our land, and struggling with the whole idea of importing birds merely to shoot them.

Slowly, I approached the Tanat Valley on the edge of the Berwynion. These are oft forgotten hills. Not big enough to challenge the peaks of Snowdonia and a little further away from major centres of population than the Clwydians; the Berwynion draw few visitors. There are suggestions that they might be rolled into a new national park along with the Dee Valley and the Clwydians. I'm quite sure that would increase footfall significantly.

There is one fantastic beauty spot above the village of Llanrhaeadr-ym-Mochnant: Pistyll Rhaeadr is well worth a visit if you're passing through here. Today however, I was more concerned with grabbing a brew in the bustling village below the fall. Previously I'd eaten curry from a pub (which was excellent) and I'd feasted on a picnic from the SPAR whilst perched on the chip shop windowsill next door. Today I spotted the Post Office Café, Gegin Fach; its lean-to outdoor seating space was perfect for the dirty biker. The Post Office itself is as informal as someone's front room. Cushions were piled on one table, another hosted a large handbag, sanitiser and wet wipes, whilst a third was empty. The chatter of locals filled the room and it all felt very homely, rather like visiting your mother. Tea and cake arrived as I sheltered from showers in the suitable outside space. All in all, a rather pleasant interlude.

I was by now, feeling the pace: my legs were tired and I was pretty worn down. The next village along the road was only a few miles, but I was heading as off road as possible and having done this stretch before, I knew there were two decent climbs still to come. To reach a wild camp would require climbing a third, bigger hill. I had enough in my legs for two hills, but not for three; I booked the pub in Llanarmon Dyffryn Ceiriog and looked forward to a posh pub meal. It's handy having the internet on your handlebars.

There is a hidden valley on this side of the Berwynion. The Afon Iwrch, just north of Llanrhaeadr-ym-Mochnant emanates from the hidden valley of Cwm Maen Gwynedd. To flow out of the cwm the river has cut itself a deep gorge. Above the gorge a fine gravel track leads the cyclist to the hidden cwm. It's good cycling country, but as the cwm reveals itself things get ugly. This time it's sheep. Sheep are an integral part of Wales and you'd have to be pretty hard-hearted not to appreciate the beauty of the Welsh Mountain sheep. But here things had been taken to another, more intensive level. The fields were large and the hedges had been replaced by fences. I watched the soil running off downslope with the afternoon rain, from the naked land. The sheep were hybrids: big, ugly, shitty-bummed, lame beasts in enormous treeless fields. But these are the sheep that provide the chunky shoulders and legs that retail demands.

The Hand in Llanarmon Dyffryn Ceiriog is a lovely pub. I sat in the bar and enjoyed the banter of the locals, a tractor or two pulled up and the young drivers came in for a drink. Family worked the bar and a few guests admired the history of the place and shuffled closer to the fire. At the rear was a more modern addition. The rooms had been built later and whilst the dining room was impressive my room was small and wi-fi free. There was nowhere for my bike: I had to hide it in the leylandii by the car park. I ate fine food: a pie to be proud of, with sides, a top and a bottom; not one of those silly bowls of stew with a bit of flaky pastry balanced on top. This is a destination pub and I shall visit again. Not however, in the shooting season when wealthy guests take over and claim responsibility for keeping the place going through the darker months. A fox, stuffed and housed in a glass cabinet with a panicked bird under its paw, growled fiercely, as though he was the enemy. But all he wanted was to feast on roadkill (kindly provided by the local pheasant shoot…)

Day thirteen – Llanarmon Dyffryn Ceiriog to the Clwydians

Heading east from the village was the famous 'Wayfarer' pass over the Berwynion, but I wasn't going that way on this trip. I probably could have, but my memory of it was one of large 4x4 created puddles; it lacked flow and wasn't any more attractive than the route I had chosen. Leaving Llanarmon DG and heading north took me up a very steep hill. Having had a good rest and a fine breakfast I was able to cycle all the way up. I passed a house (from where I'd once got water from the outside tap, and the ubiquitous road closed sign. I now just presume that 'road closed' doesn't apply to walkers and cyclists. The road soon becomes a gravel track then carries on alongside small areas of woodland managed for shooting. A fine moorland crossing followed. On the map, a tempting bridleway heads out onto the open moor, yet on the ground nothing seems to exist. I passed another road closed sign and enjoyed a great descent down to the River Teirw, yet another river that I'd never heard of. On the corner where I met the little valley road, an old chapel was being renovated. It looked like a slow job. I headed west aiming for the Ceiriog Forest. I did like the clarity of signage emphasising that this was a bridleway and motor vehicles were most unwelcome. A superb, fast and wild descent took me down to the A5. Lower down, the route wasn't always obvious. At one point the track goes left, but the bridleway leaves it and descends a steep bank which was not obvious on the ground. I sneaked around a house and cut across a field, relieved to spot the gated exit on the other side, meaning I was on the right line. Crossing the A5, I was able to sneak down an old lane, then use the pavement for a little way to avoid the busy road into Glyndyfrdwy.

A tempting bench, just past Glyndyfrdwy Station gave me views along the Afon Dyfrdwy/ River Dee and detained me whilst I gathered enough emotional strength for another climb. There are some off-road alternatives here, but given the climb ahead, the hard top of the minor road was more than welcome. I only saw one other vehicle before I descended to the bridleway which traverses the northern side of Llantysilio Mountain. This section is shared with the Triban Trail. It's a good route, some undulations require the odd push and one neighbourly dispute required me to lift my bike over a locked gate on the bridleway.

In Llandegla village I knew I'd stop at the community shop and café. The service is always lovely, and the food is grand. I took my food across the road to the church yard where I could sit in the sun and dry my tent on branches of yew. It's a great shop, the alcohol range is phenomenal (I wondered if each volunteer had ordered in their favourite tipple!) My tea and cake, to follow my sandwich and pop, was delivered in person to me in the graveyard! I recommend the shop in Llandegla, personally I prefer it to the loud café at the nearby trail centre.

Heading north from Llandegla is charming rural riding. There was a bit of pushing, but I loved taking my time up a small limestone gorge. The clingy limestone mud reminded me of places I've visited as a climber, a few years ago now. It smelt like Cheedale, felt like Water-cum Jolly, names of routes and climbing partners slithered through my head. It felt odd, this little bit of White Peak, here in north Wales, but I loved it.

Through Graianrhyd village, there was a climb, and then the most wonderful, but short, single-track bridleway with views across the Cheshire plain leading me to the woodland on Nercwys Mountain. There's a mountain bike trail here, but it's not exclusive use and I was surprised to encounter families walking towards me. It's a good job I wasn't going too fast!

Maeshafn is the sort of village where you want to chat to people and you feel people want to chat to you. I say this because twice I've stopped for water and on both occasions the reception has been marvellous, to the degree where I had to make my excuses and push on. It reminded me of when I was a kid: my Mum would have the kettle permanently on and would seek out people to feed and to whom she could offer cups of tea. Workmen in the street, the Postie, even the refuse collectors (they were known as bin men in those days) would be plied with tea. I sat in Maeshafn on another occasion and waited on the bench in the middle of the village. And waited. I waited for a mum to appear with tea. A couple of folks passed the time of day, but no tea was forthcoming. I was forced to continue my journey.

I wasn't looking forward to the climb up through the woods toward Moel Famau. The last time I'd been here I was tired; it was late and two electric bikes had cruised past me making my climb feel evermore laborious: the hill seemed to go on for ever. On this occasion however, I cruised it. It was easy, the track was good. I had it to myself and I felt strong. It was very satisfying. The Clwydians give probably the best riding in Wales. The tracks run fast and free to the north. Some are grassy, some are rocky, and some are gravel. There's an odd wet bit, but it really is good. It's not always obvious which tracks you can use and sometimes you can be surprised by a permissive bridleway sign appearing on what you thought might be a footpath.

As I top out on the Clwydian ridge the sun is low and closing in on the horizon. Marmalade skies colour the vale below; it looks soft and comfortable. Ahead, the hills feature lengthening shadows and sunlit hedgerows. An odd white sheep punctuates the landscape. Lemon-coloured, coconut-smelling gorse mingles with purple heather. I pose for a selfie, then pose my bike for a photograph. These are smashing hills on a bike. To be up here, late in the day, not in any particular rush and with no one else around, is a privilege.

I descended to Siglen Uchaf on one of those permissive bridleways. It was grassy, well-marked, smooth and fast. I'd enjoyed this run before, but to find myself flying down it as part of this long journey was really special. It leads on to a sort of balcony route heading towards the north coast. The Clwydians were being kind to me: it had stopped raining. I could see for miles across Wales to the mountains of Eryri and I could see north to the sea. I could see all of the Vale of Clwyd laid out before me.

It's an area I've cycled many times before and I was reminded of grand days out with Graham, Richard and Sally. We once met the 'talking' cyclist who was well known amongst some of our acquaintances. I remember being thanked for having a bell rather than a shout. I've talked to dog walkers, DofE groups, horse riders and other cyclists here. It's also known as the 'Liverpool alps' as it's very accessible from the towns and cities of the north west. Never mind any of that, it's a brilliant place to ride a mountain bike. Exactly what the absolute best route is, I'm not sure, but this 'balcon' whether heading north or south would be part of it.

I can't tell you where I stayed that night, but I did find an empty barn. I nervously entered and checked the view; I was out of sight. There was a dry stage to sleep on. I felt a bit guilty, but I'd found my barn. Sometime later a bike came past, but the rider had no idea I was there.

I'd never actually slept in a barn before, not like this anyway. I'm not sure why I wanted to really. I think it stems back to reading the books of travellers who have found barns a useful place to stay. Ursula Martin certainly makes use of a few in her impressive 'One Woman Walks Wales' mission. I just never seem to find nice remote ones. I'm sure they are there, but they don't appear for me at the right time and place. I often peer into barns, just to check them out. They usually have muddy or even shitty floors. Damp straw and leaking roofs. They can be open-sided. I've used a couple of these to seek respite from the rain, but no more than that.

I have slept in odd places in the past. As young climbers we'd seek out shelters that were warm and dry and close to the crag. I remember sleeping in the ladies' toilets in Malham, in the woodshed in Stoney Middleton and the awful draughty rugby stadium in Keswick. I'm not sure if it was just down to the cheekiness of youth, or whether it was the complete confidence of my companions, typically Duncan or Paul. I was never comfortable. I didn't want to upset anybody; I didn't want to get caught and I never really slept well. I still keep an eye out for spots like these though, even today. It's sort of a habit that hasn't gone away, but I doubt I could do such an impudent thing nowadays. I'm happier finding a secret camping place, away from habitations, behind a wall and on the other side of a wood. That's where I feel most at ease.

However, I did survive my illicit barn night and I did sleep well. I think I was tired, this having been day thirteen. There was just one nagging thought: could I get home from here the next day? I'd cycled further in the past and I only needed to get to Llandudno. From Llandudno I'd be able to catch a train down the valley to my village or, preferably (if I timed it right) Sally would be able to collect me at the end of her school day.

Day fourteen – The barn to Llandudno

I left my barn nice and early, slightly fearful of being caught. It surprised me during the night that even there, far from anywhere, a stream trickling by or the wind in the trees could sound like a quad bike. I'm often on edge, even when I'm camping, just waiting for the quad bike to come and ask me what I think I'm doing there. It didn't happen that night. The morning of my last day on the trail dawned bright. The birds sang loudly, particularly for this time of year, as the morning sun's angled rays highlighted the jewels of dew in the long wet grass. I packed up in good time, not long after first light and continued north, heading towards the end of the Clwydians. Still fantastic cycling on brilliant tracks. I reached the bwlch above a settlement called Bwlch, then headed west and descended down to the oddly named

Aifft. Enjoying the descent, I couldn't help thinking that it might be the last one of the route.

I drop the saddle for one last time, straighten my legs and roll onto the downhill section. I bend my knees slightly and move my centre of gravity further back. Heavy feet, light hands, look ahead, heavy feet, light hands, look ahead. My legs ride in tandem with the front suspension, the saddle bounces below me. My tyres work hard. The bike flows, it knows what to do, all I must do is position myself and relax. I really need to enjoy the 'now' as most of the time spent on a trail like this is spent in ascent. This one last descent is mine and mine alone. I grin broadly, the grin of champions.

The track levelled out, but remained high: a level shelf, cut into the hill with gorse and bracken either side. The views of the day remained, and I revelled in my lonely trek. I crossed the A541 to the 300th gate of the trip. I'd heard complaints about the number of gates on the Trans Cambrian route so, given that I was cycling all the way around Wales, I thought I'd count the gates. I'd equipped myself with a clicker and hung it from the handlebars and as I left the road on to a bridleway, I clicked it for the 300th time. This was a side gate to a main gate. The track led to a workplace where the bridleway veered leftwards and up a hill (another push!) As I closed the side gate and pondered how much time I'd spent over the two weeks opening and closing gates, the main gate opened. It opened electronically, automatically, for a car to pass through. I had a dilemma now. If I'd waited, I could have gone through the automatic gate and this would have been gate 299 not gate 300. But technically I'd opened and closed it, so I counted it as my 300th.

Incidentally, pondering the time I'd spent opening and closing gates, I concluded that, if I'd taken a minute to open and close every one of those 300 gates that would have been a total time of five hours. If, on the other hand, it took two minutes to open and close a gate then the time taken would have been ten hours. I suspect the truth was somewhere between, but of my fourteen day journey it meant that I'd spent the best part of one of the day's opening and closing gates!

Continuing, I pushed my bike through some scrappy, forgotten woodland and across some fields. A grown-out hedge line took me to a lane which led me past a house called Sodom. I wiggled north on prettier lanes, by fields and wooded slopes. Passing under electric pylons I then rode by what I imagined to be a modern footballer's house. It had tall fences along the front, chavvy gates and high crenelated garden walls, all topped off with security cameras. It was a bloated modern house with little style and zero class. A minor road and wide track led to a footbridge across the A55, once again showing up the arbitrary nature of our footpath and bridleway delineation. I could have walked across the wide bridge, but with no one around I rolled across it, not cycling you understand, just straddling my bike. I took the opportunity to ask some builders for water in Rhuallt then rode on a country lane to Dyserth.

When planning the route, I'd mulled over which lanes to take to the coast in this area. On my previous journey, I had been further east and whilst I had enjoyed a good downhill section into Prestatyn, it had meant dashing across the A55 on foot. An experience I did not want to repeat. On this journey though, the footbridge to Rhuallt had given me a safe way across the A55 and that had led me to Dyserth with the promise of a disused railway cycle track to Prestatyn. It was a hidden gem. I did need to ask directions to find it, but once on the track it was gorgeous. It curved gently through native woodland below limestone crags and quarries. It took me past ancient monuments and industrial stories on a mirror image cycleway of those I'd followed in south Wales a week ago. I liked that symmetry.

In Meliden, I chanced upon Y Shed. What a wonderful spot that was. A fine, bustling café, full of locals, endowed with loads of information on the local history and selling fine coffee too. I succumbed to a bacon buttie and sat outside. It was soon noticeable that I was back in a more populated part of Wales. Not since the south coast had I seen so much human activity and people wanted to chat. Several people commented on my bike and baggage. One gentleman was fascinated by my Pinion gear box, oblivious to the temperature drop his wife was suffering. She had to end our conversation and drag him on his way.

Sadly, the track ended (unless I missed a turning) rather abruptly in Prestatyn. I got a bit lost, but I could see where the coast was, even though I couldn't actually see it, and headed there as directly as I could. I cut through the sport centre car park, over a grass bank and popped out on the coastal path, possibly not by the 'official' route.

What a contrast it was to what had gone before. It was urban, tarmacked, wide and lined by concrete. On the one hand, this was a fantastic traffic free, cycle and walkway all the way from Prestatyn to Llandudno. On the other hand, my goodness it was ugly! Windblown sand butted up against a curved, concrete wall on the left. To the right, concrete-edged tarmac led to a slope down to a sandy beach. I suspect choppy grey seas, grey skies and the greyness of the concourse was also to blame for my abhorrence of this place.

The over-sized family are walking four abreast along the cycleway. Portly dad with his portly son to his right, podgy mum with podgy daughter to her left. They are stretched across the cycleway. Of course, there's a line to demark the pedestrian way and the cycleway, but I'd walked along such routes myself and not noticed the lines. The super-sized family are barring my way. Two bike riders appear, coming in the opposite direction. They make eye contact with the family. I tinkle my bell and slow down behind. The other cyclists manage to squeeze between the mum and the seaward slope. I ring my bell again, a little more loudly, and aim for the same weakness in this walking front row. I'm now at walking pace and aim to the right of the mum who's stepped slightly to her left, reluctantly, just enough to let the other two cyclists pass in line. But, as I'm upon her, she steps right again, back into her line, oblivious to my presence. I nearly hit her. My evasive action sends me on to the slope, the bike takes on an unnatural angle and I just manage to stay on board and balance past the family wall. I am very close to the large mum, and she swears at me. Her large husband swears at me too. Their taunts are unpleasant, unwelcome and rather on the rude side. I think I'd shocked her; she'd certainly shaken me. Perhaps I should have dismounted and tapped politely on one of their shoulders and sought permission to proceed along the cycleway, the cycleway they'd chosen for their promenade. This esplanade is several metres wide, there is a pedestrian part, a cycle part and then the slope to the sea. There is space for the aware to coexist. As they shout at me, my blood boils, but I can't find an appropriate repost. I meekly respond that I'd rung my bell. The only revenge open for me I realise as I cycle away, slowly gaining momentum in too high a gear, is to write a book, and in it, call them fat.

Rhyl has been redeveloped. The mind can only boggle at what it must have been like before. It's as if someone with shares in concrete and none in nature has led the design. There are walls that mimic those of a prison, neatly mirroring the HMP Swansea that I passed six days ago. Here, instead of prisoners, the wall separated a deserted children's playpark from the promenade cycleway. I'm sure the £65 million has been well spent in parts of the town, but not this bit. The cycle path is ugly, its saving grace being that it's quick and separated from motor cars. There is a nice bit where the Afon Clwyd meets the sea. A smart bridge has been built for the snazzily named North Wales Coastal Cycleway, National Cycle Network 5, and a narrowing slows you down, hoping to tempt you to stop and spend some money in the café. I did.

I applauded the next section of the cycle way for contributing to the wide variety of landscapes in Wales. As someone who has studied settlement geography, I find the whole area fascinating. There is no one central business district, land uses blur and temporary buildings rub shoulders with more permanent ones. It's fascinating, but it'd be hard to quantify it as scenic, or indeed worth a visit. The North Wales Coast path shares the trod here and I can't imagine a more painful journey to undertake on foot. At least on a bike you're through it pretty quickly. It might be fascinating, but it's no place to linger. The quarries and tucked in caravan parks of Llandulas brighten the picture a little, but overall, this coastal artery is dominated by a brutalist architecture. From the hard landscape in Rhyl, past the concrete seawalls of Kinmel Bay and Towyn to the concrete flyover above, but top prize for ugliness goes to the concrete rock armour tetrapods that are piled up on the right of the path past Abergele. Yet even here, nature tries hard. There are wildflowers and sea birds. One old groyne was perch to half a dozen cormorants which brought a smile to my face. I kept riding my bike, this was pretty much the home straight. Nothing could get in my way now, except of course dogs on leads and the odd uncomfortably steep rise. I felt I needed to mind my head when I passed below the A55 by-pass: the ground was littered with debris that seemed to have been ejected from the traffic above.

Near Llandulas, I passed the conveyor-belt-topped jetty where ships dock to load stone and reached the rainbow bridge of Penmaen Head. I was now in Colwyn Bay or was it Old Colwyn (I'm never sure). The promenade here was being worked on so there was a diversion away from the coast for the North Wales Coastal Cycleway. I must have missed a sign (or one had been nicked) for I was soon lost in the suburbs of Colwyn. I wasted precious time trying to get back on track. Cursing, I hoped the coastal route would be more attractive when complete than what had gone before. Rhos-on-Sea, Penryn Bay, inland to Penrynside and the end was in sight.

As I top out on the small hill by the Welcome to Llandudno sign, I pretend that sign is for me. I can see people gathering on the promenade below, so I slip down the final bit of single track, a pathway that we'd have called a snicket where I come from. This takes me to the promenade where large crowds have gathered. They line my route home, like the dockside gatherings that met around the world sailors, like the welcoming swarms that greeted those who'd swum, run or walked our coastline. This is my crowd; this is my support. I can hear cheering and clapping, my name is chanted. Ladies are wearing grand hats, children wave flags, dogs bark happily and cats grin widely. I'm patted on the back, gentlemen shake my hand as I cruise slowly along the promenade. The crowd pushes closer to me, wanting a touch as if I am a Tour de France cyclist ascending a grand hill. I can see the finish line, I can see the actual rubbish bin from where I commenced my journey, all those days ago. The Mayor stands proud, regaled in hat and chains, and as I swing my leg off my bike to touch tar instead of pedal for the first time in nearly two whole hours, she thrusts her hand out and shakes mine with beaming congratulations. A young lady gives me a bouquet of flowers and a kiss on the cheek whilst a handsome young man proffers a magnum, ready shaken for me to pop the cork. All around there is cheering, shouting and clapping. The sun shines brightly. I raise my arms, and I feel like a hero...

Meanwhile, outside of my head, no one batted an eyelid as I dismounted and, a little self-consciously, tapped a rubbish bin. I sculked away from the heartbeat of the town, taking my sly grin with me, very happy to finish my trip here and, also, not to have to cycle around the Orme. I went to Parisella's Ice Cream parlour in the Happy Valley Gardens. I was in my happy valley, and I'd timed it perfectly. The most important person in my life was coming to meet me after work and take me home. I'd completed my expedition, no one else was bothered. I'd only been for a bike ride really. Now, what flavour?

Departure from Llandudno

↑ On Carnau

Rhossili descent ↓

Part Four
Unconsciously competent

12: A winter's loop of northern Eryri

It was February. It was dark and it was cold, but I had time in my calendar for a bikepacking adventure. I had a mission too. My mission was to travel from home in Nant Conwy to a bothy I had not yet visited: Cae Amos. I packed my bike and set off full of hope. From home, I followed good tracks past Llyn Crafnant and over to Capel Curig. Capel Curig to Bethesda journeys along the excellent Lon Las Ogwen, a long (mostly downhill) off-road and quiet-lane cycleway. The clouds were low and the air was damp; the elements were discouraging. From Bethesda, little lanes led up and over past Mynedd Llandegai. I dropped onto some cheeky tracks that led into and through Coed Padarn. I really had to focus on some of the marginal tracks; it's remarkable what people have led ponies up and down in the past. I didn't stop in Llanberis, the daylight was galloping away from me now and I had another three hills to climb. Up to Bwlch Maesgwm was splendid riding. You can just keep pedalling all the way, but it's a long uphill and I was tired. Downhill on the Snowdon Ranger was a fun bit, then it was a dash down the road to Rhydd Ddu.

Decision time.

The track I knew over to Cwm Pennant would take me to a remote place in the dark, in the rain and in the wind. If I couldn't find my way up to the bothy, which was on a track that was unknown to me, I'd potentially be in for an uncomfortable night. Discomfort comes easily in February and needs no encouragement so sound decisions must be made. It was too late to experiment with a different route. (A few months later, I descended into Cwm Pennant from the bothy, and it was an eye opener. I'm so very glad I didn't push on that night.) Instead, I followed the awesome Lon Las Gwyrfai multi-use track towards Beddgelert. It's slightly down hill, well-surfaced and was deserted. I stopped at the Forestry Commission campsite and asked for a bed for the night. The price they quoted was unsatisfactory, so I pushed on to Beddgelert and stayed in a welcoming but ageing and slightly tired hotel. On a wet, windy, February night, it was a fine place to lay my head, but why do the complimentary tea and coffee trays have to use so much single-use plastic?

The next day I scooted down the Aberglaslyn pass heading for Nantmor where there was a track that I wanted to follow across to Croesor. It's a wonderful ancient track between the two villages. The old, uneven and grooved flagstones were just above water level, whilst ancient gate posts guided my course. I had to push a little bit more than I would have liked, and I reckoned it'd be better travelled east to west rather than west to east. I was on familiar ground from Croesor.

The long track to Croesor mine does require some pushing, but it's a great old, well-made miner's route to travel. Some shepherds were bringing sheep off the hill. I stopped to watch for a while and tried to pick them out as they spread across the cwm. The dogs were hard to see and could only be picked out by following the movement of sheep. Young men ascended hill tops, whilst older ones patrolled on quadbikes. Snippets of Welsh floated across the great bowl, as sheep began to group and descend. Half a dozen men and their dogs drained Cwm Croesor of its sheep, taking them down for scanning and lambing. I took a memorable photograph of a small shepherd marching across a big hill. Sunlight tops above him, shadows below, his crook in one hand and his dog at heel.

From Croesor mine to Rhosydd mine it's a boggy push through secluded and wild country. It's surprising that the track between the two mines is not a better one, especially considering they are linked underground and both used the tramway through Cwm Croesor to export the slate they produced. From Rhosydd, once owned by the Colman's Mustard family, it's a steep, fast downhill with tyres playing unruly tunes on the rattling slate track. Through Cwmorthin, alongside a slate fence, past a ruined chapel and long since abandoned barracks. There are stories writ large across this landscape, but I'd passed this way before, and this was not the season to linger. It's possible to sneak through Tanygrisiau and Rhiwbryfdir then pick up the Crimea pass road quite close to its top. From the top of the Crimea pass there's a stunning track down to Blaenau Dolwyddelan and I flew down here, pleased to be going home. I didn't need to avoid the puddles; I went straight through every one. My feet and body were soon quite wet, but my spirits were high. Another good track led from Dolwyddelan to Capel Curig and then I was back into the Gwydyr forest searching out the late sections to the Gwydyr Mawr and Gwydyr Fach trails to give me a racing finish back to my home village.

So that was a quick winter hit of overnight bike packing. Winter's days are short, and they don't allow much faff time. A plan needs to be made and then shortened, flexed and executed (with the possibility that it may well need to change again!) Decision making is key, and I had now learnt the importance of making sound choices when bikepacking. Decision making is a fundamental skill and takes time to develop. It does, however, help to get out and practise those skills out of season and it always helps the spirit to just have a little reminder of what it's like to ride, eat, sleep repeat…

The Shepherd

13: **In camp**

I wake up in a mature coniferous forest. I had a view of the valley last evening, but this morning it's gone, all around me is cloud. The forest is damp, dripping and dewdrops sparkle like jewels on sitka needles. At the end of yesterday it was hard to find a flat spot that was away from habitation. I found a flattening on an old track. A remnant route of past harvesting or planting, which is now out of the way and green with grasses and mosses. The grass provides a pitch; though the soil is thin and the pegs are at a very shallow angle. The moss offers up a bathroom, my favourite sphagnum species is absent just here, but the rhytidiadelphus and the polytrichum have substituted perfectly adequately.

I was in an area dominated by agriculture. I'd passed through a village late in the afternoon and enjoyed a pasty from the village shop, well, when I say enjoyed the pasty, it was actually pretty awful! Ultra processed food, cellophane-wrapped and stuck in a microwave for… well I'm not sure how long. Perhaps in my case too long. But it was hot, and it was just what I needed at the time. I then had to travel further, past a few houses, leaving the last farmstead and further out of the valley up into the hills beyond the *dyffryn*.

When the land slopes (and it slopes a lot in Wales!) finding flat pitches on which to camp can be tricky. I was looking for a discreet flattening out of sight of habitation. Sometimes I might hide behind a wall, disappear around a corner or, plunge with trepidation (as on this occasion) into a patch of plantation forestry.

Coniferous forests can be really good for cover when you need to find a secret place to hide away and rest overnight. They can be awful places to find a pitch: boggy between trees with hard ground trackside. Yet, although they can provide shelter from the wind, they can drip long after the rain has stopped. Coniferous forests can be friend, or they can be foe, but sometimes they're all you've got.

I find a level dry patch with just enough soil to hold a tent peg. It's a tiny area, just big enough for my small tent. I pitch so the view is at my door. A breeze flows to one end of my tent, my needs are met, but as ever, it's not perfect.

My tent pitches outer first, or inner and outer together. For me, this is important as pitching an inner first tent in the rain can only lead to a wet interior. I have a tent with a large porch area, somewhere to leave my wet outer garments, my damp bags and somewhere I can cook that isn't in the tent but is sheltered under the flysheet. In my tent I can sit up and lie down. It's a material inner tent, not a mesh tent which is important to keep the wind out. The mesh in the door is fine enough to keep midges from entering too. It weighs under one kilogram. These things are important to me. This is my home on a journey. I'm not on a camping holiday; I'm on a journey that necessitates camping, often discreet camping so I choose a green tent. I pitch as late as I can and I strike as early as I can. As I lie down, I listen for quad bikes. I might feel guilty, but sleep will take me away. I might need ear plugs if it's windy or raining.

I place a thin mat underneath my groundsheet and an inflatable one within the tent, upon which I sleep. I choose my sleeping bag for the time of year. A quilt in summer, a two-season bag for autumn and spring, a three-season bag for winter. I always use down as it packs small and is light. It's kept in a waterproof bag which is carried inside another waterproof bag. A silk liner adds warmth and works under a quilt or in a sleeping bag. It can also be washed more easily than a down bag while it packs down small and weighs next to nothing. I make my pillow with a dry bag and the clothes I'm not wearing. I'm usually in bed early, so I have downloaded books on my phone to read.

The ground is hard and as ever, I struggle to ascertain whether it's level or slightly sloping one way or slightly sloping the other. But with darkness I fall asleep and with the light I wake. I hear a song thrush first of all, then a robin chimes in, reassuring me that in reality it probably was first up this morning. Blue tits call to each other, then it's a goldcrest with its high pitch scratch that takes up the baton, and now the chorus begins in earnest. I can hear a wren, a chiff chaff, a great tit. And maybe a blackcap, but that one is faint. A blackbird sings loud and clear and the woodpigeon warbles in the background. Morning has broken and I need to move, move before I hear the quadbike.

There's a short period of time just before the sun rises when it comes colder. I first learned this as a 12-year-old working on the markets in Yorkshire. I can remember being with David, my mentor, at the wholesale fruit and vegetable market (you know those odd photographic memories you carry around.) We sat in the cab of David's lorry waiting for the porters to bring our goods and as we both shivered a little, looking forward to our warming labours, David relayed me this temperature observation.

As you wake up in a tent, it doesn't take long to realise there's not much point laying around and you might as well get the day started. Depending on the weather, you may go outside to the loo, but if it's raining, you'll not want to leave your bed. I used to use the commercial camp food sachets for having a wee, but now I need to improvise since I make my own camp food. I can do it in an empty freezer bag. After carefully emptying it, I rinse it then keep it in a netting pocket on the outside of my rucksack so that it can be used on the next night in the next camp.

My stove hums and I get a bowl of porridge ready to rehydrate whilst drinking black tea. I simply pour boiling water on my home prepared porridge mix, gave it a stir then leave it to rehydrate for 5 or 10 minutes.

I like my porridge when camping. It's a simple dish: oats, freeze-dried fruit and some sugar. I wish I were keener on nuts but nuts for me go with savoury later on in the day.

Over breakfast I might be reading a book, I might be pouring over maps. I might just be mentally rehearsing the day ahead. When the porridge is finished, the bowl is rinsed and turned upside down. I always save a little of the hot water for this purpose. When I've drunk some tea, my mug is drained and also turned upside down. I slowly start to pack. I typically start with my sleeping bag and my sleeping bag liner. I pack these tightly in double waterproof bags. These will be in the bottom of the bag that goes on the handlebars. The rest of that bag is saved for the tent. I can get my little stove in there as well if I need to. It's a tiny gas stove which sits in a titanium pan and is partnered with a small gas cylinder. One luxury I have is a plastic base to make the stove more stable. I wrap a lighter in a small polythene bag, add some tea bags, and pack that all as one.

My pillow re-emerges as a set of clothing. I carry some clothes for a pub visit and a spare change of cycling underwear. My electrical goods are packed away, my buff and ear plugs in the same bag. It doesn't take long to pack; everything has its place in the tent and everything has its place in a bag. I repeat the same process every day, though to be fair it often takes a day or two to get back into the groove, but I know what I'm doing. I've done it many times. I never rush, methodical wins the race. But even taking my time I'm usually ready to leave within an hour of waking.

My spare clothes in a dry bag get packed first, then I slip my mug, my stove, pan and spoon in. I pack this tightly with my towel. My dinner bowl, and my electrics bag go in next, and these are packed in with my spare coat (if I'm not wearing it) with my porridge bowl last of all.

If it's wet, the inner tent will be taken down and packed away. If it's dry, the tent and the flysheet will be packed as one, last thing. An outer can be dried easily during a brief stop during the day. The worst is when it rains all day, and you have to pitch again in the rain (that's when being able to put the outer up on its own first is really helpful.)

My under-tent mat and my flip-flops go in my rucksack, bulky but light they justify the taking of a rucksack, which is also handy when you pop into a shop.

Before departure another visit to the loo is required, this time it's a bigger job and I need moss to wipe. I scratch around looking for sphagnum if there is any. I make a hole and do the business. The soft damp sphagnum is a joy to use, and I miss it when I return home.

The bike has waited patiently. I remove the dry bag from the saddle and load my bags strapping them on securely. I set my GPS, pop my phone on the handlebars, don helmet and gloves and I'm on my way once more. Repeat.

In camp

14: Conwy to Knighton

In 2023 CyclingUK, in conjunction with Natural Resources Wales, declared a new bikepacking route open from Machynlleth to Conwy. They named it the Traws Eryri (Trans Snowdonia). The route can be used as a continuation of the Trans Cambrian Trail which arrives in Machynlleth having traversed Wales from Knighton. Living quite near to Conwy and not having done the Trans Cambrian this seemed like an appealing route combination to me. But as ever, finding a way to start and finish these routes is always part of the challenge. There are good railways to Knighton and Machynlleth if you live in Shrewsbury. If you live near Conwy, then it's a little more complex. The logical thing to do then seemed to be to cycle from Conwy to Knighton and thence cross the Trans Cambrian to link into the Traws Eryri which I could follow home. All I had to do was plan and execute a route between Conwy and Knighton. To do this I wanted to vary it from my Cylchdaith Cymru route though I was certainly not averse to reversing sections of that route where that would be the best choice.

The lower Conwy valley (the northern bit) is disappointingly deficient in bridleways. They all seem to have been tarmacked and turned into small roads. Fortunately, they stay quiet and provide a quick smooth ride through a beautiful *dyffryn*. I headed south from Conwy to a river crossing at Tal y Cafn. Then, an ascent on hard-top took me into the Bodnant Estate. Technically, permission is required to ride through the estate, but I was alone and it was quiet. I took the chance and got away with it. Lovely riding followed all the way to Llyn Syberi, then lanes continued south and led to a great fast descent down to Llanrwst.

I was thinking of riders following in my wheel print when I included Llanrwst on this journey. It's a great small town with good facilities; a good place to lunch, stock up or even stay over. So much more authentically Welsh than nearby Betws-y-Coed.

You may have heard me say before, (and if you haven't you will hear me say again), that Wales is hilly. Every downhill has a payback ascent and the one down to Llanrwst is no exception. I stole my way down the cycle track which seemed to randomly cross the A470 several times for unobvious (but usually car related) reasons, to a climb past Coed Hafod. It's a tough climb, never too steep, but it does go on a bit. I've travelled it a few times now and I've always run out of drive when ascending by Moel Trefriw.

The track here is marked as a footpath on the OS map, but further investigation suggests that it's a roadway with access allowed to wheeled vehicles. I certainly received a warm welcome from horses, dogs and people at a muddy Bryn Rhug. On a fine day, this farm is a picture of days gone by, a classic, colourful Ladybird book mixed farm, with a jolly farming family and a range of smiling animals. On a wet, muddy overcast day it's more of a Pathe news black and white affair.

I had another treat as I descended to the gorgeous little bridge over the Afon Twrch. The stream flows in a wild little valley; a jewelled retreat from the surrounding pastoral land. A short sharp push took me to Moel yr Iwrch and then an unfenced lane flowed through undulating open moorland in fine style. A short road section led to ancient walled green lanes. These old lanes were probably once the main thoroughfare through the upper Conwy valley, before the modern A5 colonised the valley bottom. I met no-one. I passed protected curlew nests, off-grid farms and abandoned buildings. Rough, tussocky moor stretched northwards, and large improved fields blanketed the valley side to the south of me. This moorland district is a silent foil to the bustling peaks of Eryri.

Rhydlydan has a pub at which you can camp, but like so many Welsh villages, no one was home when I arrived. The filthiest, smelliest farm I've encountered in Wales was negotiated quickly (whilst holding my breath) before I cycled through Glaslyn on the pavement. Glaslyn is a village sliced by the major trunk route, the A5, with an unhelpful 50 mph speed limit. I passed through Cefn-brith and then had to negotiate a roadworks crew. A team of seven men with seven vehicles (no brides in sight) were resurfacing this barely used country lane. Once again, I was irritated about the way we pander to our metalled roads whilst ignoring our overgrown and unloved bridleways. We need to redress this balance.

Cerrigydrudion was, until it grew a by-pass, the highest village on the A5 between London and Holyhead. Today it feels like an outlier within Conwy County, far from coastal suburbia, a place with a droving history and stables left over from the days of the London – Dublin turnpike. It's on the edge of Mynydd Hiraethog and is the main village in an area known as Uwchaled. Queen Victoria, George Borrow and the Romans have all stopped here. I can imagine the square bustling with horses; the clatter of hooves; the clank of metal clad carriage wheels; the shouts of coachmen, stable boys and local traders; all creating a rural cacophony of *Saesneg* and *Cymraeg* in this busy, remote *pentre*. On my visit, all I heard was the sound of a rapidly approaching diesel engine as an American style pick-up forced its way passed me and pulled up on to the pavement outside the village shop. I bought cake and looked for the next hill.

I didn't need to look far.

The next hill Mwdwl-eithin was thankfully off the road, though that did come with some pushing. This is an area managed for game shooting and on a previous trip, whilst in a subtle camp with Graham and Richard, we'd heard the rumble of a quad bike. The gamekeeper was doing his evening rounds. As is form on these occasions, Graham and I sharpened our elbows and nudged Richard forward to work his charm. We then had to spend the night scaring foxes away to keep our side of the verbal agreement. Better that than having to strike camp and move, though I fear I may have slept through the night and missed the advances of any wily foxes on the moor.

There is, as reward for the climb, a great downhill to Maerdy. I've never stopped here but The Goat Inn always looks tempting. Don't, on the other hand, be tempted by the mapped bridleways on Mynydd Mynllod. I have tried them and wasted time. They don't work. On a reconnaissance trip, I struggled across tussocky moorland looking for bridleway clues, only to be disappointed. I diverted towards a well-mapped, well-used path to the south, the one I now took on this journey, but to get there I had to cross a field of fodder beet. Beet is a round root vegetable used to feed livestock in the winter. Its rounded top protrudes above the surface (you may have seen sugar beet, or swede doing the same thing). To ride across a field of beet is like riding the worst cobbled street ever. Each beet shrugs off the most cross-country of tyres with ease. It's bump to bump, slip to slip, stagger to stagger, I do not recommend it.

Hengaer-uchaf to Tyfos turned out to be the best track to take. My journey there had been on familiar tracks, but thence onwards I was on new ground. It's always a balance on these trips between the known or recommended safe options, and the speculative or unknown options. If only bridleways marked on maps were all passable, or even existed! From Coed Gaerwen, at the top of the hill, I was on uncharted (for me) territory and route-finding decisions had to be made on the move. I'd retreated down the track through Hengaer-uchaf on my earlier exploratory trip, so I knew the climb that lay ahead. At least I knew there was a track, and it was passable.

Farming often seems like a life on edge. With ageing parents, a divorce and illness amongst his flock, it was difficult to see the good times that the young farmer there hoped would be ahead. The price of lamb was high as we chatted, but he expected it to plummet before his were ready. Today's fluctuating prices are completely out of the farmer's control. He hoped the few beef cattle he'd bred would yield a profit to tide him over. Small farms are small businesses, and small businesses have increased costs. Fuel, fertiliser and general household bills are all constantly on the rise. Long gone are the days when the wool cheque made up the larger part of a hill farmer's annual income. I was pleased that I hadn't just cycled on up the tempting lane ahead and had stopped to say hello and enjoy a chat. I've always found farmers in Wales who spend a lot of time working alone, keen for some human contact and an easy half hour passed here whilst I learnt a little more about another way of life. I did lose a water bottle unfortunately which was rather frustrating. Frustrating because it was my fault. The kindly farmer had supplied me with water, he'd invited me into his kitchen to wash and fill my water bottles. I met his 89-year-old father just back from tending the flock. But absent mindedly, I left my full water bottle on the windowsill outside his back door. I only realised when I got to the top of a big hill, and I wasn't going back!

I think this was about the eleventh climb of the day. It was hard work. My bike felt heavy. My legs felt unconditioned and my spirit needed rousing. Some of the hills on that day were fairly minor but still required effort. A couple of them had been massive. To get to camp, I needed to ascend out of the habited valley one more time.

I found a secret spot amongst some trees, pitched camp and slept. In the morning it was damp, and I was enveloped in cloud. Striking camp can be hard or easy. If it's dry you can take all the time in the world. You can lay your kit out on the ground, and it doesn't particularly matter what goes where. If you've got companions you can faff because they will faff too. You can watch the sunrise. You can listen to the birds. It's a really nice time of day. On the other hand, it can be wet.

I wake to low cloud and a clinging dampness. Not sure to what degree it's a heavy dew, low cloud or indeed drizzle. I'm hidden amongst trees which have given me shelter, but now I need sun, and of that there is no guarantee. Everything is wet: my tent, the ground, the trees around, the air and even the view; everything is wet. I can strike camp without striking my tent. My tent is the last thing to pack, well the outer is anyway. Yet again I'm pleased that I have a tent that pitches and strikes outer first. With the outer still pitched I stay sheltered and get organised. I pack everything up, all my kit that needs keeping dry, like my sleeping bag, my pillows and electrics. I can pack away my inner-tent and remain sheltered by the outer. I put my last layer of clothing on. I then slip my wet feet into wet socks into wet shoes. I pull on waterlogged over-trousers and slip on my so-called, waterproof jacket. I need to move now, create some warmth from within.

I've eaten porridge, but it's a race against cooling for the next hour or so. If I'm lucky the sun will beat down on me and dry my modern fabric clothing. If I'm unlucky, it'll rain more and I'll have to warm up my clothing in the same way one warms up a wet suit, with body heat.

My journey continued across the Berwynion and down into Cwm Rhiwerth, with more great downhill off-road mountain biking. I slipped, uninterestedly, past the downhill mountain bike centre at Llangynog, closed due to tree disease. It remained quiet in the village. Its inhabitants either asleep or absent. Then another climb.

Never get complacent about the wonder of our verges as you grind uphill. Take a moment to appreciate this refuge of native woodland, forever squeezed in beside the tarmac and the fence or hedge. On this May time journey, I saw bluebells opening between the greater stitchwort. There was cow parsley, dog's mercury, red dead nettles and broad-leaved willow herb. These wildflowers are the slow uphill cyclist's companions. Take some time to learn their names, it'd be rude not to.

I passed the invisible Carreg-y-tair Eglwys, though later I found out it was a mere standing stone rather than the expected church. Llyn Efyrnwy appeared and got closer as I paced down the hill. The hotel was busy, but the café below the dam was quiet, welcoming and friendly. I stopped for a late breakfast and it morphed into being an early lunch. I probably stayed longer than I should have.

Cycling over another hill towards the Dyfnant Forest, I passed what seemed like a walking yoga group, then encountered horse riders bearing maps in flapping cases. As I passed the third pair, I enquired as to what was going on. Despite spending so much time as a bikepacker on bridleways, it's surprising how few horses I actually see. Their infrequent appearances are therefore noteworthy. I'd spent some time talking to a 'horse-packer' on the Highland trail 550, but something else was going on here.

This was horse orienteering. I thought it was marvellous and the riders were trotting around on the forest tracks, maps in hand, looking for checkpoints. I was able to speak to a marshal and he told me how far people had travelled to join in, and that their biggest problem is actually space in which to park their horse boxes. I hadn't thought of this. It looked to me like a wonderfully healthy, environmentally sound pastime, but that's not reckoning on the 40 or more horse boxes that arrive at each event. There are international competitions across the home nations and competitions exist in Wales, England, Scotland and Ireland. But it seemed that parking at base dictated more than anything else exactly where the activity could take place. It's nice to see something different though.

I didn't stop at the Cann Office, neither for a 'can' (old English for tankard) of ale or to post a letter as many have done before me. This intriguingly named hostel looks well worth a visit, but not quite so early in the day. Perhaps I should have paused here to reconsider the route options ahead in a little more detail, because I then went the wrong way. Bridleways were clearly marked on my map, and it should have been easier but...

The best laid plans of men and mice. It seems so easy to look at a map and choose a well-marked bridleway, but sadly it doesn't always work out. I followed the Afon Gam towards some hills around Nant Wythan that were littered with tracks and bridleways. The sun was out and I remember lying in the sun on a grass verge, attractively dotted with greater stitchwort, and closing my eyes for a post brunch nap. Just then, all was well. A friendly farmer stopped to say hello and check on me in my prone state. Further up the valley, another farmer stopped to check that all was well when I'd stopped to tighten up a bolt on my saddle. The morning was proving friendly, what could possibly go wrong?

On Mynydd Pantceiliagwydd, on the boundary of some access land and a coniferous forest, I met the third farmer of this *nant*, and the furthest one up the hill. We were travelling in opposite directions and I was able to open a gate for him. "I suppose you're trying to follow the bridleway," he said. "Yes" I replied, then whipped out my map and showed him the bridleway I was trying to follow.

"It's not there."

"What do you mean, it's not there?" I retorted.

"It's just not there," He said. "It's gone."

"But if I just turn left here it'll be on my right. It's clearly marked as an unfenced track with green bridleway dash all along it."

"No, it won't be. What you have to do is follow my road across my land, my private land. That's what I see people doing."

He talked me through the route on the map and showed me where it didn't exist, and he showed me where I could use his road. His wife was with him equally friendly and keen to chat, she was there to open the gates because there were so many. There were many more gates ahead.

We passed the time of day discussing farming and how the land was managed and what opportunities there were for nature. I could see rough grassland, manicured grassland, conifers and a small, fenced area with native samplings. It was an interesting patchwork quilt of land use hereabouts. At one point we heard a curlew, all three of us drawing breath to listen. We were all excited. The curlew is such a rare sound now, one we all long to hear more. A sound of my youth, walking in the Dales; a sound of the farmer's youth, living here. A sound slowly disappearing. The curlew's story is a complex one as it has specific environmental needs at different stages of its life and it's a ground nesting bird. According to this farmer, there is not enough habitat and there are too many badgers: the badgers eat the eggs and it's illegal to control them. Whilst I thought the story may be bit more complex than this, I wasn't going to argue. I did need to use his home-made road after all.

With the farmer's permission I rode into the forest. He was right, there was no sign of the bridleway at all. So, with his blessing I followed his track to its end, where I had to cross a field. This was a modern field: blank, bare, improved grassland, with thin mud across its surface making cycling difficult. At the field boundary, where the bridleway was clearly marked on the map, traces of it remained in the landscape, but it was clearly impassable. The farmers road restarted and I followed it, not quite heading in the direction I wanted but it gave me the least line of resistance. I followed the farmer's second track to its end where I cut left across an open grassy field; but this one was cyclable. It took me to the top edge of the conifers on Mynydd Careg-y-big. Two bridleways are mapped here, both taking diagonals through the conifers, but neither were traceable on the ground. I pushed across a muddy, heavily gouged track through the forest to the other side. It wasn't far but it felt it! From there I was able to join better forest tracks, then a farm track and a gated windfarm track which was helpful apart from each gate being locked. Each locked gate required me to lift my bicycle burden over.

More wind farm mayhem followed whilst I sought out the non-existent bridleway on Mynydd Pistyll-du. Hidden from view, I ground to a halt in some scrub between the wind farm and a sheep field. Here I found a flat bit of ground and camped for the night.

There was something strange on Craig y Llyn-mawr. On the rocky summit sat an abandoned 4x4. Later when I checked its provenance online, I found out it had no MOT. I have no idea how long it had been there or how long it might remain there. It wasn't destroyed, just parked badly. It's a rocky, wild summit, with craggy edges giving texture and character. It has everything a small remote top should have. It has a place in this land of hills. Except that is, someone left their 4x4 on top. Strange.

Beyond this slightly bizarre landmarks peaceful lanes took me down to Caersws. It's a place that serves the traveller well and, on this occasion, I took time out at the Seasons Café. It's a great comfort, water and chat stop, and I was in time for a second breakfast.

From Caersws to Knighton, my plan was simple. I would reverse the Chylchdaith Cymru route. Someone else had done the hard work of plotting this route and I had borrowed it for my long around Wales journey. I actually quite like reversing routes, they can seem completely different when travelled in the opposite direction. Of course, when you think about it, they are. The bits you went fast on previously are now slow, whilst the bits you went slow on are now fast! Point to point riding has a lot more going for it than you might think. Complete your journey then turn around and do it the other way. It's like doing a new route, but you know where all the turnings are.

I reclimbed the gate in the Llandinam (formerly Penrhyddlan and Llidiartywaun) wind farm (I can feel English readers flinching at, and skipping over, those names as I write – Use the 'note on Cymraeg at the start of this book then, go back and try harder!) I managed to avoid the racing motorbikes as I dashed across the A483. I had a great view from the Two Tumps. I puffed my way up the hill out of Felindre and cruised, once more, along the Offa's Dyke over Llanfair Hill. I raced down the Jack Mytton Way to a well-earned overnight stay in the Castle Inn in Knucklas, complete with speciality Thai food. That was Conwy to Knighton (well, Knucklas) completed.

In the morning I'd commence the Trans Cambrian Trail.

15: **Bored on The Trans Cambrian**

In good spirits, I left Cnwclas, just outside Knighton. I was well rested and well fed. The hill ahead held no fear for me. It would be a steady climb and then I'd be on the tops for most of the day. I don't mind a steady climb and a bit of pushing. What I hadn't realised was that I needed to go up, then down, then up again! That seemed a little unfair. The turn back left for the second climb was a stiff one but it was softened somewhat by the character of the lane. It was an ancient tree-lined, bluebell-furnished, celandine-carpeted bridleway. It was a pleasure to push this in the footsteps of the ancients. Robin, chiff-chaff and mistle thrush provided the soundtrack.

About an hour and three horizontal kilometres after starting, I topped out on Goytre Hill. This is the eastern end of a long plateau and the way ahead is clear. Clear that is, apart from the beckoning clouds and the stirring showers. The top was marked by the singing of skylarks, some rather benign cows and a flock of wind-blown sheep.

This tabletop landscape undulated away to the west. There were more skylarks than I could shake a stick at and I saw two lapwings, one wheatear and scores more sheep. This is a heavily grazed landscape. The sheep trods provide the least resistance for bulky mountain bike tyres, but there are few flowers, bushes or shrubs. Instead, the area is dominated by bracken, a large acreage of bracken. I know bracken can give the hills a textured, chestnut sheen which draws the eye in the autumn, but close up it's a lifeless, ugly fern. Each dry stem is bent and broken by westerly winds, in an easterly direction. It's like an army of bent cocktail straws impaled across the hillside; faded and disregarded.

Good tracks led me across the same route as the Heart of Wales Line Trail and a section of Glyndwr's Way. I lingered briefly near Bwlch Gwyn and sat under a couple of Scots pines. Sitting here, I was aware that at one time trees just like these were planted to show good places for drovers to stop. Maybe on this very spot a team of drovers and their herd sat and rested, maybe they even made a 'wild' camp and maybe that was perfectly normal. What changed?

It's a good, fast run down to the community shop at Llanbadarn Fynydd, though if you do pass this way, be aware the shop is around the corner on the right, just out of sight. I have to say I was surprised to be fording a stream, I simply hadn't spotted it on the map. Obviously when I looked again it was as clear as day. I could have detoured south to a bridge but I'm a purist at heart. Some people will take the ford straight on and pedal through it. If the water is low, that'll work fine, but I do like to keep my feet, socks and shoes as dry as I can, for as long as I can. So for me, it was shoes and socks off, flip flops on and I paddled through. Very refreshing. And another rest whilst I wiggled my toes to dry my feet.

I then had to regain plateau height, so it was steady pedalling up another hill, allowing for more verge study – hazel, hawthorn, holly and a random blackthorn or two. Ivy, honeysuckle and bramble. Apparently, according to Hooper's rule, the more species there are, the more ancient the hedge. Ribwort plantain waves a punk hairdo, fern fonds unfurl, dock leaves chaperone the nettles and foxgloves wait for their moment to flower. Greater stitchwort dominates, but in the wet bits, mosses rule. Mosses with names like glistening wood moss, bank haircap moss, tamarisk moss and big shaggy moss. Successful bikepackers should embrace the verge experience.

In a field to my left were eminently cute lambs. They were running around in a gang, getting caught on the wrong side of the fence, playing king of the castle and running back to Mum when they were scared. The riding, it has to be said, was pretty unremarkable. There's a nice short section of downhill single-track in one of the cleared forests, but this section is not a highlight of the Trans Cambrian Trail.

From the self-service, honesty box café (must bring cash next time!) at Bwlch-y-Sarnau it's steadier, mostly road, cycling to Rhayader. I like Rhayader: it has nice feel and seems welcoming. There are plenty of shop-based distractions and this is a place that does seem to welcome bikepackers. It should do, this is bikepacking central with routes emanating in all directions.

I suspect if Rhayader is your goal you'll be very pleased to see it. It's not the hardest day of bikepacking, but it does have its tough bits and is quite long for Wales. I nipped into the shop in Rhayader for snacks, then cadged some water off a nice family who were out in their garden planting up their newly assembled raised beds. Then it was onwards, it was a dry evening so I had no excuse not to camp, hence I needed to find a place out of town to pitch. My journey though was soon delayed. Firstly, I couldn't manage the steep hill out of Cwm yr Esgob, I needed to pause by the attractive barn and rest a wee while. Then, further up (near the top actually) I was detained by a very chatty farmer. He'd come up the hill to fix a fence but preferred to share his woes with me. It's a tough job, with little thanks and he had a bad back so fixing a fence was not what he needed to be doing that evening, but if he didn't do it, no one else would. He told me his lad was on the hill, bringing some sheep lower down ready for a big gather in the morning. He recognised I'd be camping on the hill, and was cool about that, even suggesting the best place, which was very nice of him. I met his lad close to my pitching spot. They both warned me that the area was ripe with ticks and informed me that they were losing lambs to Lyme disease.

It was a good camp, quiet, remote and I was safe in the knowledge that I wouldn't be told off having chatted amiably to both farmer and son.

Day two of the Trans Cambrian started well with a fantastic mountain bike descent back down to river level. After Rhiwnant though, it deteriorated. It's one of those tracks that has suffered very badly at the wheels of 4x4 drivers. It's so irregular to ride that I don't think I'll bother with it again. The road on the other side of the valley can be reached quite easily by a bridge at Lanerch Cawr. Yes, it would mean missing some interesting ruins, some sweet nature spots and the occasional good bit. But it'd be better than having to push up rock steps, sneak through puddles hoping they aren't too deep and trying to tip toe across bogs. It's not quite so bad in the other direction, heading southeast that is, as you have gravity on your side. There is still a need to circumnavigate big puddles, but the rock steps are more fun. Beside it's on my Cylchdaith Cymru so it has to be done!

The Claerwen dam is impressive. Apparently under the outer skin it's concrete and the stone surface you see is merely cladding. It was faced by Italian stone masons just after the war, as the British stone masons were busy rebuilding our towns and cities. These leftover prisoners of war were very good at their trade, and they have done a grand job. There is a large car park, information boards and a welcome, clean public toilet. I remembered sheltering from a very heavy downpour here when pedalling the Cylchdaith Cymru.

I met a local in a sort of traffic jam. He was waiting patiently in his pick-up, behind a vehicle leaving the gravel road by the dam. I joked about the jam and asked if he'd come far. Turns out, only from home. The gentlemen in question lives in one of the remotest houses in Wales. It's along this track and above the reservoir, a lonely house called Nantybeddau. I wanted to ask so many more questions, about how he came to be living there and what it was like. I wondered how long he'd been in residence and whether or not I'd be able to sleep in one of his outbuildings? But it just didn't seem appropriate and, when I looked up, it turned out the jam was gone. I was now the one delaying him. He was patient, but I needed to let him go. Maybe I'll meet him again one day.

And then it was back to the sheep-wrecked landscape, back to the miles of *molinia*, back to the grinding into the headwind. The only accompanying sounds were from the odd meadow pipit. The only movement was from frequent wheatears and occasional ponies. The cloud was down, and drizzle came with it. It was one of those days when there was nothing to do but pedal and maybe occasionally seek shelter for a bite to eat. It's a long gravel road and progress is easy depending on the wind. This is classic mid-Wales gravel alongside the Claerwen Reservoir.

The Teifi pools are a well-known spot in these parts. It might be interesting one day to explore on foot, but then again it probably wouldn't. It'll be what you see from the road is what you get, I'm sure of it. Still, after the featureless moors I had just passed through, the Teifi Pools are a veritable beauty spot. I've passed through here before, there's a great bothy nearby though it's one that gets abused due to being far too close to a metalled road. The descent to Strata Florida is excellent mountain biking, though not all the bridleways marked on the map in these parts are ridable. The Trans Cambrian carries on the roller coaster tarmac lane. I marvelled at the antics of the 4x4 off-road brigade. It's a devastation they seem to revel in, carving tracks and attempted tracks up every roadside bank. It just looks like mindless vandalism. Though of course in the context of the landscape their imprint is relatively small. Either side of the road is pretty desolate with over worked ground where only poor grasses now thrive. I still don't think that excuses their toxic behaviour though. This might be the green desert of mid Wales but it's a special place to many people and it's a great place to ride a bike.

Temptingly close to Pont-rhyd-y-groes, the route swung right into the Hafod estate. I took a short cut from Rhos Tanchwarel down a bridleway that doesn't feature on the official route. It's taken by the catchily named Borth to Devil's Bridge to Pontrhydfendigaid Trail. It's good.

Some neat forest riding conveyed me beyond the Hafod estate and to the quiet Cymystwyth road. The road took me uphill past the lead mining settlement of Cwmystwyth. This is a spectacular valley with the bare remains of its industrial past everywhere. Lead has been mined here since the Bronze Age. The main company was the Cwm Ystwyth Mines Company which operated the mines from 1848 to 1923. The company employed over 1,000 miners at its peak and produced over 100,000 tons of lead per year. The fact that the spoil heaps lay bare to this day, 90 years on from their abandonment, tells a story of how toxic the spoil remains.

To finish the second day of the Trans Cambrian there is another hill, it's a stiff one as well. The surface is good, but it was a long push for me, before I disappeared into the forest by the Afon Diliw. I could have carried on to the Bluebell Pub in Llangurig. I could have carried on to the Glangwy campsite. But I'm always keen for a bothy night and just off route hereabouts is the Nant Rhys bothy.

I like to stay in bothies when the opportunity arises. Membership is peanuts and I recommend you chip in too. To be fair, I tend to seek out midweek evenings off season. It's a funny business bothying. You tend to hope that you'll get the bothy to yourself, but of course part of the joy of bothying is meeting other people. So, on the other hand, you do want there to be somebody else in residence. On this occasion the bothy was empty, but it was a good place to spend the night as more rain was due. Sadly, on my own I couldn't be bothered collecting wood. The forest around the bothy would have been well picked over and the landscape was pretty sodden. I'd have had to put in more effort than I had spare to search for dry wood. Shame really because a bothy without a fire is a dark, damp hovel, but as soon as you light a fire, it's a dynamic, vibrant, welcoming home in the hills.

From the bothy it was conifers; oppressively lining the route and hiding the view. Then more climbing than I expected, before a big swoop down to the Wye Valley. The water from the Cymystwyth area would flow down to the Irish sea at Aberystwyth, whilst the water here would take a long overland journey to join the Severn estuary. Last night's teeth cleaning water would eventually head out towards Ireland. This morning's wee, would be off to see the Severn Bridge.

I turned left then right heading into the Hafren forest. I hurried through a sour smelling farm, but contrastingly the valley beyond is rather attractive. Birch saplings are leading the natural regeneration of a purple moor-grass dominated marsh. There are also saplings growing through bracken and peeping above the gorse. All in all, it's the valley of optimism. Once you pass the smelly farm, of course.

I paused at the forestry car park below the delightfully named Cwm Ricket. I ate my snack and sat quietly, listening, watching and biding my time.

I stop to remove a jacket. I can't resist a sit and a look back at the day so far. I'm mesmerised by an invisible goldcrest singing its high-pitched simple tune. There's a blackbird chuntering and a handful of large white butterflies busily enjoying the hot sun of this afternoon. There's a throng of tiny flies and it feels as though summer is on the way. I've seen yellow pimpernel to add to my tally of flowers. Tormentil is here too, but the verges are still dominated by stitchwort, bluebells and common dog violets. I sit and watch as a group gather for what looks like a nature walk. Enthusiastic yet relaxed, happy yet purposeful. They all have grey hair and a spring in their step, maybe it's a University of the Third Age group; they are active, interested and interesting. I envy them their camaraderie, but I'm ignored, like a Douglas Adams S.E.P.

I remounted and slowly wound my way up the road towards Staylittle.

An old man on an old motorbike gently passed me gently. His dome-shaped helmet and Biggles goggles marking him out as from a different era. It was like I'd stepped back in time. Another bike came, then another. By the time the fifth one was in view I was off my bike, coughing and spluttering, because the exhaust fumes were horrendous. It's good to see how far we've come on the control of emissions from internal combustion engines. The old bikes, and it's the same with old cars, are cute and nostalgic, but they also remind you of how deadly those fumes are.

From Staylittle the route really picks up its game. You could argue that the Trans Cambrian, brilliant riding though it is, does pass through some tired countryside. The intensive farming of the first section giving way to the desolate Claerwen area, followed by the conifer plantations of the eastern legs. There is mine waste, reservoirs and off-roaders causing havoc. But this last section has some interesting moorland, deep fertile valleys and enough native woodland around to keep the birds interested. Of course, the whole landscape has been shaped by people, it's just that in some areas the textures, shades and brush strokes have been kinder. Glaslyn feels remote. It's a Montogomery Wildlife Trust Nature Reserve. At the right time of year, you'll see blooming heather, cotton grass and quillwort. If you're very lucky you might hear a golden plover or glimpse a hen harrier. This moorland is now being managed for nature; I'll watch how it develops with interest.

The descent from here is legendary. The steep slatey track down from Bwlch y Graig requires just enough control and just enough speed. It might be a bit tricky when wet, but on the day I was here, it was brilliant. I'd been looking forward to this and it didn't disappoint. Bikepacking is about the journey, but that's no reason not to whoop it up a bit when you get such a fine descent as this. There is one gate (a shame) but it means you can look back at the way you've come (which suddenly doesn't look quite as steep as it felt) take your break and love the next section. It's shallower, but grassy, oh my, it's wonderful. If you don't arrive at Ty'n-y-fedw with a big smile on your face you're doing something wrong, or you're on the wrong bike. The joy should even get you most of the way up the next hill too.

Gorgeous wheeling took me through the Afon Hengwm woods up to Rhiw Goch from where a fast smooth downhill would have taken me straight to Dovey Junction. However, I turned right to sneak off straight into Machynlleth and was a bit disappointed by the up and down nature of the last bit of road.

Machynlleth welcomes the rider with shops, takeaways, cafes and pubs.

Machynlleth is a once proud town that today is a little lacklustre. Once it was the capital of Wales, now it looks like it needs a burst of enthusiasm. Clearly the local economy is languishing behind that of other places across our islands. I know there is community, and I know it's a mixed one. People speak fondly of the town, but I suspect, like all our towns, its retail sector is being gradually corroded by the twin evils of online shopping and supermarket food deliveries.

I needed some gas for my stove, but it wasn't easy to find. You'd expect there to be at least one outdoor shop in a place that borders the Eryri National Park. Can you imagine a town in the Lake District without an outdoor shop? Transplanted to Cumbria, Machynlleth might have its wide pavements thronging with south-easterners eager to spend their cash on superfluous outdoor gear. Here in the heart of mid-Wales however, it's a choice between the Spar or the Co-op. There is the odd independent shop, some charity shops and some takeaways. The hotels look tired. Such a shame as clearly this is a fascinating place with an intriguing history. A lady with a push chair tried to direct me to a place where I might be able to buy gas; a gentleman on a bike guided me around the back streets to the shop (imaginatively called the Store) in a converted school. Here, a pleasant young man served me the fuel I needed and then it was back to the main street. There seemed to be a disproportionately large number of speedy drivers in hatchbacks with loud exhausts. They weren't the only ones who seemed to be in a rush, pick-ups and white vans also took no quarter; a speeding tractor split the town in two. Motor vehicles dominated the town centre and made crossing the road something to be avoided. Machynlleth really does need the Welsh shift to default 20 mph.

I stayed in the Toad Hall Hostel. It's a quirky place. It ranges somewhere from being a place of cast-offs to a museum. There was no one to quiz about the eclectic mix of items on show or the history of vehicles in the garden. But if you fancy a glimpse, you'll see transistor radios, doors, scout tents, kayak moulds, rugs and plenty of other bric-a-brac.

So, that was the Trans Cambrian trail, the most famous bikepacking route in Wales. On the one hand, it was boring. Day one was through sheep-cropped oversized fields and meadows of bracken. Day Two was through the depleted Cambrian desert. And day three was spent visiting conifer plantations. The naturalist might struggle for stimulation (though the naturist would find plenty of solitude). On the other hand, I enjoyed it; it's good riding with very little on the road, but it's not as interesting as the Conwy to Knighton leg and it shouldn't be as good as the Traws Eryri, but the Traws Eryri has a personality crisis…

Fording the Afon Ithon

16: Disappointed on the Traws Eryri

The Traws Eryri trail, from Machynlleth to Conwy, came into being in 2023. Prior to launch, Cycling UK and Natural Resources Wales (NRW), who'd worked together to plot the route, put out a draft for consultation. This is the route I followed except for a few places where I knew of slightly more traffic free variations. The final version of the route, the now 'official' version, changed considerably and the route is currently more tarmac and gravel than mountain. It's proving to be very popular though, and is being enjoyed by scores, if not hundreds of riders.

I'd arrived in Machynlleth having cycled from Conwy to Knighton and then by way of the Trans Cambrian Trail. I'd cycled previously in a southerly direction from Conwy to Machynlleth on my Cylchdaith Cymru journey and I was interested to see how it would ride heading back north. The consultation route threw in one or two interesting variations and one or two oddities.

I'm awake early, woken by a song thrush and the creaks of the old barn that is Toad Hall. I doze a bit longer, but this is wasted time; I can bank it and rest later in the day when I might need it. The forecast is good, my breakfast is a massive portion of kids' cereal followed by a bacon butty. Unfortunately, my washing is as wet as when I hung it up and it needs strapping on the exterior of my bags, in the hope it'll dry as I ride. I head down to the garage and drag my bike away from its one-night stand with a vintage car and set off north from Machynlleth.

The Traws Eryri follows National Cycle Network route 8 on a minor road alongside the Afon Dulas to Corris. I had to negotiate bridge works to escape Machynlleth, but a riverside cycleway, with its own dedicated bridge, took me the right way. I stopped briefly in Esgairgeiliog as my eye caught the old Forestry Commission Camp. It looks like an abandoned prisoner of war camp and may have been used as a borstal at some time in its life. It also stands out for being on flat land, a rare commodity in these parts and seemingly squandered on a run down and disused site. As ever though, with the old relics there is art here. The corrugated iron huts are not unappealing to the eye and a few moments here were treasured.

Corris on a sunny day is a gorgeous place. The residents are friendly, the houses are cute and well kept. There's a deep river gorge painted several shades of green by damp loving mosses and crossed by a proud stone bridge. The tightly packed terraces would have served the needs of slate quarrymen and their families well. A strong community of people living and working together seems to continue to this day. Clearly the residents are happy, and the small houses suit, though quite where all the cars go is another matter. Nothing's open of course, I'm too early for the pub, the café or even the occasional post office. The village might look different in the darker days of winter when the sun will struggle to penetrate this valley. Each property passed showed signs of being a damp one, but everybody, with no exception had said hello. I like that.

The section of the Traws Eryri from Corris Uchaf to Abergynolwyn was one that I was particularly looking forward to. The finished, official version has taken a different route. The official Traws Eryri now follows the A487 north to Tal y Llyn. At a late stage in planning, the permission to ride my next section was withdrawn, which is a great shame as it's rather good.

To be fair it's a big climb, but it's ridable and the *igam-ogam* track heads up a nice gradient to Briddellarw below Tarren y Gesail.

It's a reasonable assumption that someone who studied geography in Aberystwyth in the 1980s is going to be an interesting person. Particularly if, after university, that person did some travelling then came back to settle in Corris Uchaf and has spent most of their working life as a dry stonewaller. That, indeed, was the case when I met a lean Stevie Haston (a climbing legend) look alike jogging steadily up the same climb as me. We got along nicely and chatted as we ascended; him on foot, wiry, lean and with a spring in his step; me on the bike, working hard for every pedal stroke. We castigated Thatcherism with reference to the state (and profits) of our water suppliers and sewage discharges, the price of utility bills, the uselessness of our trains and a Post Office on the edge. Contemporary clowns are merely jostling to be the second worst. We shared a dream of a wilder Wales, whilst appreciating its history, culture and the landscape legacy of upland farming. We agreed that we now need a happy medium between grazing and places for nature.

The descent to Abergynolwyn was a belter. It's a good track, at a good angle and it flows really well. At the bottom the proposed route suggested a detour on forest tracks across the valley. I ignored that and I took the delightful little, tree-lined lane down to the village, crossing the Tal y Llyn Railway on the way.

Abergynolwyn had placed itself handily for a lunchtime stop on the proposed Traws Eryri, but it will probably come too early on the modified official route. The leaseholders of the community cafe were all too keen to have a chat and pass the time of day. To be fair, there wasn't much else going on in the village at the moment and there was definitely an air of second homes about the place. I pigged out with beans on toast and perfect poached eggs, followed by carrot cake. I guzzled lemonade then sipped on coffee. Afterwards, I sat in the garden in the sun and listened to house sparrows busily chatting amongst themselves. Abergynolwyn is one of those places where the station is a little out of the settlement. It reminded me of a story I once came across whilst reading about Dent in the Yorkshire Dales where the station is famously four miles away from the village. When one visitor, from across the Atlantic Ocean, asked why the station was so far away from the village a local replied "'appen they wanted it near the railway line." It would appear that a similar scenario has presented itself in Abergynolwyn.

I left Abergynolwyn on the most wonderful bridleway. It sits above an oak-filled gorge on a narrow shelf and at first, it felt like cycling through the tree canopy. It then passed through meadows and across rough slopes which were grazed by clean cute Welsh Mountain sheep. Birds were singing. I picked out the rattle of a wren which interrupts its own charming and surprisingly loud song. A greenfinch wheezed; a willow warbler sang descending notes whilst a song thrush experimented with variations on its theme, every one repeated at least twice. Meanwhile a flock of jackdaws, hung around like a gang of bored teenagers and picked away at the odd juicy worm. Unfortunately, the first fifty metres of this bridleway is recorded as a footpath, so the official Traws Eryri remains road bound.

Craig yr Aderyn (Bird Rock) will, I'm sure, have been described somewhere as a beetling precipice. Perhaps an overused piece of purple prose, but it does work rather well here. The stoney outcrops weave left and right across the hillside and crescendo at an apparent Matterhorn-like summit. Of course, on the other side it's probably just a grassy slope. I enjoyed cruising along the quiet, flat lane whilst craning my neck to visually explore the crags above. Crossing the valley could be deemed flat and boring tarmac. But actually, if you sit up in the saddle and look around you, your bike is a fine vantage point to appreciate the man-made beauty of this valley. It has margins of native woodland, hedges criss-crossing the flood plain and there are little copses of trees here and there. The land is still worked, but all feels a bit more sympathetic. There was an absence of cars and delivery vans as I passed through which made the whole place much more bucolic.

A thousand-foot climb starts at Bryn Gwyn. You need a good relationship with your saddle for this one and if it's sunny, there is little shade. I was lucky and had some assistance from a westerly wind which helped me along somewhat. I chunked the hill into three sections. Part one to the first cattle grid and sheep fold. Here was a good place to sit. I hadn't gone far to be fair, but it was a flattening with shelter from the wind and with shade from the sun, which was actually quite hot that afternoon. Loins suitably girded, it was time to climb again. It's a steady haul up the Ffordd Ddu on a good surface, so steady I had time to look around whilst gaining height slowly, but surely. I had time to watch a pied wagtail alight on a fence post, then dash across the sheep pasture searching for the best place to pick for insects. I could breathe in the scent of gorse; some say it smells like coconut. I wondered what those who smelt coconut for the first time, on its import to these islands, thought that tough nut smelt like when smashed open?

As I rounded the sharp bend by Foel Tyr gawen a great view of Craig yr Aderyn opened up. The way I'd come was lain out below me, the inland cormorant colony on the crag stood out clearly, whilst the coast drew a border line heading south. I didn't want to stop though, it's a long plod up the thousand-foot hill and I carried on climbing. There were golden drops of tormentil in the lush green verge interspersed with a flourish of savoy blue germander speedwell, both species adjusting their height to that of the surrounding vegetation in a clamour for sunshine. I heard the *chee-ow* of choughs above me as I paused briefly on a patch of sheep-cropped grass. My tired legs cried on up the tarmac heading for the horizon.

The tarmac tilted ever upwards and I ground my way up, slowly but surely. From time to time, I had to practise the avoidance of insects. Not the irksome, head buzzing, stinging kind, but the rambling kind. More than once a beetle or a bee, stepped out in front of me, bound it seemed for a suicidal destiny. Our worlds so far apart, the insect couldn't imagine the deadly crush that might arrive as it crossed the hot, black desert. I slowed, swerved or speeded up. I had two wheels to think about though and I worried about the course of my rear one. I had to practise the avoidance of insects crossing the road.

There's a stand of eucalyptus trees on the horizon. It's strange. I don't know why anyone would have planted such a group of trees in this exposed location. Maybe they give some shelter to the nearby sheepfold, but it's an odd species to choose for such a role. Still, they're a landmark and, once reached, they meant I was at the top of the thousand- foot hill.

It's open country now and fine wheeling with no one around. I'm accompanied by a visiting wheatear which perches on a dry-stone wall, hiding its white bottom whilst chirping a tuneless dirge. The locals are meadow pipits and they flit through the air, ducking and diving in pairs at great speed. A red kite passes over; the locals ignore it, so little is the threat posed by the carrion eating hawk above them. And then, again, I'm negotiating pools of despair, carelessly left behind by the 4x4 gang. Further on, I can hear the RAF practising above, the whining of a Spitfire like Texan T1 plane is the backdrop as I visit a World War Two crash site. Twenty young Americans lost their life on this hillside in 1945 when their Flying Fortress came down here. I trust the modern planes are safer, but the whirring noise is wearing, and war continues elsewhere.

This section is part of the official Traws Eryri and rightly so; it's classic off-road cycling, but at the end of a particularly good downhill to the Afon Arthog, I diverged again. The official route heads along tarmac past Llynnau Cregennen then down a very steep road to the valley bottom. The lakes are worth a visit, but I chose the off-road route past Pant-y-llan. I was familiar with this route having come the other way on my Chylchdaith Cymru journey. It's along pretty green lanes, past pretty cottages, and it really is a very pretty place. There is a sting in the tail though. It's a properly steep bridleway down to the valley floor. It's also narrow and comes with unsteadying tree roots as well. As I neared the bottom I looked right, up the most perfect of pathways. A beautiful rustic gate guards a flagstone path, bordered by drystone walls, which leads to an old cottage with views across the Mawddach estuary.

I've waxed lyrical about the Mawddach trail before, so I won't dwell on it here. Just be sure it's a great linking route for some excellent mountain bike journeys and a fine route in its own right, on a different day with a different aim.

The route, both proposed and official, now ascends from this valley, up and over to the mountain bike centre at Coed y Brenin. I was tired. Camping prior to this would have been too soon and once again I'd failed to locate the campsite near to the Mawddach Trail. I simply couldn't face another climb to find a remote spot to wild camp. Instead, I went soft and cycled into Dolgellau for a lovely B&B night. A bed can be the most wonderful thing sometimes. I also prefer a pub meal to a rehydrated tent meal, but I'm sure that's just me!

I cycled north from Dolgellau (avoiding the climb to Llyn Cwm-mynach, a way I'd travelled previously) along the NCN 82 towards Coed y Brenin. I was well aware, having ridden this before, that I was taking the soft option, but I don't mind admitting I wasn't feeling strong. Typically, on these long routes I get a second wind after about day four and I settle into a nice groove of pedalling for seven or eight hours a day (with rests of course.)

On this journey however I felt unfit and had little spare fuel in the tank. So, the familiar and gentle ride along the Nant Ganllwyd was just the job. The Afon Ganllwyd is another one of those beautiful rivers of Wales with which I wasn't familiar. I took every opportunity to peer down upon its lively form. It was spring and the trees were just coming into leaf. I looked over the fresh green shades that adorned the riverbanks, perfectly framing the white, grey and blue waters below.

I picked up parts of the Minotaur Trail heading to the visitor centre. I enjoyed the little bits that slipped off the main track; a hump here and a bump there all along the way helped to keep me interested and smiling. Wouldn't a national plan to link these up across Wales be grand.

I could have stopped here if I so desired. There is water, showers, toilets, café and a bike shop. I'd paused here before when bikepacking, but it's confusing. It's all electric bikes and urban people, too many SUVs and loud 'look at me' conversations. I passed through silently and slipped back into the anonymity of the woods.

Escape was hampered by signage overload, but I found route 82 and followed 'the Council Road' north.

If you descend this way (as you might do on my Chylchdaith Cymru or the Sarn Helen Trail) you will be going too fast to stop at the Llwyn Du Bloomeries. But as I was ascending the hill, slowly as usual, this was a welcome respite, and it's a point worth stopping at. The Bloomery is an ironworks dating back to the 14th century. Dozens of people would have worked this site making iron and steel for horseshoe nails, hammers and weapons. The process consumed large amounts of charcoal, which is why the woodland site was a good place to be. The charcoal makers, a separate occupation, would harvest branches from trees in a process called pollarding. You can spot trees that were once pollarded by looking for those with a slightly outsized trunk below a fine spray of branches.

The oak hereabouts is covered in lichen. Other trees have it too, but the oak holds the most. This is *Usnea flammea*, occasionally called old man's beard but a much better name is knicker elastic lichen. If you can find a branch on the ground with some lichen on, then gently tease the central stalk of the lichen and you'll see it stretch; you might even see the 'elastic' inside. It is, as you were probably aware, an indicator of clean air and it thrives on the old growth in these western forests.

The track from here is both an NCN route and as I mentioned earlier the Sarn Helen Roman road. Don't expect it to be an easy ride. When descended, it's pretty rough in places, but on ascent I was pushing up some sizable rock steps, chuntering once more about the adverse impact of motorised traffic on these stony lanes. Though it should be noted, climate change and more dramatic weather events have also taken their toll on these rocky roads.

It's worth the push though. At the top of the hill, I was rewarded by a fantastic wild hillside, full of saplings and new growth. To the west I could see the whole of the Rhinogydd and further north there was Yr Wyddfa beckoning me towards home. I could also see, very clearly, the Trawsfynydd nuclear power station, undisguisable from a large castle such as the one at Caernarfon (or so its architects would encourage us to believe.)

As I crossed this hill above Bronaber I noticed concrete and brick building bases. A little research revealed that below this hill, on the site of the contemporary holiday village, was a prisoner of war camp. There's a lot to discover here for the war time archaeologist. This site was an artillery training camp and a prison for Germans in the First World War whilst in the second, it became a camp for Italian prisoners of war. The accommodation has been significantly upgraded for the modern holiday village!

I really enjoyed the Llyn Trawsfynydd round. On the map it looks a little odd detouring round the lake, but it's a really good purpose-built cycle trail. It's interesting to pass close by the power station which is in the process of being decommissioned, but as is often the case, around the industrial site is one of the best places for nature. The track here is fringed with wonderful new growth native woodland, full of birdsong, including the 'spinning coin' song of the infrequently seen wood warbler.

Cwm Teigl is a slog, but it's way better than the road route that the official route takes from Trawsfynydd to Penmachno. The B4391 is a narrow and up-hill road with fast traffic coming at you in both directions and as it trends leftwards you are rarely in good view from behind. It's followed by the B4407 which is the sort of road motoring journalists seek out for their high-speed research. Hopefully the official route will switch to Cwm Teigl, and you'll just be facing another long hill that needs chunking. As I climbed through the cwm, I tried to pick out anywhere the angle eased so I could pause to get my breath back. Fortunately, it's a quiet dead-end road leading only to the Manod Slate Quarry.

I find the slate mining country that is passed through here fascinating. This particular quarry was home to paintings from the National Gallery during the Second World War. The entrance had to be enlarged and inside, several brick 'bungalows' were built to house them. The storage of the priceless works of art here helped our understanding of how best to store these paintings, in terms of humidity and temperature. Lessons learnt were applied when the National Gallery was rebuilt post-war.

Hopefully this section of the trail will, in time, become the official route. It could do with a little bit of work here and there and there is a locked gate to be scrambled over. The descent to Cwm Penmachno is exceptional. Stony, curvy and steep. I arrived at the bottom in full grin mode and then had to joust with a kissing gate. Road riding took me efficiently to the start of the Penmachno trail and four sections later, I was discharged on to the minor road that leads downhill passed Ty Mawr towards the Lledr Valley and the A470. Through the Penmachno woods I'd stuck to the fantastic mountain bike trails. I wasn't interested in avoiding the good bits, like a gravel biker, and plodding around the same old, same old, forest tracks.

I didn't want to follow the official Traws Eryri on to the A470 either. I've driven that road enough to know it's no place for laden bikepackers. Instead, I used forest tracks and wiggled my way (not without some superfluous climbing it has to be said) to Pont-y pant. From Pony-y-pant the Sarn Helen track leads handsomely over the hill to Betws y Coed. Hereabouts the proposed Traws Eryri route showed some rather eccentric and definitely superfluous wandering around the Gwydyr Forest, both south and north of Betws-y-Coed. It seemed to me that the best route was to use the forest tracks towards Capel Curig then the Lon Las Ogwen route down to Bethesda.

From Bethesda the Traws Eryri route masochistically goes up, down, up, down, up and down again to deposit you in Conwy with an awful train journey back to Machynlleth. Me? I just went home. I live in the Conwy valley and following routes I already knew around the Carneddau was not the order of my day.

The Traws Eryri, whichever way you go, is a fine route and it will be enjoyed by many. It's a shame the potential mountain bike version remains under wraps. If you do it as a loop from Conwy via the Trans Cambrian and back to Conwy, then the route, for all its idiosyncrasies, is a fabulous north Wales round. If, on the other hand, you start at Machynlleth and want to get back there on public transport, then the route finishes in the wrong place. Caernarfon would have been a more convenient end, and the castle is just as grand as Conwy's. From Caernarfon, the traffic-free, Lon Efion takes you to Harlech and thence a train can be taken to Machynlleth.

17: Time travelling in Eryri

I heard wren first, but the blackbird was almost simultaneous with it. Robin chipped in, then a chiff-chaff. A blackcap made its presence felt, then, on a seemingly different wavelength, the looney tunes of the song thrush began. It was all brought down to earth with the tuneless crank of a carrion crow; the morning had begun. Well sort of, it was only half past four, but it was light, and it was summer. It was also wet and warm. I tried to sleep some more.

I was camping in Waunfawr for our mid-summer bikepacking overnighter with Sally, Richard, Jules and Jess. We had endured an evening in fine 1970's style in the local inn. A room stuck in time, the decor, the ambience, even the seating all took me right back to my teen years. As too did the quality of the food and the beer.

Once on the bike however, and in fine company, life got better. A short dash up the road and we were on the quietest of lanes, followed by a super bridleway with views to Castell Caernarfon and Ynys Mon. These empty tracks led down to the Lon Eifion Cycleway, surely one of the best of our rail-based traffic free routes. I loved the seamless entry to the route with no need to go on, or even cross the busy A4871. No missing links here, just great riding all the way to Garndolbenmaen. But first, lunch.

We pulled into Penygroes with a couple of venues in mind. There's a vineyard which looks very nice, but possibly a bit upmarket for a trip of this nature. There's a community cafe which sounded just right. We asked directions from a local woman, elderly with a smiling face; we slipped in some Welsh as this is the heartlands of Cymraeg. "Yes, it's nice there, but come to the bakers with me, they do lovely coffee." We could hardly refuse. She took us to meet Barry and Rita, and we stepped back in time.

This was a baker, albeit with less stock, which took me back to the 60's. I remember one in Cawood, where I met Alan Pulleen on the way to infant school every morning (we walked in those days). British bakers were simple, they sold good bread, sliced or unsliced, and simple but tasty cakes. The fanciest cake was (and some would argue still is) the vanilla slice (vanilla slice sounds so much more exotic than custard slice!). Here in Penygroes was a simple, but very appealing vanilla slice. This cake is so much more than the sum of its parts: cold custard, soggy flaky pastry and a bit of thin icing on top. It knocks the French fancies flying in my book!

"We make everything here," claimed Rita, who's working hours were midnight till 5 pm, daily. The pasties and pastries had us tempted. Whilst not 1960's prices it was still very good value. Barry had a cake to bake (whilst the menu advertised his special Barry's Burger) so was slightly stressed, but he hid it well. The shop was full of customers needing pasties microwaving, whilst juniors waited to collect lunchtime orders for their workplaces. Pop, pasty and cake did us nicely. This is no place for TripAdvisor: step back in time, see the Pepsi sign Barry and Rita brought back from the USA, hunt the café for all the different menus, admire the rolling digital board that promotes cheesy chips, and meet the locals. Our lady had already stepped up proudly to the counter to announce she'd brought some people. I hope she earned a good discount.

The Homestyle Bakery was not what I expected of Penygroes, but this is an experience rather than a pure eatery. A subtle one all the same.

We continued along the very amenable Lon Efion (NCN 8) to Garndolbenmaen. This is one of many silent villages I've passed through on my travels across Cymru. Beyond is a peaceful land too. A place where trees are growing and it feels like nature has a chance. There was an appealing looking by-way (actually a 'road used as a public path') on the OS map across Bwlch y Bedol but it wasn't there on the ground. Instead, we followed a good track just to the north, which took us to the bothy: Cae Amos.

Cae Amos was, from the 1960's until 2015, the Welsh base of the Leeds University Mountaineering Club. It's now under the management of the Mountain Bothy's Association and is seeing considerable work undertaken. At some time, in days gone by, it would have been a home. A small farm, probably a mixed farm. A family would have lived here long before personal transportation revolved around the motor car. This is our glimpse into how we lived in the 18th Century.

We were lucky that the area around the bothy had dried out in recent weeks, but heading north-east from here might be a bit of a chore under wetter conditions. We though, rode past the impressive ruin of Llywyn-y-bettws easily and down through Chwarel y Plas to Cwm Pennant.

Unfortunately for us, we picked the wrong way out of this valley. The by-way from Brithdir to Cwm Trwsgl is, despite being reasonably graded and well-marked on the map, not such a good route. It's a long, untracked, bracken-infested push, and it pretty much finished us off for the day. Our bodies were saved only by a glorious swim in the small llyn in Cwm Trwsgl. It might have been a bit weedy and tricky to enter, but it was great; cooling and refreshing. We camped on a dry, flat meadow at the head of the llyn where we were surrounded by rocky peaks and an old quarry. It was a ragged wild feeling land and a perfect camp, apart from the tick infestation. We discovered during next the next day that we were all covered in minute tick nymphs. It took a couple of days to find and remove them all.

The remnants of slate quarrying in Cwm Trwsgl are from the grandly named Prince of Wales quarry. Sadly, this was an unsuccessful venture. It opened in 1873 and closed in 1886, one can only wonder at the tough and unprofitable lives of those unfortunate enough to try and work here. This then is the 19th Century representative for our time traveling bikepacking journey. We then pushed our bikes up through the quarries to Bwlch-y-ddwy-elor and entered the Beddgelert forest.

It was nice to get to the forest because it meant we were going downhill for a bit. There are some clearings in the forest which give the riding a lovely open aspect and the descent to Rhyd Ddu is as classic as it gets. The forest was planted in 1926 giving us our 20th century contribution to this journey through time.

Rhyd Ddu is a small village, but it has the all-important cafe. The Ty Mawr is lovely. The service is friendly, the food is great, and the ambience is delightful. We took pleasure in parking our four bikes in the space it would take one car to fill and spent an hour or so enjoying a good breakfast before we had to start the ascent of the Snowdon Ranger path. The Snowdon Ranger path has recently been tidied up and it's in good order now, so this all-purpose path is our 21st century contribution to the time travelling journey. We were surprised that much of its 300-metre height gain was cyclable too.

The descent from Bwlch Maesgwm towards Llanberis has recently been improved. Traditionally, on this descent, elite mountain bikers would thrill at the need to bunny hop, at speed, over awkwardly placed diagonal drainage ditches. The rest of us panicked and slowed down for each and every one of them. These have now been removed and the full flow of this journey is open to all of us, bikepackers included. I think the only thing wrong with this descent is that it's over too quickly. To get full value do stop a while, take a few photographs, admire the view, and watch out for walkers. Try not to do as Sally did and get a blow out, completely unfixable, meaning she had to walk. I'm blaming the cheap tyres that were provided with the bike when it was bought. Fortunately, she wasn't too far from the end of the route so I was able to head back to the car then pop round the hill and pick her up from the base of the track in Llanberis.

Jess, Jules, Richard and I didn't take the tarmac down to Llanberis but contoured around, and up a bit, on a lovely bridleway with great views over the village and Llyn Padarn. The enormous Dinorwig slate quarry across the valley stands as a World Heritage Site and a monument to the history of north Wales. This was a very successful quarry and dwarfs the workings we saw earlier in Cwm Trwsgl. It was a steady roll back to Waunfawr and our cars now. Or it would have been except the heavens properly opened. This was rain plus! We were soaked to the skin in no time at all, so glad this came at the end of the weekend. There was no hiding place. We just had to buckle down and get on with it. I took my glasses off as I couldn't see through the rain splattered lenses, but then I couldn't fully open my eyes as I slid into the maelstrom. Sometimes it rains, sometimes it drizzles, sometimes it's a mizzle and sometimes it's a short sharp downpour. We really should have more words for different kinds of rain. It's key to check the temperature. If it's warm, or warmish, then I'll just get wet and wait to dry out. I do pull a cag on over my soft shell just to stop the worst of the precipitation and to stop me losing heat to the wind. When it's colder, I wear full waterproofs: leggings and all. They don't keep me dry, but staying warm is the key. Two or three wet days and nights equal a hostel or hotel night in my book.

I squinted and freewheeled as fast as I dare. We hit a tarmac road, but a very quiet, dead-end one. Only a farmer with his trailer, hurdles placed to gather sheep, blocked the way. I slowed. I saw him bob between his truck and the trailer. I crawled up to the obstruction. There was just enough room to sneak through. As I arrived the farmer turned and stepped out. He nearly jumped out of his skin poor soul. I couldn't do anything; I knew I wouldn't hit him, but the noise of the storm perfectly covered the sound of my approach. Apologies all round, nobody's fault and some very British sorry, sorry, sorry, ensued.

We reached the cars soaked to the skin, relieved. I raced to load the bike and get back for Sally who was pushing her bike downhill in the same storm, but with no one to chat to. Jules did ask how we'd be feeling if we had to camp again, but camping in the rain is just another painful lesson to learn.

Our wonderful journey, that unexpectedly took us time traveling, was a varied and really enjoyable weekend ride in very good company. The tick count however, was astronomical. Exactly where they all came from, I do not know, but I have never had so many on me before. Perhaps mid-summer, once the bracken is up, should be considered closed season for bikepacking!

18: Notes from the Triban Trail

I'd wanted to do the Triban Trail for a while. It's a classic round of north-east Wales. I had done some of the sections before, but there were other interesting bits that I liked the look of, and they linked the whole into a fine circular route. I had four days to play with, but the friend with whom I was meeting to ride the trail only had two. We solved this problem by meeting in a pub at the end of my day one, a sound idea if ever there was one.

I added an extra day at the beginning by cycling from home in order to join the trail. Most of day one was spent cycling to Llanfihangel Glyn Myfyr where the pub was. In doing so, I joined the Triban Trail near Llyn Alwen en route. Richard, on the other hand, had spent his day supporting refugees in Stoke on Trent, attending choir practice in Cheshire, then driving across to Llanfihangel GM to meet me for a late dinner!

The route officially starts in Ruthin, but starting from Llanfihangel's finest hostelry, The Crown Inn, meant we could have a couple of beers and an evening meal. Then we'd enjoy the fine campsite in the pub garden and leave Richard's car tucked out of the way on a side road in the village.

Inevitably, the route starts with an uphill plod. We set off slowly with me ticking off the July species list: herb-robert, meadowsweet, shiny-leaved geranium, wood avens, cow parsley, rosebay willowherb and knapweed for starters. Richard was just thrilled to be on another adventure. He's been retired for nearly 30 years and hasn't wasted a day. The section past Mwdwl-eithin was familiar to both of us and once again we enjoyed the fine riding (and pushing) hereabouts. The descent to Ty-nant Major being particularly enjoyable and interesting. We were pleased not to have troubled the gamekeeper on this traverse, as we had once before.

Neither of us had visited Bettws Gwerfil Goch before and we half hoped that there might be a shop, pub or café, but of course there was nothing. No people, no services, not even a moving vehicle. The churchyard provided some comfort with benches and bushes on which tents could be dried. Here, we ate the lunch items we'd carried. Richard is quite famous for always being able to produce a sandwich from his rucksack, or one of the many carrier bags he perpetually recycles. He'll empty his fridge before leaving home and create butties for the entire journey. It's quite remarkable how long they keep (or don't!) Nothing gets wasted.

A lovely bridleway took us south from Bettws Gwerfil Goch through woodland and below Craig Arthbury to Ty'n-y-ddol. It's not clear, as you pass by, what this well-kept place is, but it turns out that it's a Buddhist Retreat Centre. More interested in a bacon butty than a meditative retreat, we carried on and made a small detour to the Rhug Farm Shop. It seemed rude to go so close and not pop in, besides there are surprisingly few cafes and shops along the Triban Trail. The service here hasn't always been great and it's certainly not a bargain bistro, but I do believe that we should contribute to the local economy as we enjoy our bikepacking journeys and this was today's only opportunity. Not only that, the food is excellent.

After lunch it was back to lanes which guided us around the 'big house' of the Rhug estate.

We were climbing again, slowly. I continued my July list: wood vetch, bird's-foot trefoil, wood sage, clover, wild carrot, foxglove, elderflower, lady's bedstraw, yarrow and red campion.

There's a pleasant tree-lined cycleway through Clawedd Poncen, just north of Corwen, which follows a disused railway line but again, this is a village without services. We could have detoured to Corwen, but we knew they even charge you to go to the toilet there and whilst we were keen to contribute to the local economy, spending a penny to have a wee gave us little incentive to visit. We nodded respectfully at the Ifor Williams trailer factory, a company that flies the flag for Wales across the land. They are Britain's largest manufacturer of trailers (up to 3500kg that is) and probably the most mispronounced as well.

The bridleway on the north side of Llantysilio Mountain beckoned us and it did not disappoint. The beginning is a fine grassy track bordered by bracken, but as we headed north-west it opened out to sheep and pony grazing. Here and there, we heard stonechats clacking and ravens cronking. Looking to the north-west we had a fine view of the Clwydian Range, our goal for the next day. By now, we were on familiar terrain: classic, rolling bikepacking country with fine grassy tracks interspersed with dips into dells followed by short sharp pushes, and one annoyingly locked gate (reported).

A funny thing happens in the late afternoon when you start thinking about where to stop for the night and you notice that the place you're in is not so promising for an overnight camp. Here, on Llantysilio Mountain, it felt public, and as we crossed the A542 even more so. But something always turns up. It's little mantra of mine, something always turns up, and I haven't been wrong yet. On this occasion it was actually the campsite in Llandegla and given the agricultural and populated nature of the place through which we were riding, it seemed appropriate to patronise this tidy, friendly farm campsite.

We'd overtaken a few DofE kids and passed the time of day with them wondering if they would be heading to the same place and of course, they were. We enjoyed watching them stumble in. It's remarkable how big those rucksacks are compared to the thin legs that carry them. We were amused by the arrival of one young lady who said hello and hugged each of her friends before even thinking about removing the rucksack that seemed to be the same size as her!

Being in Llandegla village it was only a short ride to take breakfast at the wonderful community café in the village centre. It's a favourite stop of mine and I prefer it to the noisy trail centre café (we're of that age!) which is further out of the village (though they do excellent food there too.)

I'd copied the Triban Trail route north from Llandegla to Maeshafn on my Cylchdaith Cymru route. I like it. The limestone smells of Cheedale in the White Peak, reminding me of climbing days gone by. From Maeshafn though, this route headed north instead of west and pretty soon we were at Loggerheads (the place, not with each other.) I was a little too enthusiastic on one of the downhills here and crunched my rear wheel a little heavily. Fortunately, Richard the fireman, charmer, sandwich master and all-round thoroughbred, is also quite handy when it comes to fixing things. He sorted me out and kept me going. Choose your friends wisely.

With a delicate back wheel and a clock that wouldn't wait, we needed to adjust our plan on the Clwydians. We'd both ridden most of the routes here and we wanted to get to Clocaenog to stay with friends. With the words of Jerome K Jerome in mind *"We did not succeed in carrying out our program in its entirety, for the reason that human performance lags ever behind human intention."* We modified our route accordingly and raced down to Ruthin on a marvellous downhill and some quiet lanes.

On the horizon, sunlit white windmills stood out against a blackened sky. They were spinning frantically in what, sadly, seems like a vain attempt to save the last vestiges of our planet. All we had to do was ride our bikes up to the village of Clocaenog. It's amazing how motor cars flatten out journeys. I had no idea just how uphill it is to the village from town. Not only that, but the best bit was overgrown and required a push. Even the detour to the hillfort of Pen-y-gaer was a bit of a letdown. Fortunately, we have good friends in Clocaenog. Kenny, Jules and Jess welcomed us with open arms, food and beer. Kenny ran Richard back to The Crown for his car, then fixed my back wheel sufficiently to get me home. This was the dream pit stop with warmth, a well-managed chef, enthusiastic barman, entertainer and topflight mechanic. Again, choose your friends wisely.

With Richard's two days over, he drove home in the morning whilst I persevered with the Triban Trail completing it after rounding Llyn Brenig. I then set off on lanes and overgrown bridleways heading home. There may be a little too much lane on the Triban Trail, but they are quiet lanes. The linking of Llyn's Brenig and Alwen with the Clocaenog Forest, Llantysilio Mountain and the Clwydians can only make for an excellent route, and I thoroughly recommend it to you. I never did find out how it got its name though.

Richard in the Clwydians

19: A couple's adventure

The Kerry Ridge and the Shropshire hills

It's not often I get to go backpacking with my wife Sally, but when I do, I love it. She is my best friend and we have a lovely time together. Don't get me wrong, we enjoy our own space, but when we're together we work well as a team, even if it can be a bit Michael Caine at times: *"It's a very difficult job and the only way to get through it is we all work together… And that means you do everything I say!"*

Sally is a teacher, so we are limited to the school holidays for our adventures. We'd been sea kayaking in Scotland earlier that summer, then both had to work. However, we had a few days to spare before she had to go back to school. I suggested the Shropshire Hills and the Kerry Ridgeway, a route from Emma Kingston's excellent 'Bikepacking Wales' book.

We stayed over on the campsite at Panpunton, just outside Knighton, which is not only a good campsite but allows you to leave your car for a few days. The route starts similarly to the Trans Cambrian but sensibly misses out the first climb from Knucklas, something of which I was very appreciative. Still, we were heading off uphill and I was looking out for flowers and mosses, listening for birds and dodging the hazel regrowth that reached out to me from the side of the lane.

The weather had been dry, and along the ridge from Wernygeufron hill the sheep shit was firm, and like cold butter, it wouldn't spread. It stuck to the bike in clods. The last time I'd passed this way was pre-bracken season, so it was slightly sad to see the giant ferns enveloping the trail and keeping the meadows quiet. But there was, against the odds of intensive farming, some wildlife. A red kite took off from a pond as we passed by, and a fox disappeared from a clearing to hide in the bracken. We saw a robin chick and wondered if it was second or third brood.

We let some other bikepackers overtake us on the heather clad moorland by Warren Hill, then we turned right leaving the line of the Trans Cambrian trail and heading for the Cider House and the Kerry Ridgeway. Along this north bound section of the route, we followed tracks on the ground rather than tracks on the map. It happens this way sometimes and the old line of the right of way has drifted across to new tracks, built by farmers of land or wind. In one particular place, we were rather glad of this as the 'official' line went through a field occupied by a bull. Now, there are strict rules about the breeds of bull that can be in fields: some are allowed alone, some have to have cows with them and others should not be seen at all. With limited bull identification knowledge between us and the lure of a well-made track that navigated around the field, we made our circumnavigation with minimal disturbance.

Whilst the Cider House is merely the name of someone's home, the Kerry Ridgeway is a fantastic old route, and it was lovely to be able to ride the length of it on this occasion. It commences at a rundown, but welcome picnic spot. We rested our bodies by laying down precariously on creaking picnic benches surrounded by nettles. We lunched and listened to bird song before ascending to the ridge itself. On this day, the Two Tumps viewpoint lived up to its full promise with distant views across Wales, even as far as Cader Idris in southern Snowdonia. Days like this are not common. The riding was great, a gentle slope on a good track led us on up the hill until we decided to dismount the ridge in search of lodgings. The descent to Ceri, the Welsh spelling of Kerry, was fine, off-road riding and all that is good about mountain biking. We stayed in a beautiful house just outside the village and walked into Ceri for our evening meal. The quiet village-bound lane was lined with blackberries and wild roses which were bedecked with the spectacular Robin's pincushion galls. In the morning, we breakfasted in a grand dining room, sharing a large antique table with other guests.

The re-ascent to the ridge post-breakfast appeared a little daunting, but actually went really well. Evenly graded, it required only the slightest of pushes near the top to regain the ridge. Back on the Ceri Ridgeway we headed east, enjoying the high wire act that is the ridge itself. Sadly, some of this ancient drove way has now been tarmacked and whilst this made for good progress past some bland plantations, it did seem a shame. Still, it didn't last for long. Dirt tracks continued the journey and we were accompanied by flocks of chaffinch as we descended to Churchstoke in time for lunch.

There is a proper old-school transport café in Churchstoke, well it's in that style anyway. It certainly wasn't limited to lorry drivers though, all and sundry were here gorging on fry-ups with chips, accompanied by big mugs of tea. We left recharged but stinking like a chippy.

The biggest climb of the route was tackled post Churchstoke lunch. We took our time, despite the afternoon's route stretching away a little further than we would have liked. To be fair though, we probably went as fast as we could! We were also distracted by views across the Welsh Marches.

At times we were on the Wales-England border and at other times we were criss-crossing it. It was by now a hot day so neither haste nor speed were available to us. Ancient fields were cornered by pretty little houses and punctuated by time-worn monuments of stone; their meanings long forgotten. Habiting the fields were placid ponies and inquisitive sheep, ever on the lookout for picnic crumbs. Over Llan Fawr and past The Rowls the tracks were good, giving plenty of reason to keep on rolling. Wonderful riding, far reaching views and all threaded with stories.

The Stiperstones was threaded with DofE expeditioners, teachers remotely supervising and families walking dogs. We passed them by and hurried across the Long Mynd, eager to make the most of our evening in Church Stretton. A fast descent deposited us, tired but grinning, in the old English market town, nicknamed little Switzerland by well-healed Victorian and Edwardian travellers. We stayed at Victoria House, a lovely town house furnished with antique furniture and original artwork. There was enough space for the bikes out the back and the breakfast was excellent. Bikepacking doesn't have to be all dirt and ditches.

Our third day began with a slow climb back up to the Long Mynd. The National Trust had placed some 'cyclists – please slow down' signs at the base of the hill. We climbed as fast as we could, pushing our bikes all the way, and we still considered our going to be slow. I can't imagine who the signs were aimed at unless an inexperienced member of staff placed them at the wrong end of the hill! Once up on the tops we knew we'd be there for a while and easy riding on good tracks led us back west.

Yet more DofE activity was present on the top of Long Mynd. Youngsters with big rucksacks were being happily greeted by car born supervisors. As we passed the Midland Gliding club, someone was taking off. The cable which pulls the glider into the air is released once the aircraft reaches a certain height. We knew it wouldn't hit us as it came back down to earth, but it really didn't look as though it would be far away. We stopped to watch and double checked our safety zone. Needless to say, the club has been there long enough to have got the distances just right.

At the end of the runway there was a straggly, slightly scruffy thicket. It was alive with a chirping and cheeping of sparrows. They seemed to watch us come close, chirping to each other all the while as if they were daring each other to stay in the open for longer. Then, at the last moment like naughty children, they all dived for cover in the bushes, still chuntering away to each other. Sparrow life is very chatty. Meanwhile harebells nodded, horses trotted by, and a kestrel ignored us from its lofty height.

In Clun, we stopped for a brew and lovely cakes. The tea shop was low-ceilinged, tiny and packed, so we sat outside at a table squeezed on to the narrow pavement. Cars passed closely, a little quicker than we might have preferred. It was my birthday, so we treated ourselves to cake as well as a fine homemade soup. I got told off (a humorous mild rebuke really) by a gentleman on the next table for calling Clun a village, but surely you can't talk to strangers in towns! Lunch passed, and with one more hill to climb the clouds began to paint the landscape a darker shade and we knew we'd had the best of the weather on a delightful tour. With views aplenty, we followed Offa's Dyke along Llanfair Hill then descended briskly to Nether Skyborry where the undulating road, with just one too many roller coaster humps, led us back to our car. As we neared Knighton, we noted a GR post box, completing a set of VR, GR and ER for this trip. This had been a lovely tour, and it had been fantastic to share it with Sally.

Along the Ceri Ridge

20: A tour of the English Lake District

In 1769 Thomas Gray undertook what he called, 'A Tour of the English Lake District'. His letters and journals from the trip are credited with being the first example of modern travel writing. My goodness, how many have followed! From William Wordsworth to Alfred Wainwright (whose initials when joined together make a fine relief cross-section of the district, especially if you add in William's wife Mary's too WWMWAW) there have been many. The district is loved, over-loved and waxed lyrical about across the World. I too am a fan. I have fond childhood memories of holidays here, of early hillwalking experiences and some very formative climbing trips. The Lake District is somewhere in the soul of most English hill goers. Keen to find out more about the magic of the Lakes one young Welsh friend asked me what I knew about walking up Scafell, except he pronounced it as a *Cymraeg* word – '*Scavecchh*'!

There have been some gentle murmurings of discontent about the continued impact of large-scale sheep farming on the landscape in the district. Indeed, I now look at these hills rather differently myself than I might have done earlier in my life. I am aware of a blandness, lack of nature and the sterility of much of our uplands. I wondered how I'd feel revisiting the Lake District, a place I have always argued to be one of the most beautiful parts of the UK. Would my newfound knowledge and understanding of upland land management mar my journey? Would it be dominated by bracken, conifer plantations and course grasses?

It was October when I left Staveley. The climb was gently uphill on a quiet country lane, a robin serenaded me with its territorial song. It sang loud and proud; my route would be largely signposted by this chorus as I passed from robin territory to robin territory on my circular Lakeland tour. A wren let out an alarm call, a crow cackled, and some wood pigeons mumbled agreement. The lane was mostly green, the damp weather enhanced the glistening moss with just an occasional red campion hanging on within the verge. The River Kent flowed belligerently below me. Its mass increased by recent rains, it barrelled through the countryside like a prop forward, stumbling side to side, but too weighty to stop. The lane led me up into the clouds. I wasn't high: the clouds were low. It was good to be cycling up these gentle slopes as the hills which would require pushing would arrive in time, there was no doubt about that. The hawthorn and wild rose looked ready for Christmas with their bright red fruits glinting in the damp air. I was pleased these ancient lanes had escaped a tarmac cladding and remained traffic free.

The route I wanted to do was the Lakeland 300. There is a better-known route called the Lakeland 200, which is a sort of inner circuit of the Lake District with some significant climbs up to, and down from, a range of cols. I'd heard plenty of tales of having to carry your bike not only up the hills, but down them too. It never seemed like a route that really flowed well for the bikepacker. So, it seemed to me that the Lakeland 300, taking a wider circle around the Lake District and spread over a further distance, would be much more amenable to the bike-based traveller. It was a good choice, but it wasn't an easy choice. Though this first section from Staveley to Ambleside was, it has to be said, an absolute delight.

I cycled between dry stone walls topped and dressed with common polypody ferns. Mosses and spleenworts hugged the sides whilst nettles and brambles bossed the verge below. A buzzard perched atop a dead tree in the middle of a field on my right, like a forgotten fairy on a discarded Christmas tree. Close by the tree stood the four walls of a ruined barn; centre stage in an enlarged modern field, its roof slates recycled, and its timbers repurposed. Gates opened and closed easily for me; the way ahead was well-signed and without obstruction, leading me nicely to High Borrans.

I arrived at a field gate, wide open and blocking the track I was riding. I soon saw why as a group of tall, well-weathered sheep trotted down the lane towards me. They were followed by an old farmer, his ancient dog tagging along behind. The vintage sheep seemed to know exactly where to go. I thought they were Swaledales and the farmer confirmed this, adding "old ones though, not long for this world, like me". Asked if they would go for mutton, he said they might, but he worried about what would follow them into these fields. His neighbours were turning to growing trees rather than lambs. "Bloody trees" he said, "there's plenty of them round here and they'll make no difference to that carbon thingy. Not whilst China is pumping it out like there is no tomorrow. Folk don't come here to look at trees, they come to see sheep and open hillsides. We made the 'Lakes' and now they want us to just grow bloody trees."

It didn't feel appropriate to argue. The 2 ft tall clover to my left nodded in agreement.

I crossed Trout Beck to my first push of the day. It's a steep narrow bridleway leading to neatly manicured hedges, recently mown verges and topiary. Troutbeck village felt a world away from the life of the farmer I had just met. These old houses are now only available to those in high income brackets. To be fair, they'd been done up lovely, but no one seemed to be at home and the café was closed. I pushed on up Robin Lane, accompanied by the singing from the eponymous birds, all staking a claim for the best bit of territory.

The bracken-covered slopes of Applethwaite Common across the valley from Troutbeck tell another Lakeland story. The slopes are blanketed in bracken. Bracken spread has previously been controlled by spraying with a chemical called Asulam which was banned in 2011 by the EU because of the risks it poses to human, animal and environmental health. The Health and Safety Executive continue to advise against its use in the UK. Despite this, 'emergency' applications to use the spray have been granted in England, though not in the more considerate nations of Wales, Scotland or Northern Ireland. There are other ways to control bracken. It needs deep well-drained soil to thrive. Its natural home is in woodland clearings and along woodland edges where it spreads by underground rhizomes that enable it to compete with the higher order seed plants. If the soil is deep enough for bracken to grow, then it's deep enough for trees to grow and trees, once established, will shade out the bracken. As long as sheep have access to the bracken-covered slopes though, they will wander through and pick out any tasty seedlings of heather, bilberry, rowan, birch or oak, which could grow and out-compete the bracken. With the development of sheep monoculture on our hills since the industrial revolution, bracken has spread to cover much of the Lake District. One farm in the north-west lakes has taken to harvesting bracken and composting it with sheep fleece then selling it on as peat free compost. It seems to me that if bracken can be harvested and used for compost then it should be. If some slopes are too steep or rocky for harvesting, then they could be fenced off to keep sheep out. With sheep unable to nibble at the tasty seedlings a natural succession to woodland could take place once more. This would not require adjusting the number of sheep as the harvested areas could support the extra sheep kept off the unproductive bracken-covered slopes. Occasionally you can see this happening, usually accidently. Imagine passing through Lakeland and seeing the steep bracken covered slopes reverting to native woodland. What a boon that would be for nature.

I opened and closed 17 gates on my way from Staveley to Ambleside. That is a lot for a lone cyclist. But these were well-behaved gates. They were easy to open and they swung closed behind me.

It was a great downhill ride to Ambleside, through woodland on a rocky trail. There were walkers, but there was plenty of space and the tracks were shared amicably. My first view of Ambleside revealed a magnificent garden centre. Here, in the heart of the Lakes, the biggest, brashest landmark was a palatial, and I mean Crystal Palace palatial, garden centre. Good to know all that traffic queuing along the A591 between Bowness and Ambleside had a worthy destination ahead of them. I passed by.

Ambleside was a different place when Thomas Gray passed through in the late 1700s on his way from Keswick to Kendal. He describes arriving in Ambleside and intending to stay, but as he inspected "the best bedchamber" he found it "dark and damp" so he pressed on, along the road towards Windermere which he describes a "fine Turnpike but some parts not made yet without danger".

The cycle path along towards Rydal Water and Loughrigg Terrace is probably in better condition than the turnpike of Gray's day, but it's also doubtless busier. Surely a contender for the busiest path in the Lakes! It is rather lovely though.

Rydal Water was flat calm. The bow wave from a swimmer seemingly stretched right across the small lake from shore to shore. Small beaches and rustic benches hosted picnicking couples or small families. Dogs were under close control, and everyone said hello politely, as they passed by. A cormorant dried its wings on Little Isle.

A quiet lane with a big downhill took me to Elterwater; a village in which to linger if ever there was one, but it wasn't for me on that day. I needed to press on. Whilst supposedly not in a rush, I felt the need to get a decent mileage covered on this first day of my trip so the oak tree on the green, the tempting hostel and the enticing pub were all soon left behind.

As I headed across the moorland track towards Little Langdale, I made a few minor stream crossings. I was reminded though of a worrying experience from a group trip in this area a few years previously. One of our number slipped when fording a stream and got trapped under his bike. The force of the water pushed him down and cemented the bike on top of him. He couldn't escape alone. It was fortunate that there were a few of us there. A couple of us were able to prize the bike up enough whilst another helped John to his feet. It was an alarming few moments and lessons were learnt. If you're crossing water with your bike always hold it downstream and if out on your own, always be especially cautious around water crossings.

Another 15 gates on from Ambleside and I was in the former slate quarrying area around Hodge Close. It was raining and I was due a lunch stop, but for some reason I still wanted to press on. I rode straight past all the best sheltered spots and ended up crouched behind an old quarry building. The industrial archaeology is largely obscured by trees, so you only get glimpses of holes in the ground, of worked faces and disused tramways. It's somewhere I'm keen to return and explore on foot. As indeed, were two groups of youngsters from Outdoor Centres as I passed through. I loved seeing them in their oversized blue, red or green water-proofs. Welly-clad feet stumbling along quarry tracks with a slightly unruly teacher herding them like an experienced sheep dog. A tall, handsome outdoor instructor (aren't they all) led the group and regaled them with tales of the past, with nature connection and inspirational adventures. As I chatted to one of the instructors (who'd been easily distracted by my bike) three of his charges started damming the small stream flowing down the path. They were in their element, exploring the properties of H2O, whilst their teacher was a little unsure if this was OK, or not. I thought it was brilliant and had to restrain myself from joining in!

The rain dragged on and I sought a better shelter, for I was now in need of a proper break. I found some respite from the afternoon rain in a barn doorway. It was a tidy barn. Firewood was piled high to dry; floors were swept and tools were tidy. The farmhouse below was immaculate and, with its carefully tended flower baskets, looked more like an ex-farmhouse than a working farmhouse. Indeed, the lack of animal manure in the barn supported that theory. I didn't expect to be disturbed. There were three oil tanks in a row. The first was rusted and a wren played underneath it as you'd expect of *troglodytes troglodytes*. A newer one was being pushed out from the wall by an errant ash sapling, whilst the third was just inside the barn door and stood proud with a lock on its nozzle.

Some short narrow steps led up to a lawn where a blackbird was searching for worms, beneath a clothesline which was waiting for a nicer day. I loved the way a sycamore had established itself, almost without anyone noticing, in another of the garden walls. It had sneakily grown into a tree whispering, 'Don't mind me I won't be here long'. Hiding behind it was an ash, one of those keys that got away. It was losing its leaves quickly, barely bothering to change colour, just shredding its clothes at the first sign of autumn. Ferns and mosses competed for space on the rough walls. The garden was a reminder that nature merely tolerates us and will recover when we're gone.

My trail passed peacefully above and out of sight of Tarn Hows and on a lovely forest bridleway from Outgate passed Bletham Tarn where I was again, impressed by the maintenance work carried out on the bridleways hereabouts. By contrast, the ascent to Claife Heights was dull, dense conifer plantation. A timber lorry driver told me that it wouldn't be replanted though, and in time, the birch would be harvested as hard wood. It'll be a better place for that.

I failed to pause at Beatrice Potter's house, and I was sad not to visit the lovely Tower Bank Arms. I needed to keep on keeping on as the day was drawing to a close, darkness arriving earlier and earlier in this latter part of the year. A cruise down to Satterthwaite meant I could try for a camping pod on Bowkerstead farm. This turned out to be a prize move given the rain and wind that night. I was also aware of a growing discomfort in my body. My legs were working fine and my lungs were bringing oxygen in efficiently, but my ears were blocked, my nose was running and there was a developing tickle in my throat. A warm night and a good sleep were most welcome.

I took a little bit of time to try and work out what the rattles in my bike bags were; the gas cylinder in the pan needed wedging in better and the dried porridge, preplaced in my pot, was rattling like the seeds in a maraca.

Satterthwaite has an attractive looking pub and a few houses that looked lived in. The event of the morning however took place in a field just before the village. An old bull was working hard and very physically to repulse the advances of a young bull on one of his herd. It was gentle, but affirmative and very powerful.

Monotonous plantation forestry, enlivened by the sight of a red squirrel, led me to the skyline above Coniston Water where a distinct change occurred.

Firstly, it was brilliant riding. The bridleway above Dodgson wood is superb and the views are tremendous, but this was a place I wanted to visit for another reason. I've been following the story of Dodgson Wood online for a few years now. The owners of the farm are working in a nature friendly way within the Lake District. They aim to produce the finest quality meat ethically and sustainably. They are clearly influential, active and busy people. They get involved with the associations, they contribute to documentaries and they sing from the fell tops about the joys of living with nature, rather than fighting it. The farm produces a range of goods such as soap, wool and food. There are also some very exciting accommodation options, and it was a pleasure to pass through their land. I saw their cattle on the hill, I saw mature juniper trees, wild fungus and spotted saplings in the undergrowth. It's just one of those places that you're pleased exists and makes you feel positive and wholesome.

To the south-east of Coniston Water there's an area of low moorland. It comes under the general and ironic name, Woodland Fell. There are some attractive properties, but this is farming land and sheep are very present. A grey squirrel ran along the top of a wall on the edge of the hillside; a hillside dominated by bracken. I am constantly reminded that despite remaining very attractive to the eye, much of our rural environment is so greatly depreciated. I pushed my bike along an ancient bridleway, in one place motorbikes had crossed and left their tell-tale deep, muddy grooves. It's not a right of way for motorbikes on the map, but of course that doesn't mean it wasn't the landowner of Green Moor out for work or even just for fun. The hillside bracken was being patrolled by a handful of sheep; they wandered through making sure no seedlings could take hold. Our current farm support payments perpetuate this and it needs to change. I entered shooting land as I climbed passed Yew Bank. Up above me I recall seeing a couple of ravens, one meadow pipit rushed away as I arrived, and a wren skittered along a dry-stone wall. Their numbers were, however, overwhelmed by non-native birds. There were pheasants and partridge galore. I really do worry about the environmental impact of importing non-native species, rearing them in their millions and releasing them into the countryside to be shot or fly free.

After a delightful lunch in Torver it was an uphill slog. I was heading for the Walna Scar Road across the Coniston fells. It's lovely country. The way took me through native woodland, on some ancient bridleways, past isolated settlements and even a climbing club's hut, seemingly in the middle of nowhere. A disused quarry gave an indication of what the native vegetation could be, were the grazing regime different. It's a big push; it's a long way. Even when I joined the Walna Scar Road and crossed the Torver Bridge, I was still pushing all the way to the summit of the ridge below Brown Pike. Then, as ever, what goes up must come down. It's a long exhilarating and fast descent all the way down into the Duddon Valley. The final part of the track is a little too stony and rocky to enjoy, but overall, it's a fine bit of riding. Leaving the Duddon valley, I arrived in another area that I was interested to see. This is the Hardknot Forest, and it's changing from plantation forest to native woodland. There's a joint wilding project between Forestry England and Leeds University here. The project has a long way to go but the fresh shoots of recovery are abundant everywhere. As I lay down for a rest in this woodland it was astonishing, compared to the previous sections of the journey, how many birds I could hear. Not only that, but I chanced upon the largest display of shaggy ink caps I think I've ever seen in one place. The rounding of Harter Fell is a good place to be and a strong contrast to the treeless Woodland Fell, the yew-less Yew Bank and the straw brown landscape of Green Moor Farm.

The descent into Eskdale was slower than I expected. On an unladen full suspension bike it would have been challenging fun. On my laden hardtail it was rollable, go with gravity, be patient, end-of-the-day tired and interrupted riding. Happy not to be on a gravel bike though.

The shadows lengthened as I sped down the valley to Eskdale Youth Hostel. For the price of a bed in a dorm, given my head cold and potential for frost overnight, the hostel was very welcome refuge. Chatty too.

In the morning my cold was becoming a pain and worse, my gear changing was dire. I'd already lost my bottom two gears and now the 3rd and 4th had gone too. I needed a plan. The route I was following went close to a settlement called Cleator, and Cleator had a bike shop. That's where I'd head.

But first to Wasdale. The way across to Wasdale from Eskdale via Burnmoor Tarn was tough going in places and ran through a rather denuded landscape. Only the sun lifted the mood of the scenery thereabouts. I could have been in the Cambrian Mountains. I passed one solitary tree and acres of matt grass and soft rush. There were some cattle by the tarn so change could be ahead. A sheep turd harboured some egghead mottlegill fungus. Not an edible species, but fungi in animal poo is indicative of organic grazing, so there is hope for this bleak part of Cumbria.

I really enjoyed the descent to Wasdale. A few walkers stepped aside and said hello, a few bogs stepped in the way and said hello. Coffee and a chat in the National Trust Brackenclose car park was very welcome. The volunteer in charge, having relocated from Sussex, knew he was now a rich man. On this day, Wasdale was bathed in cool late autumn sunshine and it looked magnificent. Great Gable stood proud, I could see the tops of the Scafells, new growth woodland was sprouting, and the paths were in good order.

Wasdale Head is one of those iconic places for outdoor people. I had climbed and walked here many times over many years. Once, as a teenager, my friend and I were flooded out of our campsite and called my Dad hoping for a rescue. Start hitching, he said, and I'll pick you up when you get a bit nearer. There were two of us: Simon Collins was one of my best friends at the time, so we stuck our thumbs out and smiled. Remarkably we made it back to Yorkshire. We had some great long lifts, and many friendly helpful people gave two young lads a leg up. The most memorable lift was in the back of a Land Rover crossing the Pennines on the newly opened M62. It was slow, drafty and bloody freezing! The weirdest thing is, I can remember climbing Needle Ridge and watching someone on a nearby Hard Very Severe climb, but I have little recollection of topping out on Napes Needle. I think we just sort of touched the top and reversed back down off it. Nevertheless, we'd had an adventure.

I couldn't remember when I had last driven down Wasdale, but to follow the road on the bike, was splendid indeed. The sun was warm, the Wastwater Screes were hidden in dark shade and cars were largely absent. Looking back up the valley and across the water I took one of those pictures you might see in a magazine. My head cold forgotten, my lack of gears absorbed, I was enjoying this day.

It's always good to call ahead and talk to bike shops, they can be very busy people. I also thought if I was to visit the bike shop, I'd need somewhere to stay as camping 'wild' in town is rarely an ideal choice. I booked some accommodation in Cleator and phoned the bike shop. They'd be too busy to help me. That was disappointing but worse was to come. Just east of Gosforth my gears went all together. I was reduced to riding a hobby horse. It was lunchtime so I sat and ate and thought. Two dog walkers came by and chatted amiably for slightly longer than was comfortable, but they really did just want to help and be supportive. Then a motorbike passed by, one of those cheeky little trials bikes with no seat. I nodded, as I fiddled forlornly with my broken gears. He nodded and passed me by.

Something must have struck John about my demeanour for pretty soon he turned around and rode back to me. Now, whilst I'm not a great fan of motorcycles on the hill the riders are typically courteous and keen to chat. John was more than that, he was friendly, interested and, as it turned out, a genius mechanic. He worked as a firefighter and mountain-biked on his days off. On this morning, the sun being strong, he'd taken out his battered old trail bike to get some height and ride into the hills. He told me (and I believed him) that he avoided people when on his motor bike. If he saw people he rode the other way, kept his revs low and rode in harmony with the land by following farmers quad bike tracks. To be fair he knew the farmers too, he knew all the landowners, he was of this land. And to return to my original point, he was a genius mechanic.

John stripped down the non-standard gear cabling of my Pinion gearbox. He had the tools with him in his rucksack; how cool. The cables are a twin set that go into the gear box. This is an internal gear box mounted between the pedals. He worked out that the cables were a simple push-pull mechanism and after cutting and stripping and re-routing he was able to give me back my middle three gears. Without John I'd have been freewheeling down to Gosforth and calling out the bike rescue people. He made it possible for me to get to Cockermouth, but that still lay ahead.

I enjoyed the journey to Cleator. It was interesting and varied, a bit of woodland, a river crossing, some open moorland, a small lane and some great bridleway riding. There was a gorgeous section past Nannycatch Gate. I watched from afar, a small school group go one way then another, working things out from a map. Living here they could learn to become hikers in the evenings after study. Or they could have gone and played rugby.

Wath Brow to most people is not a glamourous setting. These villages are old coalmining settlements, and the world of work has moved on. But to me, Wath Brow had real meaning. I have a passing interest in the history of rugby, so I knew this was home to top amateur club, the Wath Brow Hornets. They've been playing amateur rugby league here since 1898! I nodded anonymously, but with respect as I passed the ground. It was good to see a substantial amateur rugby league club set up.

What shocked me most about Cleator was the speed of the traffic. The road through the village is not the main trunk route, but it is an A road. It's a road that surely can only be used by locals. They knew the people whose doors opened onto these pavements. We have become such a car-based society that I don't think we realise what we are doing. If you ever aren't convinced that 20 mph isn't right for residential areas, go and stand on the pavement in Cleator (there's an excellent pie shop here too).

My bike spent the night in the ballroom of a once grand hotel in Cleator. I spent mine in a room with a lock I couldn't operate. The shower was a dribble, but the room was clean, the towels white and the bed comfortable. But my head was stuffed, my ears blocked and my throat was dry and tickly. I slept long and deep that night. My health was suffering and I'd have struggled to camp. I think my bike must have enjoyed that particular stopover more than I was able. I imagined it dancing the night away in an alternative reality as I drifted off to sleep.

To get back onto the Lakeland 300 I'd spotted a traffic-free route. The NCN 71 ran inland from Whitehaven and I could pick it up in Cleator. Given my lack of gears this was ideal. It followed old railways which presumably harked back to the area's industrial and coal mining days. Every dog walker said hello, one so keen to chat even trotted alongside me!

I slowed down to hear his tales of long walks and bike rides, whilst Toby the dog sniffed and scent-marked his way beside us.

"Call in for a coffee," he said, "it's near the pub," but on arrival at the pub there was no phone reception. I had to cycle back up hill to get some! Anyway, coffee was ace, and I enjoyed the chat with new acquaintance and like-minded soul Graham of Loweswater. I only hoped I hadn't passed my head-cold on to him.

I had to carry on. By now I had received an encouraging message from one of the bike shops in Cockermouth. They would be able to help with my gears.

I kept off the main roads as I entered Cockermouth. Doubling back onto a traffic-free cycle way which zig-zagged into the centre of town. By following this route I think I managed to increase the actual distance from the outskirts to the market place by a factor of about three.

I arrived at the 4 Play cycle shop (dreadful name I know) in time to catch the owner. He shouldn't have been there as he was off with Covid; he was in because he really needed to sort some customers' bikes. He looked at my job and promised his mechanic could fix it tomorrow. As he spoke, I listened to his Covid symptoms: ears, throat, nose, fatigue and I slowly matched them to those of my 'head' cold. I began to suspect my head cold might be Covid. Having never had Covid, I was hoping I might be immune, but as it turned out I was not. I tried to keep myself to myself in Cockermouth, but I did need a B&B, and I found a beauty.

I'd arrived in the town at a good time. The main bridge in the town centre was closed to vehicular traffic due to the collapse of a nearby building. It gave me a rose-coloured view of a low traffic town centre, one that would be ruined when the bridge reopened. For now though, I liked Cockermouth. It might feel different when the cars return and I visit again, as it was clear by now that I would need to return. Takeaway pizza enjoyed, I collapsed into bed and slept soundly that night and in the morning, after a lovely breakfast, I made my way back to the cycle shop.

The mechanic in 4 Play bikes inspired me. He knew what I was talking about, he understood the problem and he knew how to fix it. Sadly, given the Covid, my Lakeland 300 journey would have to be interrupted here and I would need to take the bus to Staveley to fetch my car and pick up my bike. I'll return to Cockermouth in time and resume my journey. I suspect my fond traffic-free memory will get shattered when I come back to the town, the place where Ben Stokes played club cricket and William Wordsworth was born. A town near the Lake District.

21: A winter bothy trip

Glentrool Tour

The Knowledge and the Fireman make good winter companions. We like to undertake a winter bothy trip around November time. We get the last of the autumn colours, a few flowers hanging on, quiet tracks and silent bothies all to ourselves. It's a time to travel at a gentle team pace; to chat and to look around. Twice now we've chosen the southern uplands of Scotland. This is a good place to go for bothying as it's the home of the original bothies. This year's trip took us to Glentrool and a circumnavigation of Merrick and the other Galloway hills. Bothies have existed, as we know them today, since long before the creation of the Mountain Bothy Association. It was a comment in the Backhill of Bush bothy book that actually led to the formation of a club to save and to care for bothies. This led to the formation of the association in 1965, and the rescue of Tunskeen bothy was the first project of the newly formed Mountain Bothy Association.

You've met the 'Knowledge' and the 'Fireman' before, here the Fireman (Richard) was in his element.

The Fireman manages the fire. He arrives at the bothy last, he's the first to fetch wood, he carries and drags more than anyone else. He chops and saws, he prepares the wood into neat, size-ordered piles. He doesn't stop. The Fireman lights the fire, feeds the fire and tends the fire. All evening, as long as we have wood, he tends his flames. He puts damp wood to dry and the production line of wood for his blaze seems never-ending. As he exhausts his fuel he sits and watches, sips a whisky and revels in every flame dance. The Fireman likes nothing better than to watch nature's TV.

He is also a charmer. On other trips, we've had to make a sneaky camp and then listen out for the dreaded gamekeeper-bearing quadbike. If it does arrive (and it has done more than once) the Fireman feels sharp elbows in his back; the stage is set, and the Fireman turns on the charm. The thing is, the Fireman loves people, so the sight of a human to chat to is always welcome. He steps forward gladly and disarms the stranger, turning him around to our point of view. The gamekeeper leaves, we promise to scare the foxes away and we'll be gone in the morning before his guns arrive.

The Fireman does, however, have a weakness. I remember cycling with him and the Knowledge on another occasion. We passed a few walkers and the odd cyclist on our way. The Knowledge and I led the way, then stopped. We knew we had to wait for the Fireman. Not content with brief hellos to our passers-by he would have been, we knew it, drawn to a halt by the female team of three. We both knew he'd need a conversation a little deeper than the mere passing of the time of day. We waited with good grace for the appearance of the smiling, now purring Fireman.

As I write, Richard, our Fireman is 79. He leads on the hills, slowly but surely. He's the last one of us to dismount and push. A life of adventure in the mountains, in summer and winter, has given the Fireman resilience. He doesn't always make life easy for himself: he often carries too much, carries it awkwardly then forgets where things are. But he's strong. His replaced hips seem to be performance-enhancing and he's never without a positive, appreciative attitude.

We left the White Laggan bothy in good time that morning. It had been a splendid evening after our drive from Wales and Cheshire. We'd feasted on the goodies we'd brought, drank a little whisky and sat around the fire chewing the cud. Daybreak was grey, but there was no rain, having exhausted itself through the night. We'd headed to this Galloway Forest Park knowing the conifer plantations, boring as they might be, would shelter us from the worst of the weather. On this day, the wind was light and the forest tracks gave welcome firm ground to cycle upon after the nighttime downpours. We cycled past remnants of red campion, occasional hawkweed and bright pink herb robert. In-between the weary flowers, hanging on grimly at the end of a long season, bright green mosses flourished, punctuated by the odd grandstand of cladonia lichens. Along the woodside fringe we passed shaggy moss (both big and little), haircap moss and glistening wood moss. The mosses were laid as a carpet around the willow and birch saplings waiting for their chance to supersede the pines from Scandinavia and North America.

In some ways it's quite a dull ride north from White Laggan and I sought comfort in the patches of native plants, the odd raven, buzzard or wren. I saw one kestrel too. We were watched over that day, by Craiglee, Craignaw and Dungeon Hill to our west and hemmed in by the Rhinns of Kells on our east. The latter presented a most unattractive backside when seen from this angle! The forest tracks took us easily, with few hills, to the Backhills of Bush bothy. This former MBA bothy was looking a little unloved. The MBA pulled out of its care around 2010 due to continuing anti-social behaviour at the site. This was once one of the most remote homesteads in Scotland and was inhabited by a shepherd and his family, right up to 1949.

Unfortunately, the development of the forest and its associated roads have made the bothy accessible by private vehicles and with accessibility comes poor behaviour. A very disappointing and sad fact. Scotland Land and Forestry still maintain the building as a bothy and it was perfectly habitable on this occasion, but it was adorned with a box of mugs, unused wine glasses and several bin bags of rubbish. It looked like some sort of party event had taken place, and the perpetrators had come well-equipped, but neglected to remove their waste. A sadly common occurrence which will be unfathomable to anyone who's reading this book, I'm sure.

I'm sitting down for lunch. I've found a flat spot with a bit of a backrest and I've got my mat out, my water is to hand and my treats are within reach. Graham points out that there is a mouse behind me. I turn to my left and I can just see the mouse over my shoulder. I turn to my right, and I can watch the mouse creeping and crawling under my bike. It veers off right at the last moment and then cuts back left to lick my sandwich box. I only make the slightest of movements to move it away from the sandwich box and it starts to eat the spore capsules of the haircap moss. I can see its tiny little bony fingers, quite long, grasping each seta as it nibbles the haircap tops.

It was a tiny little thing, miles from anywhere, a wood mouse, also known as a field mouse, they are the same thing. I couldn't help but wonder how it managed to sustain itself. Just to keep warm and eat enough food to keep its racing metabolism functioning looked like an enormous challenge. I didn't know mice ate the spore capsules of moss, but they do. I enjoyed watching the mouse eat lunch while I chewed on mine. I had a little fancy in my head that the mouse felt safe and secure, knowing I offered it no threat and as long as it sat next to me it wouldn't become lunch itself for a bird of prey or a passing fox. Both of which we'd seen that morning.

There was one gap in the forest track, but it gave a good downhill for mountain bikers to a splendid sheepfold. We needed to remove boots and socks to cross the Kirreoch Burn, from where we followed a forest ride. The ride was wet, boggy and full of machine-made waterfilled ditches. The plod was at times balancing on tufts, at other times tiptoeing across boggy bits and occasionally we had to make wee jumps using our bikes in the manner of a hurdle. However, we made it without any major soakings.

Flowing into Loch Doon was the unusually named river: Gala Lane. The term Lane is a local one and applies to a tributary, though another source suggests it's a meandering, even loitering waterway. The Gala Lane that entered Loch Doon was however, on that day, a rather lively beast. We stood awhile on the bridge to comprehend its tumescent antics as it bullied its way north. We had had overnight rain, so the river was rampant as it tumbled down a series of falls and into a ravine below the bridge. Rainbows slipped through the mists created by the water spray and the sound of the hammering water shook our inner selves.

Beyond the bridge we passed a house called Starr. Here, we saw our first other humans of the day: two smiling, chatting dog walkers, striding with purpose as their hounds wagged and sniffed along the track. Juxtaposed with their energy was a portly gentleman sat in his car in the loch side car park. He ate a large lunch whilst remaining in his driver's seat. Feeling fit and virtuous we cycled away from Loch Doon, first west to Loch Riecawr and then south to the Tunskeen bothy. Forest harvesting meant we nearly missed the track to Tunskeen: on the map it's alongside a forest which now doesn't exist. I posed on the Rocking Stone (which didn't rock) for photographs. We rode past the ruin of Slaethornrig and some good cross-country mountain biking led us to the gorgeous little bothy. Tunskeen is a small bothy in a wild and remote setting below Tarfessock, Nick of Carlach and the Maiden's' Bed. If nothing else, the Galloway hills are a great place for interesting hill names.

The bothy is well-sheltered, has clean (though peaty) running water in streams close by and a supply of firewood from the nearby remains of forest. It was in very good order, as near spotless as a bothy can ever be. Despite being small, there was plenty room for the three of us, and our bikes. The Fireman was soon at his work again and the results were excellent. More fine food, a wee dram and some good natter led to a lovely twelve-hour rest. Bothy life.

The morning dawned bright blue, stunning. We headed back along the rough track to a major forest road. Once again, we were surrounded by the blue tinted sitka spruce and the north American Douglas firs. Occasionally a lichen-coated goat willow decorated the trackside, whilst the effervescent birch saplings made their presence known too. The odd rowan, hazel and alder brightened the mood, especially on the single-track sections we found east of Stinchar Bridge. We chose a sunny spot hereabouts and snuggled into heather sofas to enjoy our morning snack. There was quite a cool wind blowing now and we knew we had a road section to cross the bealach into Glentrool. As we lunched, several laden timber lorries raced past, assuming they had the roads to themselves. They made me nervous. But when the time came, the road over the top was quiet and the few vehicles we did encounter gave us a respectful distance and allowed us the right of way.

Alchemilla mollis, not to be confused with *Alchemilla vulgaris* (obviously!), and Oxford ragwort made the roadside meadow buttercups and pinkish yarrow look a little out of place in this wild landscape when really, they should have held the upper hand. The moor beyond was brown, dead grasses and downbeat heather gave a matt sheen to the landscape made worse by the scattering of siskin sown conifer saplings. We summited and descended at speed to the Bell Monument. In remembrance of David Bell, 'The Highwayman', "who knew these hills so well, 1907 to 1965". So, not that sort of highwayman then! In fact, David Bell was a cyclist and did much to promote the joy of cycling in Galloway. He must have been one of the earliest mountain bikers as he recorded taking his bike up Merrick. Bell was also a trained botanist, he often enhanced his cycling diaries, which were published in the Ayrshire Post, with observations from the natural world. Clearly a man after (or before) my own heart. There used to be an annual David Bell Memorial cycle race organised by the Ayr Roads Cycling Club, but I couldn't find any recent details of whether the event continues or not.

After one harrowing near miss at speed by an ignorant car driver, we gladly re-entered the haven of the forest. We passed through a very dangerous quarry, or so the signs would have us believe; it looked rather benign to us. Fortunately, the quarry didn't leap out and get us and we found another sunny, comfortable spot for our lunch.

Forest roads led quietly down towards Glentrool village. We passed two dunnocks whistling to each other as they foraged amongst the Somme-like destruction of a felled conifer plantation. In another patch of forest, a group of long-tailed tits kept in touch with each other by rapid little chirps as they darted from treetop to treetop. Glentrool village was closed. The seasonal visitor centre was firmly locked and bolted. There was nothing there to detain us. We did enjoy the beech trees lining our approach though, indicating as they did, that the character of our journey was about to change. It was a pleasure to follow the autumnally embraced minor road, with zero traffic, which took us down to Newton Stewart.

Newton Stewart was a sad place. It had a fast road through the middle, so was unwelcoming to cyclists and the handful of pedestrians present. It felt like a car-wrecked settlement. The odd take-away, run down hotels and a sprinkling of small shops cowered along the roadside. I wondered how this town would thrive in days to come. It had made good money when the wind turbine builders were in town, but seemed to be struggling to find its contemporary identity, industrial, agricultural, arboreal or touristic? However, the cheap hotel we settled in was very welcoming and accommodating of our bikes (not for the first time they were housed in a spare bar area of a hotel). We ate overpriced bar food in the pub next door, but again the welcome was sound. Clearly Newton Stewart is a town of friendly people, it just seems to be a place that's lost its sense of purpose and it's not alone in that. We showered and slept long. Breakfast was excellent.

The way back to our car was uphill. The Fireman led the way, the Knowledge and I crept along, chuntering, behind him. To be fair, it wasn't quite as uphill as the profile on our phones had indicated it might be. Given that the angles were much gentler in real life, we quite enjoyed ourselves. It was a remarkably beautiful day; the sun was climbing slowly into a very blue sky giving sharp and clear shadows that highlighted the shape of the land beautifully. We had glimpses of deer and watched a pine marten try to get into someone's house. I supposed they must feed it, nevertheless, that was a lovely broad daylight sighting. The views stretched away down to the Solway Firth and across to the English Lake District and because the pedalling was on good forest tracks, we made pleasing progress towards our journey's end.

Alongside the Black Loch (I couldn't help saying Llyn Du inside my head and wondered if it should be Loch Dubh really) was the most marvellous pencil-thin tall sculpture carefully built with small sandstone blocks. We did not resist a photo stop, but we struggled to get the best angle. I took delight in noticing the moss growing on the shady north side and the map lichen growing on the sunny southside. I gripped the edges of the blocks, and they reminded me of days (now long gone) when I revelled in the matchstick edge climbing of north Wales slate.

The landscape here compared favourably to that further north. Rolling hills set off south, covered in both native and planted woodland. To the north, hills called Milfore and Curleywee were featured and promised hidden secrets, with walks of interest. We passed them by, slowly ascending our hill.

Finally, we topped out 360 metres above sea level with a promising run down to the car 160 metres below us. We unintentionally startled three woodland cattle grazing on the track side verge. We stopped and pondered. We thought we might be able to slip by them to one side, but as we approached, they ran. Clearly, we did not want to continue careering downhill at pace with three cows leading the charge, so we sat down for a brew whilst the bovines found a place in which they were comfortable, and we could pass them by. Our descent was interrupted again, this time a large tree blocked the track and forced a ditch crossing diversion. Grinding his way up the hill was a gravel biker. He ignored us and passed us by with no flicker of acknowledgement. Strange. We sped down to the car.

A most satisfactory expedition was completed. Much of the route was boring, but we liked it anyway. The bothies were lovely, the weather had been grand, and the tracks were good. But for me, it was time well spent with two good friends: the Firemen and the Knowledge.

Bothy life

22: **The best bike for bikepacking is the one you already own**

This is a phrase you will come across in your early considerations about bikepacking. It should be a phrase that piques your interest and enables you to go to the next step of planning your own trip. It is a true phrase.

I started bikepacking on a full-suspension mountain bike. I'd been doing some half-hearted mountain biking in the winters. Mostly I rode just to get outdoors when I couldn't go rock climbing (my former first love). I'd meet up with friends and we'd do a mix of trail centres and natural trails. I found that whilst I really enjoyed a flowing, well-built, trail centre circuit, I actually preferred the exploratory feeling I got when on natural trails. To be a bikepacker you'll need to love natural trials. I should add that I'm not a very good bike rider: I worry on the fast downhills and struggle with the long up hills. I lack the skill to ride rock gardens and an inch of air feels like I'm flying. For me, the ride was about getting out on horrible days, meeting friends and getting some exercise. The fun was never in the actual bike riding. I'm fortunate to live near the Gwydyr Forest Trails here in north Wales and whilst I can't remember the last time I rode the trails in one, I do enjoy a home run down the fast, finishing sections of these trails; Pen y Parc, Reid ar Ras and Reid Rydd. It's like a seductive reward that I've earned by working hard on a journey. In fact, learning that you can use bits of trails and link them to forest tracks and bridleways to go where you want is a step towards a true freedom of the 'road'. Bikepacking is journeying. Travelling through the land, across horizons, vales and passes. A bike will take you far, quietly and efficiently.

So, if you have a bike, even if it's a full suspension mountain bike, get yourself a saddle pack and away you go. The saddle pack has become synonymous with bikepacking. Graham reckons a small one is fine, but my experience was one of an unpleasantly swaying pack. I really didn't like it. To be fair, whatever you do, however you pack, there always seems to be a rattling coming from somewhere in your luggage. But adding in the sway of a saddle pack is not my preferred option. I soon switched to a hardtail mountain bike. If you aren't too bothered about the rough stuff and you want to travel longer distances and quickly over gravel tracks and small lanes, then a gravel bike will be worth considering. Myself? I reserve the right to drop on to any available single track and to seek out smile inducing descents.

The advantage of switching to a hardtail meant that I could use a rack on the rear of my bike and still keep full dropper post functionality, making the riding of single tracks and stony downhills all the more pleasant. You can ride these trails on a drop-handled barred gravel bike, but it's so much nicer with some front suspension and wider grip handlebars.

My first hardtail had 650B wheels and tyres, that is 27.5" x 3.00". Quite why 27.5" is referred to as the metric 650B and the 29" wheels retain their imperial measurement I have no idea! Welcome to a world of secret codes and hidden meanings. Don't let them put you off! I love that bike, and I still have it; I call it my fun bike: it rides well, and cost less than £1000. If I were a bit better on the maintenance and mechanics side, I probably would have stuck with it. But I'm not. I am utterly useless at mechanics, maintenance and even cleaning the bike. I've gone for a Sonder Broken Road. It has a titanium frame, 29" wheels and a pinion gear box.

The Pinion gear box is heavy, but the weight is low down on the lightweight titanium frame so, as a combo, it works. Remember any bike with a load on will be heavy to lift regardless of whether or not it started out as a lightweight option. It's something to think about as you surely will have to lift your bike over some sort of obstacle at some point on your bikepacking journeys. The gear box is internal which removes the need for those hangy down bits at the back (a 'rear mech derailleur hanger' in biking code!) It removes the need for a chain and loads of finger shredding cogs (the code word is 'cassette'). I have a carbon fibre drive belt linking the pedal action (crack arms and bottom brackets) with the rear wheel. No gears to adjust, no chain to break or go rusty and there is less tweaking required of the gear cables. The gearbox has an oil change once a year (I take it to the shop, obviously). The cables will need changing too and mine actually work so much better after being changed than they did when they were new. The gear change is by rotating the handlebar grip and is so light that it's really easy to do.

I have 29" x 2.4" Maxxis Recon Tubeless tyres. The last pair wore out without me ever getting a puncture. In fact, there were 12 punctures that I knew nothing about, so good is the tubeless system. That bit is a no brainer.

I have front suspension, a dropper post and hydraulic brakes. I've changed the handlebars for On-one Geoff handlebars. These are more swept back than flat bars, but give more control on descents than drop handlebars. I find them a good compromise, plus you've got more mounting options. I use a leather Brooks saddle, which I've loved from the first moment I sat on it. The smooth leather just feels right to me, but I know it's not everyone's cup of tea.

My rear rack is from Tailfin. This is not a cheap option but it's worth it. When coupled with their own AeroPack it's about as perfect a system as you can get. There is no sway, the bag is easy to put on and take off, you have mounts on the uprights for extra water bottles, mini panniers, or your pump. It's light, it works, and you can still use your dropper post.

I have two water bottle holders in the frame, again trying to keep the centre of gravity low. I use a less-than-half frame bag under the crossbar and a small top tube bag on top of it. On longer journeys I add an extra top tube bag just in front of the seat post. I take two stem bags, and I strap a dry bag on the handlebars. I keep looking for a better front-end system, but the simple strapping on of a dry bag works. Do make sure your cables are loose and won't be compromised though. The one I use is an elongated one from Ortleib which is 13 litres (though it takes as much kit as my 20l AeroPack pack!). I strap this on to the handlebar with Voile straps.

That gives me plenty of baggage. The bag on my handlebars takes the tent, blow up sleeping mat, sleeping bag, sleeping bag liner and stove and pan. One stem bag is used for a water bottle and the other for snacks (fortunately the bags are Eccles cake shape). The top tube bag takes my glasses collection. The rear top tube bag harbours a bike lock, multi tool, spare brake pads (only on long journeys), my head torch, some cable ties and a few first aid bits. These items will fit in the frame bag on most journeys. The extra top tube bag is only needed when I'm out for at least a couple of weeks.

Tent: I use a Terra Nova Laser Competition tent. It packs down small, weighs less than 1 kg and works all year round in the UK. I do on some occasions have to pitch my tent when it's raining. This is so much easier if I can erect it outer first, or at least inner and outer together. I then need to be able to get in the tent and keep the inside of it dry. For this I like a big porch. I can ditch the wet gear in the porch as I crawl into the tent. I have gear in waterproof bags so that they can stay in the porch once I'm in the tent and dry. I then remove from the waterproof bags the stuff I need inside the tent, like my sleeping bag and sleeping mat. I've learnt that in the tent everything has its place. It's not necessarily about being tidy but it's a matter of knowing where everything is and where everything goes. There can be days when I need to pitch my tent in the rain, strike it in the rain, ride all day, pitch in the rain again, strike in the rain again and repeat. This is one of the specialities of bikepacking in the UK; you have been warned! To be fair it's rarely that bad and you can often find some shelter and most bikepackers (me included), will not be averse to using a bothy, a barn, hostel or even a B&B. In fact, carrying the internet on your handlebars in the form of a mobile phone means some sort of accommodation can usually be found even if it's off route a bit.

Sleeping bag: I use a Montane two-season down sleeping bag that I bought in the 2001 Foot and Mouth Disease lockdown, making it over twenty years old. I really like it. It works for me for all of the spring and autumn. In the deep winter, I might take a three-season bag and in the height of summer I might take a lightweight quilt instead. I always take a silk sleeping bag liner which is easier to wash than a down sleeping bag. It weighs next to nothing and packs small, but it can give me an extra layer when it's cold or a sheet to hide in if I want to use my bag like a quilt. Flexibility is nice to have.

Sleeping mat: I'm currently using the Cloudbase blow up mat from Alpkit. I've used it lots, fixed one puncture, and been very pleased with it. Some of these mats are too narrow and some have tubes that seem to repel your body. The air 'lumps' in this one help me to stay on it. I do have further insulation underneath my tent. I use 4mm closed cell foam padding underneath the ground sheet. This is like an insulating tent footprint. It's dead light and easy to carry in my rucksack. I can also pull it out to lay down on at lunch time. I've cut into two pieces, each one nearly a metre square, folded and kept folded by a Velcro strap. It's not something you see in the shops, and I had to purchase it online.

Pillow: I simply use a dry bag. I always have one as I keep most things in them. My sleeping bag especially, but also spare clothes. I just stuff whatever clothes I'm not wearing into the bag then wrap it in a T shirt.

Stove: I use a tiny gas stove. Mine is the Kraku from Alpkit. This is coupled with a titanium pan and is only used for boiling water which I add to homemade couscous or freeze-dried rice meals. I make these up myself as it's cheaper than buying them. I put together an Italian mix, an Indian mix and a Moroccan mix. Several meals are carried in small freezer bags so that I can eat whenever and wherever I need to. I actually prefer real food though and if I can pick up some rolls, an onion, one or two butcher's burgers or some halloumi, I choose that. I carry chilli sauce too. I've started carrying a small titanium frying pan (an Alpkit Mytipan) in which I can do the frying, make an omelette or even just heat up a tinned meal. Eggs are easy enough to carry in an egg box (I put them in my rucksack so they don't get squashed).

I do enjoy my camp breakfast. I take porridge. I buy the cheaper oats and then rehydrate with boiling water in a bowl with a screw top lid. There's no need to cook these oats, they are lovely after only about five minutes. I add dried fruit, freeze dried raspberries, strawberries and blueberries and lovely brown sugar. My biggish bag of porridge goes in the AeroPack bag on the rear rack, whilst the smaller bags of savoury food, along with my butter box and plastic jar of jam, go in the under-bar frame bag.

Also, in the AeroPack bag on the rear rack is a change of clothes for evenings in pubs and hostels, a change of biking under-clothes, towel, soap, toothbrush and paste, mug, power pack and charging leads, breakfast bowl and dinner bowl.

Rucksack – In my rucksack I carry a pair of Croc flip flops. These are really handy for evenings indoors, nipping out of my tent to go to the loo and for wearing whilst wading through rivers. They are tough, I can walk or cycle in them and they dry instantly. Also in the rucksack are my closed cell foam pads (the ones that go under my groundsheet), a warm coat for stops and my Personal Locator Beacon should I need to call for help in an emergency and I'm out of phone signal. I also tend to chuck a roll of duct tape in here too.

Dry bags – Most waterproof bags will let you down at some point. It might even be your own fault for letting water in when you opened the bag, it might be that you didn't close the zip fully or that some stitching is leaking. If a bag is waterproof, it means it keeps the water in and anything in the bag will be sat in a puddle. Managing your kit in constant rain is a pain. I like to pop important things into their own waterproof bag. This can make things a bit bulky sometimes, but keeping the sleeping bag and electronics dry is really important. I take an extra one for slipping over my saddle too.

What to wear?

I come from a climbing and mountaineering background. So, if I'm in the hills I tend to walk or climb in climbing and mountaineering gear. I already own such gear. This is gear that has been designed over many years to make spending time in the hills more comfortable. Much mountain biking gear copies mountaineering gear, certainly in the use of high-quality modern fabrics.

Others come from a cycling background and are comfortable wearing lycra. There probably aren't many bikepackers who choose to wear (like I do) walking trousers, walking boots or shoes, base layer and a fleece with a soft-shell jacket. To be fair, the fleece doesn't stay on long as it's usually too warm, but the base layer and the soft-shell work very well. The soft shell doesn't really need to be bike specific. I roll up and tuck in the hood of my soft shell to prevent it acting as windsock.

It's important that clothing is as breathable as possible, as most of us tend to work up some heat on ascent. It does, however, need to be windproof too as on descent the wind can pierce your layers in chilling fashion. None of this clothing needs to be bike specific and in the same vein that the bike you've already got is the best bike for bikepacking then the outdoor clothes you've already got are also the best clothes for bikepacking too. In fact, I like to use kit across disciplines as it's an easy way to lower your environmental and carbon footprint. Sustainability starts by using less kit for longer. I was slightly aghast to notice recently that I had different water bottles for sea kayaking, walking and biking. Use fewer, use it for longer and use it for more things. All that said, there is of course, some excellent gear purposely made for cycling as well.

I do wear cycling undies. The padding is welcome even when using an expensive leather saddle. Quick drying shorts will suffice in the summer but in the winter, I wear lightweight soft-shell trousers that I inherited from working at a large outdoor centre. A wicking base layer is requisite for all outdoor activities in my opinion.

If I'm out for more than three days I'll take spare socks, spare cycling undies, and spare base layer.

Hands

I always wear gloves and it's as much about gripping the handlebars with sweaty hands as it is for keeping my hands warm. My preferred gloves are fingerless, leather and non-padded. I just find that with reasonable handlebar grips I don't need the padding. Padding seems to come as standard though and I find it hard to find gloves that don't have it. I wonder if this is because a lot of cycling design comes from road cycling where you're in a similar position for longer periods of time. When mountain biking, I'm rarely in the same fixed position for any great length of time. Besides, I quite like to sit up and look around me!

The fingerless gloves I use do keep my hands warm enough on descents and being thin, they dry quickly if it rains. Sadly, because they are thin, they do wear out rather more quickly that I would like. If it's cold, a cheap pair of ski gloves are hard to beat for bikepacking. The drawback comes when it's raining, and they end up saturated. I use waterproof work gloves when rain comes down, particularly in the colder months, but these are hard to dry out when on longer expeditions so ordinary cycling gloves, maybe with smart screen fingers, are as good as anything.

Footwear

I don't like to be clipped into my pedals. I'm not looking for the extra pull that SPDs might give me. Cycling shoes are not the best choice for me. There are specialist cycling shoes that aren't clip in and with over-shoes these are very good. Over-shoes, however, will soon wear out if you spend much time walking up hills (and you probably will!) Walking boots or walking shoes, which for me are multi-purpose, do the job perfectly well and I already own them. When bikepacking I do spend quite a bit of time walking alongside my bike so footwear that I can walk in is very important. I actually like a bit of space in my shoes too. The ability to wiggle my toes is essential for keeping feet warm. Most of the time I use walking shoes they do get wet, but they dry relatively quickly too. In the winter months, I'll switch to walking boots, the drawback being they take longer to dry, but they keep your feet drier for longer as well as keeping them warm. I do make sure I'm wearing good socks or even waterproof socks such as those from Sealskin. I did see someone doing the Highland 550 race in sandals and I don't think this is a bad idea at all. The battle between keeping feet warm and dry and having to dry out your shoes and socks is one of the biggest challenges on long British bikepacking trips. I might even try wellies next!

Headwear

I wear three hats. A helmet, for the road bits and the down hills. It's hard to imagine not wearing a helmet, it just seems such a sensible thing to do and given they are so light there really is no excuse for not wearing one. I think it's normal to wear a helmet when cycling now. That said, I also always have a woolly hat with me. My head sweats in a helmet so when stopping it's good to have a different hat to put on. I cool down quickly if stopping for lunch or adjustments so having a warm hat to hand makes a lot of sense. Well, most of the time it does, but I have also started carrying a sun hat. On those long uphill bits on sunny days, I can burn and suffer in the heat. A lightweight sun hat which covers my neck and ears and fits neatly into my crossbar bag has been a godsend. I hang my helmet on my phone mount and switch to the sun hat when I'm going uphill or bumbling along slowly.

The woolly hat is also useful in camp in the evening, or in the mornings. Sometimes I set off still wearing it under my helmet, so one with a pom-pom is not ideal.

Eye protection

I carry four pairs of glasses. One pair are my plain safety glasses, which I wear most of the time. They are quite special though as they have reading inserts in the bottom corners of the lenses. This means that they can act as spare reading glasses too. I also carry poor visibility glasses and sunglasses with reading inserts. But I also like to have proper reading glasses as well! I like reading.

Waterproofs

Many cyclists don't like carrying waterproofs, but the harsh reality of bikepacking in the UK means that I'm rarely without one. Through the summer months, I always take a waterproof jacket to put on when it rains. In the winter months, I'll add waterproof overtrousers, but in the summer if my legs get wet, then they'll dry out soon enough. In the winter it can be cold and covering up the legs is, for me, a sound plan. Whilst I doubt anyone chooses to cycle in the rain there is a strange satisfaction to making progress as the precipitation chases you along. I don't mind a bit of rain, but I do need a plan for drying out. Three days and two nights of rain will usually send me looking for a B&B or a hostel to dry out and take stock.

The 'big' jacket

I always have a big jacket. Some sort of synthetic down jacket. If it's synthetic it doesn't matter if it gets wet, it still works when wet and you can throw it in the washing machine if necessary. Down doesn't work for UK bikepacking. The size of my jacket will vary with the season, but I always have it handy when I stop. My rucksack is the best place for this, not hidden away in tightly packed bags. Slipping off some outer layers and slipping on a warm jacket feels great.

Dressing for dinner

I take a change of clothes for the evening. We're not talking black tie here, but something that makes me mildly more presentable in public. I carry some lightweight trousers that roll up small, a T shirt and some cotton undies. I might put these on in the tent (just to get out of sweaty cycling gear, particularly if it's cold) or I might just get in my sleeping bag. But if you decide to hostel/hotel/ B&B or just stay in a bothy having a change of clothes makes life a little more comfortable.

What else do I carry? – bits and bobs

Of course, you need a few 'bits and bobs' otherwise packing would be so boring! Bits and bobs are crucial to the whole faff process of getting ready for departure. In the bits and bobs category are ear plugs. So many times ear plugs have saved me, be it heavy rain on the tent, flapping bits of the tent or a snoring companion in a bothy. I keep them in my power pack and recharging bag as I tend to need them at similar times. My neck gaiter usually starts off in this bag, its main use being as a blindfold on light evenings and as a barrier to early morning sun. It can stray though. In hot weather it becomes very useful as a piece of cloth that can be dunked in passing streams and puddles then used to cool down my neck. On short trips I might take a hip flask, filled with one of my favourite tipples. Unfortunately, on longer trips refilling a hip flask is tricky, so if I took it, I'd end up carrying an empty hip flask after the first night or two.

I take a towel. A lightweight pack towel. You can get quite big ones nowadays and they are great after a swim or wash. Soft items like this and spare clothing, are great for anti-rattle when packing harder items in the bags that you strap onto your bike.

I have a head torch and bike lights. I always take a powerpack or two and charging cables. I carry a couple of plasters, a wound dressing, some aspirin and some pain killers. (It's worth doing an Outdoor First Aid course rather than your normal workplace one.) I don't really carry any bike spares: I've worked hard (and spent a fortune) to eliminate the need for them. Maybe some brake pads would be advisable for longer trips but topping up and checking tyre sealant beforehand is important. If anything does go wrong, I don't have the skill to fix it anyway! (I have tried learning, but I lack any sort of mechanical aptitude whatsoever.) Other people might tailor these to their bike and their mechanical abilities. However, I do have bicycle breakdown recovery just like you might with a car (from ETA Services). In the summer it's important to take some sun cream and insect repellent. If I'm cycling in Scotland between the end of May and the end of September, I always take a midge net as well. These days you can do all your shopping and payment on your phone, but it's worth secreting a bit of cash and a cash card somewhere in one of your bags. I have my wife's phone number written down too, just in case I were to lose my phone.

Most people will be using a GPS device on the handlebars to navigate. I use a Wahoo and it's pretty easy to get along with. I also have the relevant Ordnance Survey maps on my phone to check frequently and get the overview of where I am, where I'm going and what there is to see.

Snacks and water

Instead of energy bars I might carry hot cross buns, butter and jam; much nicer. Of course, one of the 'golden' rules of bikepacking is never to cycle past a bakery, café or pub! Finally, you'll need water. I carry a couple of one litre bottles and a half litre bottle and fill them as I go either from mountain streams, cafes, public taps or by just asking people in their gardens. I like to fill up before going into camp so that I have enough water for dinner and breakfast. I've never felt the need for a water filter using this system.

My Bikepacking Kit list

No list is cast in stone. I'm constantly changing both my mind and my kit. The speedy might forgo many of my luxury items, there are others who'll carry more. I'm journeying, not racing.

Wearing

- Soft shell walking trousers or quick drying shorts in the summer
- Socks, cycling undies and base layer
- Thin fleece
- Waterproof/s
- Soft shell jacket
- Gloves
- Warm jackets
- Cycling shoes/ boots
- Helmet

Handlebar bag

- Tent
- Sleeping bag
- Sleeping bag inner
- Sleeping mat

- Stove, pan, fuel, spoon, lighter, tea
- Bendy plastic chopping board

Rear rack bag
- Spare fuel
- Mug
- Spare socks, undies and base layer
- Lightweight evening trousers, cotton undies and T shirt
- Thin fleece if not being worn
- Phone and power pack, ear plugs and neck gaiter
- Pack towel
- Wash kit, and sponge
- Bag of porridge
- Dishes
- Wooden spoon and eating spoon

Below bar bag frame bag (and sometimes in an extra rear top tube bag)
- Snacks
- Camp meals
- Head torch
- Cash, card, bus pass and written important phone numbers
- Plasters, wound dressing, aspirin and painkillers
- Bike lock
- Food prep knife
- Butter and jam
- Spare gloves and woolly hat
- Sunscreen, insect repellent, midge net
- Camera phone tripod

Little top tube bag
- Glasses collection
- Sun hat

Rucksack
- 4mm closed cell foam pads
- Flip flops
- Warm jacket
- PLB
- Duct tape
- Waterproof(s) if not being worn

Handlebars
- Phone
- GPS
- Bike light

Stem bags
- 0.5 l Water battle
- Snack

2 more water bottles

Postscript

I look back at the horizon. I'm happy. I started the day beyond that horizon. When I'm walking, I rarely trouble the horizon, but when I'm bikepacking I can ride to the horizon and beyond. I'm reminded of being in a Rupert Bear annual when Rupert would trot across several ridges to meet his chums for an adventure. I feel as though I've done similar. I've crossed ridges that I never would have in a day's walking. I've crossed bottom pastures, traversed meadows, ascended through woodland, climbed to the sheep walks and appeared on windswept moors. I've swooped down into valleys anew, not just once, but again and again. One of the things I love most about bike packing is to go over the horizon.

I urge you to grab a bike and set off on your own adventure. Yes, you will spend more time pedalling slowly up hills. Yes, you will spend some time walking and pushing the bike, but you will also have smiley descents. You will see birds and flowers, smell the soil and trees, you will get hot, then wet then cold. You will notice moss, ferns, and lichens that you never knew were there. You will hear birds, livestock, tractors and chainsaws. You will meet people and you will see places. You will feel alive, and you will feel at home. A bikepacking journey can cross horizons.

Bikepacking is about getting there, not being there.

Your author

Mike Raine is a regular bikepacker with a background in nature, walking and climbing. Mike is the author of Nature of Snowdonia (Pesda Press 2020) and The Mountain Leader – *a practical manual* (Pesda Press 2023). He runs further training workshops for outdoor leaders and supports the work of several conservation agencies. www.mikeraine.co.uk

www.ingramcontent.com/pod-product-compliance
Lightning Source LLC
Chambersburg PA
CBHW070611170426
43200CB00012B/2659